Identity under the Guise of Celebrity

Hollywood Hollywood

WITH ESSAYS BY

Fred Fehlau

Anne Friedberg

Michael Lassell

AND

David Robbins

CURATED BY

Fred Fehlau

INITIATED AND SPONSORED BY

Pasadena Art Alliance

IN COOPERATION WITH

Alyce de Roulet Williamson Gallery

Art Center College of Design

THE EXHIBITION CATALOGUE IS MADE POSSIBLE IN PART BY
A GRANT FROM THE PETER NORTON FAMILY FOUNDATION AND THE
SUPPORT OF THE SIMPSON PAPER COMPANY.

JAMES ABBE
TED ALLAN
ANGELYNE
MAX MUNN AUTREY
SID AVERY
JOHN BALDESSARI
NANCY BARTON
CECIL BEATON
CINDY BERNARD
JOHN BOSKOVICH
JOHN BRUMFIELD
CLARENCE SINCLAIR BULL
KATHE BURKHART
NANCY BURSON
ROBERT COBURN
ROBERT COBURN II
EILEEN COWIN
LOUISE DAHL-WOLFE
JIMMY DeSANA
MAX DUPAIN
JOHN ENGSTEAD
JOHN FLOREA
MICHAEL GLASS
GREG GORMAN
EDMUND GOULDING
PHILIPPE HALSMAN
RICHARD HAWKINS
PAUL HESSE
GEORGE HURRELL
PAUL JASMIN
LARRY JOHNSON
TOM KELLEY
DOUGLAS KIRKLAND
JEFF KOONS
LOUISE LAWLER
RUTH HARRIET LOUISE
ROBERT MAPPLETHORPE
CHRISTIAN MARCLAY

ANDREW MASULLO
ANGUS McBEAN
MARK MORRISROE
WILLIAM MORTENSEN
JANE O'NEAL
RUTH ORKIN
THERESA PENDLEBURY
JACK PIERSON
FRANK POWOLNY
RICHARD PRINCE
EUGENE ROBERT RICHEE
HERB RITTS
DAVID ROBBINS
MATTHEW ROLSTON
CHARLES ROSHER
ANNE ROWLAND
RENÉ SANTOS
ROCKY SCHENCK
BONNIE SCHIFFMAN
CINDY SHERMAN
LAURIE SIMMONS
ALEXIS SMITH
ALICE SPRINGS
JOHN SWOPE
DAVID TATTU
TIM TATTU
ANDY WARHOL
WILLIAM WEGMAN
CHRISTOPHER WILLIAMS
LASZLO WILLINGER
BOB WILLOUGHBY
GARRY WINOGRAND
MAX YAVNO
BRUCE YONEMOTO
NORMAN YONEMOTO

This publication accompanies the exhibition *Hollywood, Hollywood: Identity under the Guise of Celebrity*, October 20-December 20, 1992 at the Alyce de Roulet Williamson Gallery, Art Center College of Design, Pasadena, California.

Library of Congress Catalogue Card Number: 92-061647
ISBN 0-937042-09-9

Editor and Designer: Fred Fehlau
Line Editor: Buzz Spector
Printing: Typecraft, Inc., Pasadena, California
Paper: Simpson Kashmir, 100 lb. book and 80 lb. book. Courtesy of Simpson Paper Company, San Francisco, California.
Published by: Pasadena Art Alliance, 145 North Raymond Avenue, Pasadena, California 91103

Photography Credits: Photographs reproduced have been provided by the artists, galleries, institutions, and photography archivists as noted in the accompanying captions. Photographs for which additional credit is due: Squidds & Nunns, courtesy of MOCA, Los Angeles: p. 38; Natalie Boehm, courtesy of Art Center College of Design: pp. 40, 41 bottom left, 42, 44 left, 45 bottom right, 47 left, 48 right, 49, 53 left, 55 upper row, 56 right, 67 right, 68 right, and 73; Douglas M. Parker Studios, courtesy of Margo Leavin Gallery: pp. 60 left and 62.

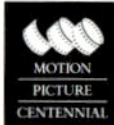 *Hollywood, Hollywood: Identity under the Guise of Celebrity* is presented as part of the *Motion Picture Centennial*, a six-year, nationwide, multi-institution observance and celebration of the first 100 years of the moving image arts.

Front cover:
CINDY SHERMAN, *Untitled Film Still (#52—on bed in slip)*, 1979

Back cover:
PAUL HESSE, *Marlene Dietrich*, 1950

Table of Contents

Lenders to the Exhibition   # *Donors*

American Fine Arts, Co., New York
Angelyne, Incorporated, Los Angeles
Ron Avery, MP&TV Photo Archive, Los Angeles
Sid and Diana Avery Trust
Roy Boyd Gallery, Santa Monica
Eli and Edythe L. Broad Foundation, Santa Monica
Linda Cathcart Gallery, Santa Monica
Robert Coburn II
Galerie Crousel-Robelin, Paris
The Jimmy DeSana Estate
Anne and David Fahey
Fahey/Klein Gallery, Los Angeles
Feature, New York
Rosamund Felsen Gallery, Los Angeles
Richard Green Gallery, Santa Monica
Pat Hearn Gallery, New York
Alan Hergott and Curt Shepard
Donald Hesse
Mr. & Mrs. Michael Hopkins
Deborah Irmas
Tom Kelley, Jr.
Jan Kesner Gallery, Los Angeles
Marsha Kleinman
The Kobal Collection, New York
Richard Kuhlenschmidt Gallery, Santa Monica
Max Lang
Margo Leavin Gallery, Los Angeles
Los Angeles County Museum of Art, Los Angeles
The Robert Mapplethorpe Estate
Robert Miller Gallery, New York
Mirage Editions, Inc.
The Mark Morrisroe Estate
Museum of Contemporary Art, Los Angeles
Jorge Pardo
Stuart Regan Gallery, Los Angeles
Marjorie Richardson
The René Santos Estate
Shoshana Wayne Gallery, Santa Monica
Barry Sloane
Stanley Soble
The John Swope Estate
Marjorie and Leonard Vernon
Councilman Joel Wachs
Daniel Weinberg Gallery, Santa Monica

Peter Norton Family Foundation
Simpson Paper Company

Anonymous
Vern and Marsha Bohr
Betty and Brack Duker
Mr. and Mrs. Robert S. Dulin
Mr. and Mrs. Gordon Fish
Paula E. Foley
Peggy Phelps

Anonymous
Alice O'Neill Avery
Ann and Olin Barrett
Linda Brownridge and Edward Mulvaney
Mary F. Buckingham
Betye Burton
Susan and John Caldwell
Martha Marsh Chandler
The Honorable and Mrs. James Cobey
Sallie and Harry Colmery
Mary Louise Crowe
Kathryn and Gordon Files
Harriet Fullerton
Jim and Liz Greene
Carol F. Henry
Adelaide Hixon
Joan and John Hotchkis
Mrs. Preston Bixby Hotchkis
Jane Hulick
Sally and Bill Hurt
Mr. and Mrs. George D. Jagels, Sr.
Patricia Ketchum
Virginia C. Krueger
Hannah and Russ Kully
Anne and Eldridge Lasell
Claude R. Logan
Judy and Paul MacCready
Jeannette McCarty
Barbara and Terry Maxwell
Helen Candler Miller
D. Harry Montgomery
Elizabeth Morton
Jane V. Palmer

Valerie and Larry Read
Gloria and Ed Renwick
Dorothy M. Scully
Howard and Gwen Laurie Smits
George and Gretel Stephens
Rea S. Taylor
Lois Ukropina
Biji Wilcox
Alyce de Roulet Williamson
Maybelle Bayly Wolfe

Deborah Booth
Virginia Reynolds Cartwright
Robert A. Rowan
Eileen and Fred Schoellkopf
Mr. and Mrs. Kyle Smeby
Jane B. Stott

Foreword

S I X   Y E A R S   A G O , the Pasadena Art Alliance wholeheartedly embraced a plan to initiate and fund a biennial exhibition, with the goal of encouraging a fertile climate in Southern California for the exploration of contemporary art within an historical and social context. This new program continues our long tradition of supporting artists, art institutions, exhibitions, and educational opportunities for the community, as exemplified by our involvement with the Pasadena Art Museum and, subsequently, the Baxter Art Gallery at the California Institute of Technology.

After successful completion of the first exhibition in 1990, we launched a search to locate a curator whose ideas would offer substance to, and challenge for, the general public, as well as revelation or insight beyond a survey. Certainly words of appreciation are due those curators whose proposals presented us with the formidable task of selection from excellent alternatives.

It was from this impressive field that Fred Fehlau—artist, writer and teacher—was invited as curator. His commitment to the exploration of ideas through substantive visual documentation fulfilled the mission of the Pasadena Art Alliance. Upon accepting our offer, he assumed his first curatorial assignment.

Work on the catalogue and the exhibition has been a collaboration imprinted with growth and friendship, involving numerous participants. From the beginning, Art Center College of Design has been most generous and enthusiastic about presenting this exhibition in the inaugural year of the Alyce de Roulet Williamson Gallery. For making this possible, we gratefully acknowledge the cooperation of David Brown, president. Special appreciation is reserved for Stephen Nowlin, gallery director, whose support and good counsel have always been available.

Owing to the generosity of the Peter Norton Family Foundation, as well as the Simpson Paper Company, with the assistance of Richard Giacchetti and Judith Kermeen, and enabled by James Allin Cross, Fred Fehlau was able to design a catalogue more inclusive and enriched than first envisioned. To them, we convey our appreciation. Typecraft, Inc., and particularly Harry Montgomery, deserves thanks for maintaining excellence in the catalogue production. We also extend our gratitude to our members and friends who granted additional support.

Above all, the association with Fred Fehlau has been a pleasure throughout. His insight and integrity are admirable, his curiosity contagious, and his patience remarkable. We are also indebted to his assistant, Jean Rasenberger, for the work she contributed to the project. We thank them for working with us to transform our goal into reality.

—L I N D A   B R O W N R I D G E , *president, Pasadena Art Alliance*

Acknowledgments

A PHOTO BOOTH SELF-PORTRAIT by Andy Warhol and a publicity photograph of Nanette Fabray by Paul Hesse seem, at first, to have nothing in common with each other. The former is a deadpan, self-reflexive critique of identity and its representation. The latter is part of a complex system of studio-driven celebrity promotion. It is not my intent to further reinforce these differences or to separate their respective practices; they already *are* different. However, it is far too simple to say that one production is critical and the other commercial, or that one is personal and the other professional (whatever those two terms really mean). Both are highly mediated, calculated, and manipulated images with shared codes of meaning. Both rely on complex narrative structures, both propose characterization and identification, and both understand the intricacies of irony and parody. Given the relationship Southern California has to filmmaking, it seems only appropriate to place these two—the film culture of the present and the past, and the critical production determined in part by that culture—together on the same turf. What we find is that they sometimes share more than each would care to admit. As for the overriding presence of celebrity in the construction of identity, we find ourselves constantly reminded of our distance from, knowledge of, or association with, fame. And so we are presented with a series of images that are either familiar, look familiar, or look as if they *should* look familiar. All of the photographs in this show pull, in some way, on the strings of recognition that place us (or exclude us), along with the famous, within the frame of the camera.

The production of this exhibition has not been easy. Not only has the work been gathered from many diverse sources, but the documentation of some of the images and photographers has been difficult to authenticate. For any errors or omissions we may have made, I offer my apologies. My thanks go out to all the galleries and institutions who not only lent work but guidance and information. I would especially like to thank Sid Avery of the MP&TV Photo Archive and David Fahey of Fahey/Klein Gallery for their help with the more historical aspects of the show. I would also like to thank the staffs of the Eli Broad Foundation, the Los Angeles County Museum of Art, and the Museum of Contemporary Art for their assistance.

I am grateful for the three fine essays contributed by Anne Friedberg, Michael Lassell, and David Robbins. Each provides a different point of view to this complex subject and succeeds, better than I could ever have done, in extending the range of interpretations given to Hollywood, to its production, and to its representations. Buzz Spector, as always, lent valuable editorial guidance. And for her tireless help with the catalogue and exhibition, as well as for the many valuable discussions we have had, I cannot thank my assistant, Jean Rasenberger, enough.

This exhibition and its catalogue have been generously supported by a number of individuals and organizations. The Art Center College of Design, Pasadena, contributed not only the gallery space but tremendous financial and organizational support. I also thank Stephen L. Nowlin, gallery director, and the installation staff under the direction of Julian Goldwhite, for all the help they have given me. I owe a debt of gratitude to Harry Montgomery of Typecraft, Inc., who printed this fine catalogue; and to Simpson Paper Company, who generously donated the paper. And for their grant towards additional catalogue support, I thank Peter Norton and the Peter Norton Family Foundation.

None of this would have been possible without the Pasadena Art Alliance, the sponsors and initiators of this exhibition, under the leadership of Marsha Bohr and Linda Brownridge. I am honored to have been chosen to curate this show for them. More specifically I would like to thank the Exhibition Committee, chaired by Sallie Colmery and Anne Lasell, all of whom have worked enthusiastically on all aspects of the project's concept and production. The Committee's guidance and friendship, as well as their impeccable editorial assistance and coordination, have been invaluable.

Finally, I am grateful for the cooperation and support of all the artists and photographers who lent not only their work but their ideas and support for the exhibition. I hope they find that this grouping of images, unconventional as it might be, draws a different picture of this all too familiar face we call Hollywood.

—FRED FEHLAU, *curator*

THE THING ABOUT MEDIA IMAGES is how they nag at us. Both affirming and rejecting, we see ourselves in these images, projecting deeply into their fantasies. The celebrity portrait is a consideration of how we daydream about a life outside of our day-to-day world. In this sense these images are theatrical, full of narrative possibility, and full of the inclusion of ourselves as players in that narrative. In our gaze is a reverie that beckons the image, and us, into (back into) a celluloid life.

What became more and more apparent as I pored over image after image with Fred Fehlau was how familiarity itself played into my interpretations. Familiarity allowed me to already "know" the image and its course of identification. But what nagged at me was how awkward these images continued to be, a process that frustrated the image's sense of transference. Why was this Garbo more beautiful than that Garbo? Why did this Doris Day portrait read as more camp than that one of Rita Hayworth? More than genres of seduction and desire, more than a process of projection into the theatrical space of the photograph, it was the effect of familiarity that drew my attention beyond the spectre of recognition.

The failure of these images to "perform" allowed me to consider them as something other than historical enigmas, examples of codified image-making, or even reflexive quotations. Indeed, looking at the photographs in this show became a process of deciphering, to coin a phrase from Artaud, the "hole in appearances." It is our failure to foreground disassociations, misconnections, etc., that provides us with a history of the missing, a failure that disrupts the machine of familiarity permeating our self-imaging. We come to understand this oversaturation of familiarity as a process of hollowed recognition. Indeed, this show is a recognition of ourselves as being a deeply affected people and how our identities revolve so heavily around the structures and genres of Hollywood, despite its confines and endless repetitions. I cannot thank Fred enough for asking me to assist him on this project. It has been an opportunity to reconsider the photographic portrait from the extraordinary perimeters Hollywood cuts through our lives.

—JEAN RASENBERGER, *curatorial assistant*

Here's Looking at You, [Kid]

BY FRED FEHLAU

"I am told that as I marched down the aisle, an actress on the screen asked another character a question, and I answered her, in a very loud voice. So, as the movies began to talk, I began to answer questions posed by two-dimensional fictional characters thirty times my size."

—Gore Vidal in *Screening History* [1]

"As we have a collage vision fostered by the rapidly escalating demands on our attention, so we have collage personalities, made up of fragments of public people, who are in turn made from fragments themselves—polished, denatured, simplified. Similarly, the self-exposing and self-asserting gestures we learn from the famous become licensed for our own use."

—Leo Braudy in *The Frenzy of Renown* [2]

THE COVER OF THE MAY 1990 ISSUE of *ArtScribe* magazine carries a photograph of Meryl Streep, cigarette in hand, staring to our right. Added to the usual cover lines, the phrase "Recognition maybe, may not be useful" is printed across the image. Beneath it is printed the name "Louise Lawler." The photograph, the phrase, and the name do not signify each other; rather, they float somewhat independently in this small pool of references. Streep, of course, has made a career of maintaining the strictest character acting techniques, playing such diverse roles as a southern lawyer, a Victorian English maid, a Danish immigrant to Africa, and an Australian mother accused of murdering her own baby, while managing to become a familiar celebrity, outside of those characters, in the world at large. The image, a publicity photograph taken by Maureen Lambray, shows Streep *as* character. The phrase, with the word *maybe* rather than the words *may be*, refers to Streep's characterability, her changeability, her "facelessness." And the use of Louise Lawler, as caption, as identifier, as "author," places this identification of Streep (and Lawler) into a wider field of interpretation. Who is *in* the picture, who *made* the picture, as well as who is *reading* the picture, become a series of responsibilities shared among Streep, Lawler, the actual photographer, and ourselves.

Portraiture is perhaps the most readily manipulated of photographic practices because we understand and respond to the image of each other so quickly and with such varied experiences and interpretations that meaning is impossible to control. A photographic portrait attempts, successfully or not, to locate an identity, to join an image with a referent. [3] Only one thing is really necessary; the subject, or the characterization of that subject, should in some way be recognizable. The photograph (and the photographer) presupposes that the viewer be familiar with the subject *before* it appears in front of her/him. The difficulty lies not in producing an image—any image will do—but in determining the relationship between the viewer and the subject (and between viewer and photograph and between subject and photograph), the availability of each to the other, the use of one by the other, and the slippery cross-referencing of one identity over another. Thus, a celebrity portrait relies upon the ability of the viewer/audience to recognize that celebrity or, at the very least, to recognize the character that celebrity portrays. Every viewer has both an individual, i.e., private (her/his own memories of or identifications with the subject), and a collective, i.e., public (the sum total of the distributed information on that subject),[4] relationship with any given image. One viewer's relationship necessarily differs from another's. That difference, that specificity, "defines" both the image and the viewer. One understands oneself through the recognition of, identification with, and resistance to, celebrity.

[**THAT WAS THEN**] Between 1901 and 1914, 74 percent of the biographical essays in the *Saturday Evening Post* and *Collier's* magazines concerned politicians and business people. By 1922, more than half came from the field of entertainment.[5] This proliferation of publicity material was due in part to the emerging Hollywood star system, when previously anonymous "players" became headline personalities in their own right. Mary Pickford was perhaps the first to truly establish her name as a "site of knowledge."[6] (In the early '20s, Pickford had a yearly personal budget of over $50,000 just for publicity photography.) These photographs, and those later produced by the studios, found their way into such new publications as *Photoplay* and *Vanity Fair*, magazines that defined the language of celebrity and glamour for an increasingly sophisticated audience. Actors became known for the characters they played on and off the screen. That identification, according to Richard deCordova, "extended well beyond the film." He goes on to state, "What the [star's] name designated above all was a form of intertextuality, the recognition and identification of an actor from film to film."[7] Charles Rosher's photograph, *Mary Pickford in "Tess of the Storm Country,"* 1922, presents this double identity—Mary and Tess—as one. Pickford looks directly at the camera, toward the viewer, as an individual in costume on a set, rather than merely as a player or object viewed from a distance. That she is "Mary," not "Tess," is more the point. James Abbe's *Charlie Chaplin in "The Pilgrim,"* 1923, presents not only actor but director and celebrity as well. Recognized by both the public and the industry as a talented storyteller as well as an endearing character, Chaplin quickly seized upon the power of (his) personality and utilized it to its fullest potential. Like Rosher's *Pickford,* Abbe's *Chaplin* is both Chaplin and his role, both inside and outside of the photograph and the film.

[**WITNESS TO THE ACT**] We "know" celebrities through the press. The paparazzi act as the scavengers for our social experience, recording and collecting contact with the famous. Their frontally lit, presumably candid images, usually taken outside of restaurants and theaters or through covert observation, are both mutually beneficial publicity and an extreme violation of privacy. Madonna, in her film *Truth or Dare,* 1991, acknowledges the voyeuristic and exhibitionistic nature of this attention and exploits it to full measure. Ostensibly a documentation of the star on tour, the line here between choreo-

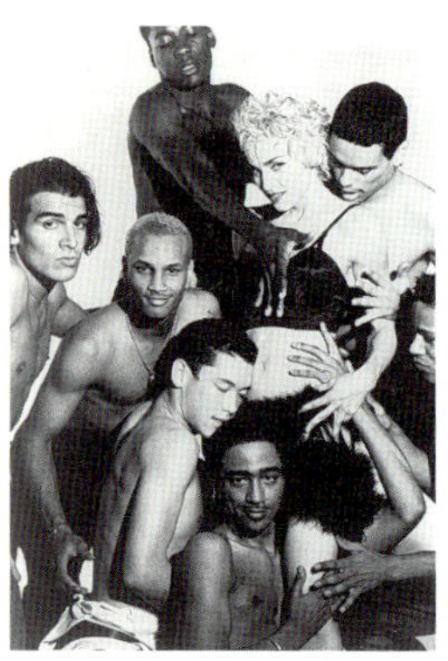

graphed and candid is completely erased; every action becomes an assumed pose. Madonna moves seamlessly between stage and dressing room, playing with and playing to the camera. The camera itself rarely comes to the audience's attention, remaining outside the action, sometimes addressed, but not seen. The supporting characters in the film—dancers, producers, assistants—are more or less comfortable with this arrangement. Some self-consciously acknowledge the camera, flirt with it, and camp it up. Others ignore it or are annoyed and critical of it. They, like the film viewer her/himself, realize their own exclusion, or at the least their difference, from the subject in real view: Madonna. Watching the film forces one into an uncomfortable pact with the star: you can see her, but you must remain outside her cinematic space. Much like performers viewed through one-way mirrored compartments in peep-shows—as depicted in *Paris, Texas*, starring Nastassia Kinski and Harry Dean Stanton, where the actor[8] strips and dances in front of brightly lit mirrors—Madonna, in *Truth or Dare*, plays for an unseen audience hidden by the darkness of the theater.

Ruth Orkin's *Lana Turner at Famous Party Given by Marion Davies, Esther Williams, Fernando Lamas, and Ben Gage*, 1952, sets up a similar stage of privilege and exclusion. Lana Turner stands, back to the wall, in conversation with another woman seated at a table in front of her. Three men, also in conversation, ignore the two women. The camera is outside, away from view; no one in the photograph addresses it. The table not only blocks Turner spatially but also prevents any intimate contact with her. Orkin's position in all of this is also unclear. Presumably she was invited, but in what function—participant? witness? audience? John Swope's *Elsa Maxwell, Tyrone Power and the Duke of Windsor*, 1942, also ignores the camera while acknowledging its necessary presence. Swope, a freelance photographer for *Life* magazine and husband of Dorothy McGuire, was most certainly a guest at this function. The camera, while not addressed, is certainly in the same space as the subjects. Elsa Maxwell exits left, Tyrone Power passes directly in front of the camera while the Duke of Windsor shoots a sideways glance back at Power. Only the photograph is able to hold all of this momentary action in place.

Sid Avery's *Jayne Mansfield Signing Autographs in front of Dino's on the Sunset Strip in Los Angeles*, 1961, presents the ultimate in star worship: flashing cameras and autograph hounds. Avery stands back, recording both the center of attention and the attention itself, as if a snapshot of Mansfield alone were not enough. The camera plays witness to the chaos surrounding celebrity. The site of Max Yavno's *Betty Grable's Legs*, n.d., is also a sidewalk. The concrete pads in front of Graumann's Chinese Theater are a "must see" tourist location. Fans from around the world try on the hand- and footprints in a vain and ultimately humiliating attempt to get close to the celebrities who made them. In Yavno's image, however, a figure (Grable?) cropped so that only her legs and the hem of her coat appear in the frame, stands directly on top of her own referent. She stands isolated and alone. No fans press against her. The title is plural, but there is the impression of only one leg visible in the cement. Thus, the "legs" of the title seemingly include all three as Grable's, named through the association and identification with each other.

Garry Winogrand's *Marilyn Monroe, "Seven Year Itch" Location*, c. 1957, brings us another sidewalk. But in this case, the identity of the subject is undeniable. This image, and others by different photographers at the scene, has become so familiar it functions as an iconic artifact in itself, spawning numerous knock-offs and impersonations; the floating skirt held down against the air rising from a subway grate is cemented in camp vernacular. (Theresa Russell shows how easy it is to imitate this gesture in Nicholas Roeg's film *Insignificance*.) It is difficult to determine if the film, *Seven Year Itch*, is remembered because of this image, or vice versa; the image is nonetheless lodged in the collective experience of an entire generation. Marilyn's emphatically public persona provides a counterpoint to *Greta Garbo in "Grand Hotel,"* c. 1932, a still from the Edmund Goulding film, suggesting a different sensibility, one of privacy over publicity. Garbo, one of the most secretive of stars, avoided contact with the world at all costs. In this scene, an eerie foreshadowing of her later persona, we see Garbo entering a limousine surrounded by onlookers. Her face cold and aloof, she attempts to separate herself from the crowd.

[**IN THE SET**] In a movie, one shot moves easily to another and one scene to another with little question of continuity. Even with the time-wrenching techniques of flash-forwards and flashbacks, dream sequencing, over-narration, fade-ins and fade-outs, this movement, or change of focus, is easily assimilated. As an audience, we have been well trained in the act of perceiving flow within discontinuity. The actual making of a film, however, takes place within a double discontinuity. Not only may time be interrupted in the narrative itself, but the film will most certainly be shot out of sequence, with numerous takes and delays between one set-up and the next. Further, while the viewer may perceive the actor as alone in the room, or in a space of intimate repose, the reality of the set is one of professional congestion; the director, cameraman, script "girl," grips, lighting technicians, etc., are all present and press upon the scene. Pulling back to reveal the set discloses that crowd and diverts attention from the actor, while simultaneously centering and solidifying her/his position in that frame. Jane O'Neal's *On the Set of "Impulse,"* 1989, shows a scene being shot, a close-up of one of the supporting actresses. Camera, clapboard, and crew are all present and, most importantly, dominate the set. Above their heads a curved mirror reflects the action from the (still) camera's opposing position. Read side to side, as well as front to back and back again, the photograph ricochets in a geometric tangle of site and responsibility. Everyone is there as a participant, each has a job to do, yet only one person will ever be presented visually to the audience.

In a much different way, Matthew Rolston's *Meredith Salenger and Clayton Rohner,* 1985, takes some of the characters usually found outside the scene and places them directly in front of the camera. But what at first seems to be an opening of the frame becomes instead a tightly controlled composition of event. Through such references as the clothing and equipment of the set (lights, booms, and backdrops), the time period of the photograph appears to be the late '40s or early '50s. Moreover, there really is no separation between the stars' and the technicians' inhabited space (a ladder is seen immediately behind Salenger's head). However, one is still aware that the two stars are really the only subject of the photograph, first, because they are named in the title, and second, because they are the only ones in the photograph addressing the camera in full light. The attendants, in darkness, place their attention on them, not on the camera. Much like the courtiers in *Las Meninas,* Velázquez's portrait of the Princess Margarita of Spain, their role is one of assistance, not presentation.[9] And further, these other characters, the director, script girl, etc., are not real; they are models, dressed and styled with no less attention than the stars, or the set, for that matter. The portrait(s) becomes choreographed artifice. The specificity of these references only reinforces its production. It becomes, to use Daniel Boorstin's term, a "pseudo-event."[10]

Bob Willoughby's *Elizabeth Taylor in "Raintree County,"* 1956, reveals the artificiality of the film set by presenting its incongruity and overdetermination. Elizabeth Taylor and her co-star, bedecked in enormous 19th-century hoop skirts, sit between takes in what must be sweltering heat. An electric fan stands on a stool in front of the pair, predictably aimed at Taylor. Behind them sits a group of bored-looking set technicians and assistants while, further off, standing in the sun, a crowd of onlookers eagerly waits to catch a glimpse of the action. From front to rear, the succession of subjects is arrayed in a casual yet strictly determined hierarchy of attention. In contrast, Willoughby's *Marilyn Monroe,* 1960, sits alone, isolated from the events of the set and the attention of the crew. She waits, patiently, for the sign to return to the action, for the time she may again find herself in center stage. Finally, John Florea's *Marilyn Monroe,* 1953, tells its story through manipulation of costume and set. Familiar and sexy, Marilyn stands in front of a roaring fire in pale pink long johns. Ski gear paraphernalia is strewn carefully around. Is this picture some kind of advertisement for winter fashion? a teaser for a new movie? Or are we to presume that Marilyn has just come back from a ski weekend in Big Bear? None of those things; it is a produced event—a Hollywood Magic Moment. Marilyn, her fame, her glamour, and the ordinariness of the setting work together to create this image of casual, carefree leisure, so that we, the public, the fans, the critics, can rest assured knowing that Marilyn does indeed have time to relax.

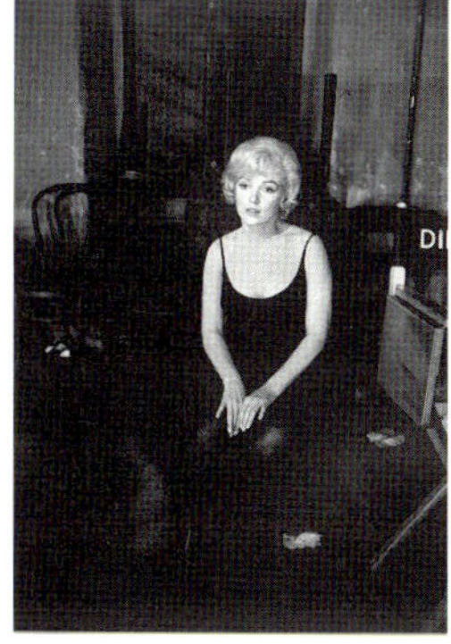

BOB WILLOUGHBY
Marilyn Monroe, 1960

 Distinctions between the "cinematic" and the "real," in terms of the experience of film, do not truly operate, dissolving as they do into the seamless space of memory. Gilles Deleuze, in *Cinema 2*, describes this mutability as "a power of the false which replaces and supersedes the form of the true, because it poses the simultaneity of incompossible presents, or the coexistence of not-necessarily true pasts." [11] Eileen Cowin's *Untitled*, 1986, takes up the construction of artifice and isolates it against a blank, black background. As if caught in the headlights of an oncoming car, the woman's movements are frozen into a single moment. Silvery skirt pulled up, she reaches down as if in pain or discomfort; the gesture is ambiguous. Cowin shifts the focus of artificiality from thing to event, from noun to verb. In making contrived what is already a contrived event—acting—she doubles the stakes in a game already weighed in favor of the photographer/filmmaker. Cindy Bernard also reconstructs the cinematic scene, in this case devoid of action. In a series of photographs subtitled *Ask the Dust*, Bernard has rephotographed the locations of crucial moments from specific movies, some recognizable and some less familiar. *Ask the Dust: North by Northwest (1959/1990)*, 1990, presents the road from Alfred Hitchcock's famous airplane chase scene. One hears (remembers) the roar of the cropduster in one's head and watches (imagines) Cary Grant (his character) run from side to side, but one sees nothing. Bernard's image is empty. A construction of produced events builds up one upon another: the film; the photograph; and the re-placement, by the viewer, of the action from the film into the photograph. All are false, or mediated, yet all are experienced as reality, or rather, as physical and imaginative continuities.

Jack Pierson's *Excalibur*, 1992, also presents a place like something out of a film, but without specific cinematic reference. A Disneyesque castle tower of the Excalibur Hotel in Las Vegas is seen through the drawn blinds of a hotel room. A sense of filmic identification, through location and association, occurs between the viewer and that dimly visible presence, of being *close to* or *in the vicinity of*, but remaining perpetually outside the implied scene. Hollywood has always understood the gap between ourselves and the cinematic. Our inclusion in the mythical or sublime offering of film, and the perversity of that gift, is the subject of Bruce and Norman Yonemoto's video *Made in Hollywood*, 1989, in which various characters—an aspiring starlet, two ex-performance artists (refugees of the New York art world, Mary Woronov and Ron Vawter), and a bisexual actor—revolve around a Hollywood mogul representing power and wealth. All share disillusionment. The starlet, rejected by the actor, turns to a gift given to her by her parents, opening up a Pandora's box capable of reflecting her image back to herself in its make-up mirror. At that moment she knows where she must go—into a world where "everyone is happy and no one goes hungry," the land of television commercials. Hollywood's mythologies and projections are transferred into the banality of TV production; moguls and film stars are replaced by the echoes of fulfillment that come with new cars, breakfast cereals, and clean, white toilets.

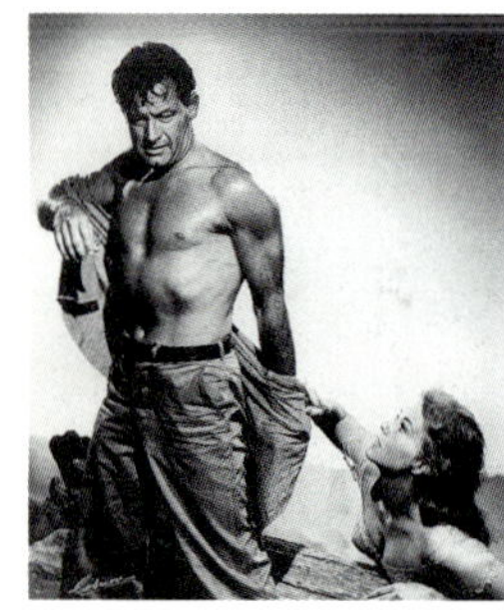

William Holden and Kim Novak, c. 1955

 Film, from the very beginning, has attempted to depict romance, and romance hasn't been the same since. Whether a joining of, or a war between, the sexes (most often a combination of the two), cinematic narrative rarely lacks a love angle. Usually arranged between a handsome male lead and a beautiful female lead or, in more recent times, between the interesting and the interesting of any gender, romance is usually a projection of an unattainable ideal rather than a reflection of an actual reality. Robert Coburn's *Rita Hayworth and Glenn Ford*, c. 1946, a publicity still for Charles Vidor's film *Gilda*, (1946), represents this ideal in full cinematic splendor. Hayworth, in a strapless dress, perfect hair and makeup, is held aloft by an impeccably groomed Ford against the white, seamless background of the studio. She faces the camera; Ford, in profile, gazes up at her. Coburn's photograph *William Holden and Kim Novak*, c. 1955, for the film *Picnic*, (1955), tells the other side of the story: same lighting and background, but this time Holden is the rugged individualist, bare chested and in denim, who turns away from a reaching Novak, the image of unrequited desire, lust, guilt, and shame.

The problem with all of this, of course, is that not all people fit the images Hollywood produces for them. Coupling takes place in spite of appearances or roles, not because of them. Richard Prince's *Untitled (mixed couple–men)*, 1977-78, questions the construction of the conventional male/female archetype. Two men, presumably two models in an advertisement or fashion layout, are cropped at mid-torso. One man looks and speaks to the other, who, in turn, gazes out of the frame. What may have been a simple photograph to sell suits becomes an intimate relationship between two individuals. Like actors in a film, the *real* relationship of these two men is unimportant; it is the interplay of characterization and cropping that produces meaning.

Relationships need not always be romantic. The play of one character off another—buddies, enemies, sidekicks, etc.—is the stuff of narrative itself. Many times the incongruity of the pairing tells the story. Robert Coburn II's *Kim Novak (Columbia Pictures)*, 1957, shows a somewhat perturbed Novak receiving a kiss from a circus seal, an image made more ridiculous by the fact that it looks so natural. Paul Hesse's *Nanette Fabray*, c. 1959, captures a perky Fabray with an equally perky terrier. Jeff Koons's four *Art Magazine Ads*, 1988-89, present Koons with somebody/something—seals with flower leis, bikini-clad vixens, schoolchildren, and pigs. The photographs (all taken by Greg Gorman) are highly styled, retouched, and obviously manufactured images of "perfection" dictated by the artificial standards of promotion and advertising. In all, Koons is the center of attention, of adulation, of desire. He is the lead. As a couple, Koons and the pig are a comic reminder of every mismatched pair in film. The similarity of their expressions only adds to the theatricality of the image. John Engstead's *Sugar 'n Spice (Peggy Lee)*, n.d., pictures Lee, first in white with pink carnations and then in leopard skin holding a cat, as two sides of a record album cover. Along a somewhat different line, Christian Marclay's *Absolutely*, 1991, pairs the head and shoulders of a sexy Ann-Margret with the tattooed biceps and forearm of Boxer's *Absolutely* album. This cross-referencing of body parts and gender produces an alternate identity, a pumped-up version of Ann-Margret's own hyper-realized presence.

[**FEMMES FATALES**] No single category of representations in film has been more closely investigated than the roles and stereotypes produced for women. Even when relegated to a secondary role in the script, a female star is often used as the primary focus of publicity. The reason is both obvious and problematic. Mainstream Hollywood seldom produces strong leading roles for women, and women, presumably, make for good advertising. More than likely, the roles women can play have been limited to a list of types: the "sexy," the "silly," the "serious," the "second woman." And when work critical of these constructions is made, work which seeks to criticize the language of stereotype, it invariably utilizes that language itself, in some ways weakening the critique. Hence, the images of the feminine in a Sherman and a Hurrell are superficially identical. We, as an audience, understand that similarity, regardless, and determine difference through use. The job at hand is to disrupt, through and in spite of critique, these constructions. Louise Dahl-Wolfe's *Lauren Bacall*, 1943, shows a youthful, underwear-clad Bacall seated gracefully on the side of a marble bathtub, looking back over her shoulder at the camera. Cast as feminine and sexy, Bacall is both subject and object. The image Bacall plays and the woman Dahl-Wolfe photographs are harmonious. One can either desire her or desire to be like her or recoil at the use (and abuse) of this desire; but in all cases there is no argument about her desirability. Similarly, Cindy Sherman's images of women in beds, like *Untitled Film Still (#6–black bra)*, 1978, use the language of seduction to question the very roles of observer and observed. What Sherman does, however, is to place herself, as an anonymous model, in that field of recognition. Both Dahl-Wolfe's *Bacall* and Sherman's *black bra* are comfortable and familiar with themselves, and we, in turn, are initially comfortable with that recognition. But the clash between pose and intent in Sherman's work upsets the balance of the stable signifier and places that familiarity, and the familiarity of *type* in general, into question.

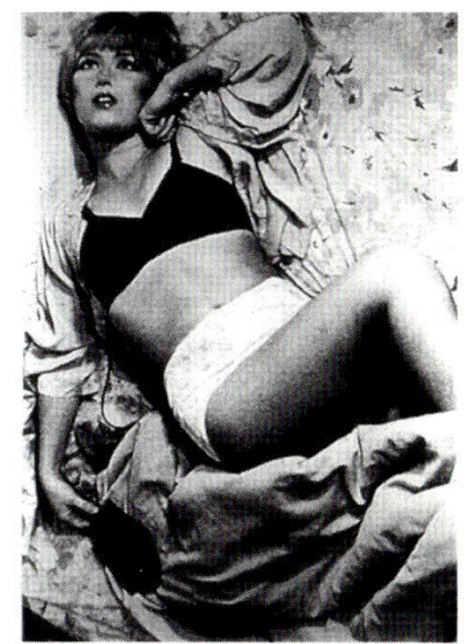

CINDY SHERMAN
*Untitled Film Still
(#6–black bra)*, 1978

Another way to upset this identification is to cause the image itself to rupture these codes of expectation. Replacing the model of the female with that of the male, through either pose or objectification, can sometimes achieve this end. Robert Mapplethorpe's photographs of men, and primarily black men, as sexual objects within the male gaze, project an incongruity between the expected and the depicted. Mapplethorpe's *Almasi*, 1981, poses gracefully on a cloth-covered stool, nude, eyes closed and face turned. Photographed in the controlled light of the studio, the image preserves all of the intent and conventions of high photographic practice. Ironically, although Mapplethorpe's images are more similar to the conservative aesthetic ideals of an Edward Weston or Aaron Siskind than to the critical arguments of a Sherman or Prince, the reception and interpretation of his subjects render them otherwise.

Cross-dressing and gender-bending are other means of upsetting convention. Rocky Schenck's *Phranc*, 1989, is a picture of an androgynous woman—a folk singer, a lesbian—styled with a crewcut, red turtleneck, apple blossoms, and a glass of milk. The mixed message of "good girl/good boy" produced by that styling interrupts any simplistic reading. Phranc (and Schenck) seems to be producing a sincere picture of wholesomeness while simultaneously questioning the very conventions of the wholesome. Greg Gorman's portrait of *Divine with Bulldogs, Personal Publicity, Los Angeles*, 1984, is a more direct and outrageous attack on convention. The late Divine, cult-star of such films as *Pink Flamingo* and *Hairspray*, both by John Waters, reverses the codes of gender by exaggerating traits usually associated with male ideals of the feminine. Big blond hair, high-cut mini dress, overdone makeup and nails complement, or not, Divine's ample voluptuousness. Through this reversal, codes of both the masculine and the feminine come under fire. Identification of, or with, Divine and the image of Divine is further complicated by this play of inclusion and exclusion.

The ability to recognize both ourselves and others in any object, human or not, relies upon our desire to see the world as a projection of ourselves. Hence, recognition is in some ways predetermined, not entirely produced. Even animals can supply behavioral attributes in these circumstances. William Wegman's photographs of his dogs, the late Man Ray or Fay Ray and her clan, invest them with the expression and condition of the human. Wegman's *Island Way*, 1991, shows an entirely plausible Weimeraner in a red wig and tropical print muu-muu, complete with a "real" woman's hands and feet. And Mark Morrisroe's *Portrait of Chi-Chi*, 1985, is an image of a Chihuahua presented as a portrait, providing personality to the sitter. Photographed frontally rather than from above, the position of the camera reinforces a directness of address. Chi-Chi's expression and posture, as well as her jeweled gold choker, anthropomorphizes her into a depiction of the qualities of the "human" transferred to the "not human."

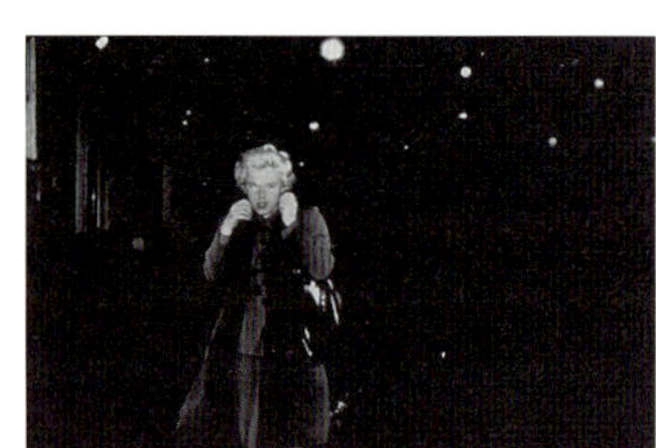

*Untitled Film Still (#54–
blond in rain)*, 1980

[**ANGELYNE AS MARILYN, MARILYN AS ANGELYNE, MADONNA AS EVERYONE**] For better or for worse, the image of the Blond Bombshell is inscribed in our collective consciousness. From Jean Harlow and Marlene Dietrich through Jayne Mansfield and Lana Turner to Geena Davis and Sharon Stone, the film industry has produced an endless stream of cross-referenced and collectively identified blond actresses. Madonna, already cross-referenced and multi-indexed herself, maintains a schizophrenic control of most of these models (her last tour was entitled *Blond Ambition*). Marilyn Monroe, however, may be the quintessential Blond. Not only does she epitomize the most stereotypical of attributes—sexy, "slightly dumb," "playful," "funny," etc.—but she supports, or is supported by, an industry devoted to this characterization. While the passage of time ultimately destroys most celebrities, it has only accelerated the cult-like worship now delivered upon Marilyn.

Cindy Sherman's *Untitled Film Still (#54,–blond in rain)*, 1980, captures that now-familiar quality of innocence and fragility. Hands held to her face protectively, Sherman's *blond* becomes Marilyn. Without this reference, the woman in the picture remains anonymous. Sherman projects our desires to know, to be like, to feel close to this woman. Jimmy DeSana's *Aluminum Foil #3*, 1986, also manipulates this desire for recognition. Utilizing time-lapse techniques, DeSana's metallic hair, eyebrows, and lips burn unnatural highlights into the print, concealing the artist's own face behind this bright layer of color. DeSana and Sherman both play with the possibility of identifying themselves, as model or as role, with another. Rocky Schenck's photographs of female impersonators further complicate this notion of self-identification. Shot in the highly mannered style of Hurrell and Coburn, these men become the women they idolize: Marilyn, Judy, and Bette. *Jimmy James*, 1989, is more Marilyn than Marilyn herself, because the Marilyn we see in Jimmy is an accumulation of all the gestures and poses we have come to know of her. Jimmy's Marilyn is a shared and quantifiably public identity; we see in Jimmy the Marilyn we already know, the Marilyn all of us have helped to create.

Aside from Garry Winogrand's *"Seven Year Itch" Location*, no other photograph has been as published and imitated as Tom Kelley's *Marilyn Monroe*, 1949, the pin-up calendar photograph of the then Norma Jean Baker. Strawberry blond, nude, stretched across a diagonal of bright red velvet, this one photograph helped to elevate Monroe, and Kelley, to instant notoriety. It also reveals the interdependence of desire and success, of the ability for that (sexual) desire to be couched in popular celebrity, and of the objectification of desire in return for fame. John Brumfield, in *Robert Posing Coyly as a Hollywood Star*, 1974, manipulates this pin-up format. The title takes the three words, *posing, coyly,* and *Hollywood,* and wraps them into one play of address. Robert peers at us, head turned from a profile body position, with a suggestive and inviting smile, ready to accommodate any need. With a doubling of sexual seductiveness—both male and female—and of pure innocence, Robert makes himself into whatever the viewer wants—a pose of possibility.

Alexis Smith's *Miss April*, 1992, as with most of her work, juxtaposes various Hollywood narrative themes to produce what amounts to a romance novella. A 1968 pin-up calendar is paired with a film still from Cardoza-Francis's *Walk with the Damned* depicting an actor with a knife in his back. A wooden sandwich spear stamped with the words "Pierce Gently," aimed at "Miss April's" derrière, mirrors the direction of the knife. The phrase "April is the cruelest month" (perhaps an allusion to T.S. Eliot's poem *The Waste Land*) runs across the top. Both the girl on the calendar and the actor are unidentifiable as individuals but familiar as type: Blond and Beautiful; Young and Serious. The result is a story of love and betrayal, desire and pain—the stuff of Hollywood B-movies.

This fascination with the Bombshell, as defined by Marilyn Monroe and Jayne Mansfield, in turn produces individuals and images whose identities are determined and referenced by them. Angelyne, the self-proclaimed billboard queen of Hollywood, is one inheritor of this image. Her press release proclaims: "'I just want to be famous for the magic I possess.'…the tradition of the Blond Bombshell is carried out in grand style, in a new high-tech form of the future!!!" With a cult following devoted to her music videos and entertainment engagements, her identity is almost entirely subsumed in its promotional effects. Angelyne exists primarily as her own billboard advertisements. Bonnie Schiffman's *Angelyne*, 1987, reclines on the hood of a pink Cadillac behind a bright blue sky. Angelyne gazes up into a mirror turned to the camera, facing her audience through the reflection. We are to see her only as she sees herself. The mirror, like the camera, provides Angelyne with the distance fame requires.

[**HEADS**] Photography allows us to traverse time, to sift through our own memories of films and their actors. Thus, the studio shot, in proposing identification above all else, is a concise tie between that celebrity and ourselves, between the past and the present. A photograph of a celebrity is a kind of notation, one that prompts memories of the pleasure of the cinematic experience, the recognition of projection and identification, and the reverie of recon-

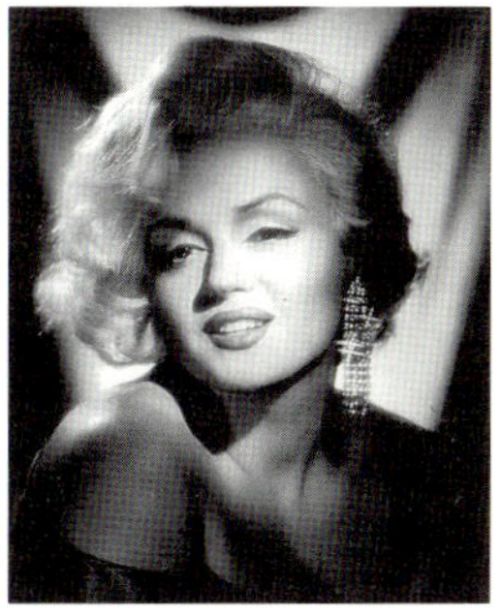

struction. Eugene Robert Richee's *Tallulah Bankhead*, n.d., and Cecil Beaton's *Orson Welles (with Bust of Shakespeare)*, 1936, both isolate their subjects in the flat, constructed space of the studio. Each stands with a plaster cast, equating pose with classical ideal. The photographs are direct, formal, and self-conscious. Not of their time, as a location-bound image might be, yet not as timeless as the staging would at first suggest, they take on the aura of the stage (or of the opera, whose theatrics freeze action into extended gesture), emphasizing delivery over action.

The tightly controlled and dramatically lit portraits of Clarence Sinclair Bull, Ruth Harriet Louise, George Hurrell, and Laszlo Willinger constitute a style unto themselves and set the standards for the now identifiable mark of Hollywood glamour. They, and the imitators who followed, elevate their subjects to immortality, imbuing them with a distanced yet enticing sexuality. Bull's *Nancy Carroll in Leon Gordon's Drama "Undesirable Lady,"* n.d., side-lit, close-cropped, captures Carroll glancing sideways, off camera, the corners of her mouth just forming a smile of recognition. Louise's *Greta Garbo*, n.d., similarly lit, tilts her head backwards in apparent anticipation. Hurrell's *Edwina Booth*, 1932, shot from slightly above, her hair glowing with highlights, stares sulkily over the camera. Willinger often staged more theatrical photographs, using props and other imaginative backgrounds. His *Susan Hayward*, n.d., also seen from above, looks out of the frame while an almost identical enlargement of her face is projected in the background. Imagined in the surreal space of photography itself, Hayward is doubled in iconic appeal. These stars rarely look directly into the lens, as if that intimacy would be too painful to bear. Max Dupain's *Greta Garbo*, 1940, expresses this isolation more than most. Eyes closed, hands over her face, she hides from the camera, maintaining her mystery by keeping the viewer just outside of her experience.

Christopher Williams's *Andra Millian, Women and Roses* (detail), 1986, depicts a woman, in this case a television actress, in the manner of an ordinary publicity head shot. The light is flat, her hair is big; she has a slightly anxious look of quiet desperation on her face. Because the print is, in fact, a publicity shot taken from her publicist's files, the image maintains, in this context, a double-edged quality of being both what it is—a head shot—and a model of itself, the image of a photograph of a headshot. Andra remains a construction, not fully an individual, yet not completely false. Andrew Masullo's *2249*, 1989-90, is a normal 10 x 8 headshot taken of Masullo, the face cut out and replaced with blunt strokes of dark and light blue paint. This negation of identity through excision and camouflage only heightens the attention on Masullo himself, present as he is despite this excision. Masullo, in this case, is represented as stroke, as hand, as production. Anne Rowland's *Untitled (Frank Sinatra)*, 1987, tackles this problem of identity in an entirely different manner. By projecting slides of famous people on her own face, partially hidden by folds of sheer fabric, she produces a composite image of both identities. Not Sinatra, but certainly not herself, the resulting image is caught in mid-transformation. Rowland's own forehead and eyebrow, peeking out from above the gauze, seem plastic in the harsh projected light. And Sinatra's famous smile, overlaying Rowland's mouth, is frozen, by dint of the pose, into a painful grimace. Nancy Burson's *Baby Marilyn*, 1988, is a computer-altered composite photograph of an adult Marilyn Monroe combined with a generic baby picture. Through a process of interpolation, or shifting of units of information similar to morphing, the two images are blended with characteristics of each, such as the shape of the baby's head and eyes, as well as Marilyn's mole, remaining in the final print. This physiognomic composite collides with the mechanisms of projection and identification already operating within the photographic gaze, (re)placing the generic with (into) the specific.

Sometimes photographers leave the set in favor of the real world. However, their presumably candid portraits of the everyday life of celebrities are as much a manipulation of situation and gesture as the glamour photographs they seek to supplant. Herb Ritts's portraits of *Jack Nicholson, L.A.*, 1986, and *Madonna, Tokyo*, 1987, project an ease and silliness more familiar to stand-up comedy than to film. Nicholson's sinister smile spreads from ear to ear, enlarged by a huge magnifying glass, and Madonna looks uncommonly girlish and carefree as she attempts to see the Mouse ears on her head.

Frequently the desire for realism manifests itself in extreme closeup, as if showing more detail might actually deliver more meaning. Abandoning the Vaseline-softened focus of the past, Douglas Kirkland pushes his camera into the face of *Judy Garland*, 1961, revealing not only her pores and blemishes but the sweat and pain of performance. Cindy Sherman's *Untitled, (#180, Michael Jackson's Face)*, 1987, brings to the surface of the picture plane a grotesquely manipulated and disfigured mask of pop hypersensibility. Jackson, already known for dramatic refigurations in both dress and mannerisms as well as through plastic surgery and skin-lightening (a change recorded by photography), is in this manifestation doubly falsified. The bulging eyes and torn flesh are evidence of a personality painfully insecure and constantly clawing at the self in its attempt to produce an image of perfection. Finally, in René Santos's *Untitled*, 1984, an unidentified black woman, heavily made up, stares out of a video-produced haze, at something outside the frame. In this image taken off the TV screen from what appears to be some daytime drama or commercial, the harsh camera lights burn patches of white into her skin. Not quite human, or, rather, rendered inhuman by the effect of television, she has become a zombie of popular representation, unknowable within the character she portrays—fittingly—masked behind mascara and lipstick.

[**PHOTO WALLS**] Like the walls of the now deceased Wilshire Brown Derby in Los Angeles or innumerable dry cleaning establishments and diners from Hollywood, CA, to Hollywood, FL, collections of head shots, usually 8 x 10s framed in cheap black and gold molding, are a familiar sight. These walls of faces test a viewer's knowledge of cinematic trivia and complicate the here/now-there/then dislocation of the referent. Max Munn Autrey's *Max M. Autrey with 11 Portraits*, c. 1947, is a rather intricate play of photographic convention. The image depicts Autrey surrounded by large black and white prints, presumably shot by him, of such actresses as Joan Crawford, Lucille Ball, and Jane Russell, each highly stylized, dramatically lit, and carefully retouched. This picture of Autrey, however, is frontally lit with harsh floodlights, the portraits themselves are haphazardly arranged, supported by an assortment of columns and props. This picture is obviously not meant to "represent" Autrey in the same manner as the other portraits. It serves rather as record, as some spur-of-the-moment snapshot of a man and his work.

Paul Hesse's *Marlene Dietrich*, c. 1950, is an altogether different arrangement of pictures. Dietrich lounges on an emerald green settee in a strapless white gown and pale pink full-length gloves, a long cigarette holder in her hand. Behind her, five black and white prints, identically framed in white plaster molding, hang on a false studio wall, the edges of which are visible and ragged. A fragment of green shag carpeting lies carelessly on the floor. The black and white portraits, photographs by Hurrell and others, all recall a Dietrich from an earlier era. The image, if cropped as obviously intended, depicts *both* the woman and the legend. The full image reveals instead the struggle for perfection within the confines of artifice.

[**DRESS UP**] Wardrobe and makeup add as much to characterization as the actors themselves, both on and off the screen. Photographing celebrities in costume produces a sense of cinematic narrative that portraiture otherwise lacks. Ted Allan's *Eleanor Powell, "Broadway Melody of 1936,"* 1936, shows a smiling Powell seated at a piano, handing a top hat to herself in miniature dressed in a tight-fitting tuxedo. Two other miniature "Powells" complete this composite image of a Broadway performance. Powell, in both the real and the imagined space of entertainment, simultaneously directs and performs to/for her own representation. John Baldessari's *Two Dwarfs*, 1990, reverses this shift of scale by pairing an image of a dwarf, a familiar player in vaudeville, with an image of a young boy in tux, black tie, and cane, performing for what is probably an adult audience. Man as little boy, boy as little man, the pairing of diminutive characters renders them subject to further control by the viewer. Laurie Simmons's *English Lady*, 1987, shows a ventriloquist's doll—a woman or a little girl—with bright red coat and oversized hands, seated in an upper-class but unadorned interior, smiling and gazing dreamily out of the frame. Costumed and waiting, she is the perfect cipher, able to be whatever the viewer wants her to be. In Alice Springs's *My Husband (Monte Carlo)*, 1987, Helmut Newton sits, legs crossed, on a sunlit outdoor patio, casually dressed in cut-off shorts, loose shirt, and a wide-brimmed straw hat. On his feet, however, are a pair of woman's open-toed, sling-back, high-heeled shoes. Newton acknowledges no incongruity and not only reflects an ease in such playful theatrics but manipulates the edge between the expected and the unexpected, and between the male and the female, found in his own photographs. And Paul Jasmin's *Kathy*, 1991, reveals an ease in undress rarely seen in public. Kathy applies makeup to her already made-up face in a gesture of defiant nonchalance. She embodies a carefree and privileged sexuality, in many ways no different from the unapproachable seductiveness of Harlow or the iciness of Crawford.

The grotesque is an identification of our darker selves, of the violent and primordial. John Boskovich's *Self-portrait*, 1986-87, pairs an image from the film *The Creature From the Black Lagoon*, (1954), with a text panel from an e.e. cummings poem. The creature emerges from a dark field—water or void—into the bright light of the print. Seen as a self-portrait, it proposes both enlightenment and danger. In a more humorous manner, Angus McBean's *Woman's Head under Chair*, c. 1940, is a surreal and disturbing image of domestic violence. The "decapitated" head, without the blood and gore, of a beautifully coiffured and made-up woman sits serenely on a marble floor underneath a wooden kitchen chair. Both images reveal the scenic distance, the cinematic space, of the horrific, fascinating in its celebration of degradation and surprising for its lack, or for the viewer's lack, of actual revulsion.

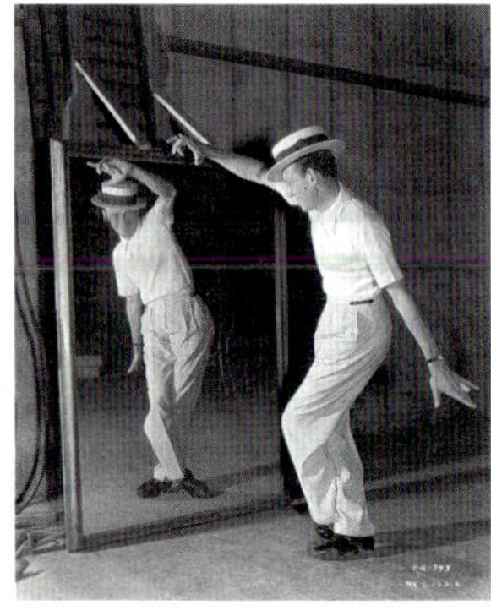

Fred Astaire, Dancing, n.d.

[**MIRRORS**] How we know ourselves and how we know each other occur in quite different ways. While we may recognize another through direct contact or through various pictorial media, to a great extent that recognition, at least visually, is frontal and exterior. Knowing oneself, in contrast, is both an interior and a reflective activity. We learn to recognize our exterior selves by looking both at mirrors and at photographs. These two image-types contradict each other—one a reversal of the other—and place the act of knowing and seeing into a series of displacements. More often than not, the photograph is the unfamiliar image; the mirror functions as the usual means of self-identification. Michael Glass and Nancy Barton's *Untitled* (from the show *Butter Wouldn't Melt in My Mouth)*, 1990, depicts a series of (self-) portraits, images of Michael gazing into a small pool of water. Reflected in the mirror-like surface, however, are images of '40s and '50s Hollywood stars—Marlene Dietrich, Langston Hughes, Bessie Smith. The transference of identification, from self to other, suggests both a lack and a longing. Not only are images of the other more familiar, they can become more desirable than one's own self-identity. Theresa Pendlebury's *Untitled ("An American in Paris")*, 1988, is a photograph of a scene from the movie of the same name mounted on a painter's oval palette. Gene Kelly is seen from behind obliterating a conté crayon self-portrait. The drawing is in full view, the mirror Kelly presumably used for reference is out of sight. The portrait, of course, was not really drawn by Kelly but by a stand-in sketch artist. Further, the portrait is one of Kelly as the character in the film, not Kelly himself. Who and what is depicted, or in this case doubly depicted, becomes a complicated negotiation between actor and role, film and video, painting and photography. In a similar manner, the portrait of *Fred Astaire, Dancing*, n.d., taken by an unidentified photographer, shows a youthful Astaire practicing by himself in front of a mirror on a sound stage. Astaire not only sees himself in character and poses to that effect; he also knows he is being watched by the camera and acknowledges its presence through the theatricality of his actions.

[**NAMES**] Actors' names are a matter of publicity and as such are as much images as the characters they play. Larry Johnson, in *Untitled (Movie Stars on Clouds)*, 1983, surprints the names of stars who have died in tragic or mysterious circumstances—James Dean, Montgomery Clift, Clark Gable, Sal Mineo, Marilyn Monroe, and Natalie Wood—over photographs of white clouds and blue skies. Each name stimulates a memory, each memory a story. Questions arise: Why Gable? Where is Jayne Mansfield? The grouping creates a cast of characters in a tragic and surreal movie, combining narratives from many different films into one. Alexis Smith's *Your Name Here*, 1975, is a standard canvas and wood director's chair with the name *Alexis Smith* printed on the backrest. Smith purchased the chair from a mail order company whose advertising included a photograph of the chair with the words "Your Name Here" stenciled on the canvas. She took the advertisement's implied promise of celebrity, and her name, itself an assumed identifier *and* a famous actress's name—Alexis Smith, the sophisticated leading lady of the '40s and '50s—and made them one. The act of reading oneself through another, in this case through an identical difference, jams recognition beyond all singularity. William Mortensen's *Jean Harlow*, 1927, contains both her face and her name. Harlow looks dreamily to our left, the name "Jean" rendered in the background over her shoulder, captioning and contextualizing the image. We see Harlow; we read Harlow. In Frank Powolny's *Tony Perkins*, c. 1960, Perkins sits before a white seamless, holding his hand in front of his face, hiding from the camera. A black and white head shot, twice lifesize, stands propped up to his left. And above, in watery light blue paint, the word "Tony" is rendered with the short blasts of a water pistol, left lying on the ground. Did Tony write his name as a means of self-identification, or is it an inscription of the photographer? Why is Tony hiding? Which face, the real or the photograph, is to be recognized? Tony Perkins, in person and in character (Norman Bates, et al.), understands the game that Madonna plays so well, that of simultaneously revealing and concealing identity as a means of both protection and seduction.

[**WHO AM I? WHO AM I?**] Self-identity, a cultural, psychological, and perhaps biological problem, is further complicated by the endless stream of images we confront daily. Photographic and cinematic images, whether found in advertising, film/television, or family albums, provide models of being and behavior. That some groups historically have been subject to depiction by others—women by men, the Third World by the West, non-whites by whites, etc.—is a further complication, both because of the misquotation or misrepresentation of one by the other and because of the scarcity of counter-representations. Thus, self-identity often is a matter of playing with, or trying on, other identities. One reads, and misreads, not only the individual but the characteristics that that individual has assumed. Philippe Halsman's *Jean Simmons, Laughing* and *Jean Simmons, Crying*, both 1950, seem at first to be simple illustrations of basic character acting. Simmons, in makeup and wig, plays to the camera with both a melodramatic sadness and an almost idiotic gleefulness. But something is very wrong; the wig is badly attached and unstyled, the tears smeared and oily, the light too hot, and Simmons seems to be wearing, or is wrapped in, some kind of shroud or sheet. The purpose of the pictures is also unclear; what is the context? Certainly they are not to be used for any kind of public display. Constructed with such obvious artifice, they lose their ability to depict emotion convincingly or to represent Simmons.

Similarly artificial, head shots of aspiring actors attempt to provide information to directors and casting agents about the various personalities or characters those actors can "be." Yet each image reveals, in a rather painful way, the actor's individual idiosyncrasies and insecurities and documents both the need for recognition and the trapping of ambition. David and Tim Tattu's *Self-portraits*, 1992, are two matted and framed 10 x 8 slicks of the actresses Bobbe Hendricks and Sigal Diamant, sent to David and Tim in an ordinary casting call. In comparing the two pictures, one sees Bobbe as the more direct, the more strident, the stronger; Sigal is more exotic, more reserved, more inviting. In this exercise of self-picturing, David has chosen the headshot of

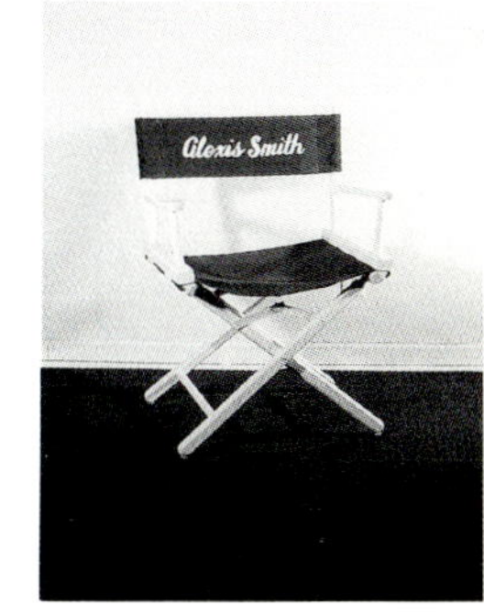

ALEXIS SMITH
Your Name Here, 1975

Bobbe to represent himself, to become his surrogate headshot. Tim has chosen that of Sigal to represent himself. No matter the differences in age, gender, or ethnic background, both brothers claim affinities to, and recognition of, themselves and each other in these two images. We see and understand David through Bobbe and Tim through Sigal. Both David and Tim also see these two women as sisters, bonded by the codes of this shared category of representation.

Andy Warhol (the creator and publisher of *Interview* magazine, socialite and social misfit, portraitist of the "beautiful people") probably understood the trappings of renown better than most. In many ways his work and his industry defined the current terms of fame and celebrity. Through his masquerade of idiosyncrasies and the deadpan images of his self-portraits, Warhol revealed he was painfully aware of the personal toll such attention takes. In his *Untitled (self-portrait)*, 1963-64, we see that already familiar face, hidden behind sunglasses and hand, questioning by its very procedure the desire to look at, by means of this most unmanipulated of cameras, the self. Warhol, through the use of these technically limited photographic materials—the photo booth, the Polaroid, the Super-8 left running on its tripod—and their subsequent translation into the graphic rendering of silkscreen, captured a people painfully in love with themselves and with the possibility and promise of fame. A portrait by Warhol became the ultimate ticket to stardom, resulting in an attention both indiscriminate and accusatory, no matter if its production was self-imposed or "journalistically" apprehended.

[*NATIONAL VELVETEEN*] Richard Hawkins's *Bruce/People*, 1991, uses as a "frame" the advertising supplement photographed by Bruce Weber for Calvin Klein and inserted into the October 1991 issue of *Vanity Fair*. In it, or on it, are taped cut-out pictures from an issue of *People* magazine from around the same time. Images of Jeffrey Dahmer, the then accused and now convicted serial killer of young boys, and photographs from Liz Taylor's marriage to Larry Fortensky, collide with or imitate the images of well-toned models, both clothed and not. This fascination with youth, as acted out by Dahmer and Taylor, reframes the Klein supplement, revealing duplicitous aspects of the seduction and fetishization of an ideal physical type. Kathe Burkhart's *Kathe Burkhart by Elizabeth Taylor*, 1989, is one of a number of works collectively entitled *The Liz Taylor Series*, all of which are simple and deadpan renderings in acrylic on paper of Taylor garnered from magazine publicity photos or film stills. The text for *Kathe Burkhart by Elizabeth Taylor* is from an interview of Taylor in the November, 1965, issue of *The Ladies Home Journal*. In it, Taylor discusses herself and her relationship with fame: "... I am disgusted by the amount of myth that now is accepted as fact. The public me, the one named Elizabeth Taylor, has become a fabrication—a bunch of drivel—and I find her slightly revolting. But I am afraid that, in talking about my life now, there is a point of privacy beyond which I simply cannot go." Burkhart, by assuming, or subsuming, Taylor's identity (by fabricating a scenario in which Taylor, by means of the title, presumes to be discussing Burkhart rather than herself), has ultimately co-opted both Taylor's notoriety and the credibility it gives her words, as well as her self-reflections, her thoughts, her emotions—an identification through a mirror-like reversal—whereby Burkhart, and the viewer, rather than the star, becomes the ultimate reference. Finally, David Robbins's *And*, 1991, similarly manipulates this confused self-identification of authorship. The framed book jackets, front and back, of Lester David and Jhan Robbins's publication of *Richard and Elizabeth* propose, through a coincidence of names, a relationship of Robbins to the production of the book, and ultimately to Richard and Elizabeth themselves. David and Robbins are both personality journalists who feed off the industry of celebrity. David Robbins also utilizes the conventions and excesses of the film and television industry in his work and writing. This rummaging by Robbins of the authors David and Robbins, David and Robbins's of Richard and Elizabeth, and ultimately David Robbins's of Richard and Elizabeth produces a complex triangle of paired identities, each dialectically related to and dependent upon the others for meaning.

[**FIN**] The mediated relationship between the famous and the audience extends into all fields of production; the model of Hollywood is only its most obvious and transparent example. Celebrities exist in sports, politics, music, and in the art world. It is as impossible to disconnect Warhol from Marilyn or, for that matter, Kennedy from Marilyn as it is to disconnect ourselves from her. For those constantly in front of the camera, there exists a break between the image and reality, a tension, described by Stewart Ewen, "between self as subject and self as object [that] places these people—perhaps above all others—in the position of being perpetual spectators of themselves, taking pleasure or pain from the wrinkle-free surfaces of their own hard shells." [12] As audience, we identify, or not, with these images, a condition of being connected in some way to these representations and painfully cut off from our own experiences. We mine the gestures, the nuances, the fragments of personality for our own use. Individually and culturally, we learn by imitation and in that learning we create a void in our selves. Photography further allows us to recognize a life never experienced in our daily circumstances, a familiarity of cinematic time, frozen, cut off from the present, dredged up from collective memories. It is the very circumstance of photographic and cinematic identification that most fully presses our selves against that lens of recognition, allowing us either to peer through or to hide behind its gaze.

NOTES

[1] Gore Vidal, *Screening History,* (Cambridge, MA: Harvard University Press, 1992): 6.

[2] Leo Braudy, *The Frenzy of Renown: Fame and its History* (New York and Oxford: Oxford University Press, 1986): 5.

[3] See Roland Barthes, "To Signify," in *Camera Lucida: Reflections on Photography*, translated by Richard Howard (New York: Hill and Wang, 1981): 34. Barthes also writes: "The portrait-photograph is a closed field of forces. Four image-repertoires intersect here, oppose and distort each other. In front of the lens, I am at the same time: the one I think I am, the one I want others to think I am, the one the photographer thinks I am, and the one he makes use of to exhibit his art. In other words, a strange action: I do not stop imitating myself, and because of this, each time I am (or let myself be) photographed, I invariably suffer from a sensation of inauthenticity, sometimes of imposture. ... In terms of image-repertoire, the Photograph (the one I *intend*) presents that very subtle moment when, to tell the truth, I am neither subject nor object but a subject who feels he is becoming an object." ibid.: 13-14.

[4] Victor Burgin discusses this difference between public and private by citing Barthes's terms, *studium* and *punctum* as being the "obvious and obtuse" meanings generated by the viewer. See Burgin, "Re-reading *Camera Lucida*," in *The End of Art Theory* (Atlantic Highlands, NJ: Humanities Press International, 1986): 76-79.

[5] Daniel J. Boorstin, "From Hero to Celebrity: The Human Pseudo-Event" in *The Image: A Guide to Pseudo-Events in America* (New York: Atheneum, 1961): 59.

[6] Richard deCordova, "The Emergence of the Star System in America," in *Stardom, Industry of Desire*, edited by Christine Gledhill (London and New York: Routledge, 1991): 24.

[7] Ibid.: 25. deCordova adds: "The star is characterized by a fairly thoroughgoing articulation of the paradigm professional life/personal life. With the emergence of the star, the question of the player's existence outside his/her work in films entered discourse." 26.

[8] For purposes of clarity, I will allow the term "actor" to denote both actress and actor, the term actress functioning as an unnecessary diminution of the individual, the practice, and the profession.

[9] See Michel Foucault, "Las Meninas," in *The Order of Things* (New York: Vintage Books Edition, Random House, Inc., 1970): 3.

[10] Boorstin, op. cit.: 63.

[11] Gilles Deleuze, "The Powers of the False," in *Cinema 2: The Time Image*, translated by Hugh Tomlinson and Robert Galeta (Minneapolis: University of Minnesota Press, 1989): 131.

[12] Stewart Ewen, "The Dream of Wholeness," in *All Consuming Images: The Politics of Style in Contemporary Culture* (New York: Basic Books, Inc., 1988): 89.

Fame and the Frame

BY ANNE FRIEDBERG

ONE OF THE KEY PLEASURES of cinema spectatorship is the confusing blur of self and other, the projective fantasy of identification with a fictive screen world and its inhabitants. But in Los Angeles, where celebrity merges with the everyday, this frame of representation is gone. Madonna sits in the back of my neighborhood cafe, Michael Douglas stands next to me waiting for his table at a restaurant on La Brea Avenue. Jody Foster soaks nude alongside me in the mineral bath at the Korean spa. While this lack of frame would seem, at first, to be a satisfying inclusion in the fictive and fantasmatic realm, it soon becomes disturbing—a transgression of important boundaries. We need to have the frame implied in order to maintain physical and psychic distance, to reassure us of our difference and to allow us to fantasize our similarity. Our identities are challenged by proximity to this imaginary celestial order.

Two weeks before I moved to Los Angeles I was in a brutal automobile crash—a traumatic form of epistemological break. In a sudden mangle of glass and steel, I went through the windshield. It was as if I had to go through that glass in order to live in Los Angeles. Normally, the windshield acts as a corrective lens framing the world as it reels by and as a transparent protective skin that keeps us from entering the frame. Once I found myself on the other side, inside *the frame, reality and fantasy slid into each other in a peculiarly confusing blur.*

The frame of the photograph, like the frame of the screen, offers a window onto an absent, mystified world. The virtual gaze of photography supplants, in Roland Barthes's terms, the "here-now" with the "having-been-there." [1] The viewer re-captures the gaze of the photographer, but in virtual fashion; the pleasure is being both *there* and *not there*, a split position of virtual closeness and real distance. Hollywood portrait photography relies on this paradox. A photo of a film star can provide a privileged view of celebrity, but in a different frame, off-screen. Artists who take on a critical or analytic relation to this style of portraiture and its subjects often address the reformulated referentiality that this re-framing implies. Cindy Sherman's *Untitled Film Stills*, for example, follow the codes of Hollywood still portraiture, that of a star caught in the frame of the everyday. In Sherman's work, the viewer recognizes not the celebrity but the codes of celebrity. Recognition follows a tacit formal contract; the frame itself can feign fame.

So there I was in critical condition with a serious head injury until, as mysterious as it still seems, I returned from comatose near-death to what could only be described as near-life in L.A. I was in post-traumatic shock, but also in a form of culture shock. Shards of glass kept coming out of my skin, rising to the surface like diamonds that couldn't be digested by the flesh. There was too much sunshine, everything was too clean, colors were too bright. I kept trying to see Los Angeles as if it were Hollywood in black and white. I recuperated at my partner's family home, one of those capacious Hancock Park houses surrounded by palm trees but designed to look like a Tudor cottage in the Cotswolds. On the other side of the backyard hedge, I was told, was the site of the house from Sunset Boulevard, *that "great big white elephant of a place" with its pool where Mabel Normand and John Gilbert, Wilma Banky, and Rod LaRocque "must have swum ten thousand midnights ago."* Sunset Boulevard *had always been, for me, the* Urtext *of Hollywood celebrity, chronicling how the fragile veneer of Norma Desmond's "celluloid self" rotted and sagged with time. Even though I knew that the house in the film wasn't actually on Sunset Boulevard and was, rather, a Getty-owned mansion that Billy Wilder rented for the film with the promise of building a pool; and even though I knew the house was torn down in the 1960s, this knowledge did little to alter the cinematic space eidetically etched in my memory. The image of its black and white swimming pool kept floating in my imagination in the intangible way of all movie images. The back hedge of the house in* Sunset Boulevard *was now a place where the dog barked at night as if he were calling across the lawns to ghosts that swam there thousands of nights before.* Sunset Boulevard *was just as far and just as close as it had ever been.*

GLORIA SWANSON
Sunset Boulevard, 1949

RE: COGNITION

In a 1935 essay, "The Scoptophilic Instinct and Identification," Otto Fenichel described the unconscious components of visual scrutiny: "In the unconscious, *to look at an object* may mean various things, the most noteworthy of which are as follows: *to devour the object looked at*, *to grow like it* (be forced to imitate it) *or, conversely, to force it to grow like oneself.*" [2] (my emphasis)

The relation between viewing and devouring is consistent with acquisitive forms of incorporation in a consumer economy where desires are elaborated in a system of selling and consumption dependent on the relation between *looking* and *buying* and the indirect desire to possess or incorporate through the eye.

"To grow like it" or "to force it to grow like oneself" are the two directions of identification: introjective (incorporating the other into self) and projective (projecting self onto other). Jacques Lacan described the construction of identity as an intersubjective process based in the misrecognition of an external *other*, a specular relation he vividly depicted as a *mirror phase*. [3] Film theorists have frequently drawn upon this model to explain the interaction between the cinema spectator and the "imaginary signifier" of film. The film star has a complex function in this regard. The screen is not a mirror. As Christian Metz points out, there is one thing that is never reflected in it—the spectator's body. [4]

In the cinema, the spectator does not identify with his or her own image. The pleasure offered is precisely this denial: the star's body is *not* the spectator's body, not his, not hers. Hence, the cinema spectator may enjoy cross-gendered identification, a kind of psychic transvestism based in the play of misrecognition. In addition, as countless films with anthropomorphic but non-human stars attest, any body—monster, animal, or robot from

Dracula and Frankenstein to Lassie and Benji to Yoda and R2D2—offers an opportunity for identificatory investment, a possible suit for the substitution/misrecognition of self.

And yet the conventions of cinematic representation—scenes cut into establishing shots, medium shots, close-ups—enforce a metonymy of the body: a face, a hand, a leg; all cut up. The film star becomes recognizable and familiar, as just such part-objects transformed into commodities: Garbo's face, Grable's legs, Bacall's voice. Celebrity photographs function as a sort of double fetish: the star is already a fetish object [5] and, once captured in the frame, the photograph itself becomes a fetish of the second order, entering circulation in a market with the exchange value of capital.

LOS ANGELES AS METAPHOR FOR LOSS OF THE FRAME

Our gaze at the screen is a one-way voyeurism, where we are unseen. Like the windshield, the frame has a protective function. To be looked at by a celebrity is a reversal of the conventions of this gaze; the frame insures that this violation will not occur. And as the list of celebrities from John Lennon to Jody Foster demonstrates, if the protective shield fails, one can pay a perilous price for life in the tabloid panopticon, the fishbowl of fame. As Andy Warhol put it: "If I weren't famous, I wouldn't have been shot for being Andy Warhol." [6]

In an age of simulation where signs of the real substitute for the real itself, the virtual pleasure of being inside the frame is marketed as a commodity. Hollywood Boulevard is lined with stores where you can have your photo taken standing next to a life-sized photo cutout of Marilyn Monroe, James Dean, or Ronald Reagan. In the souvenir photograph, it looks as if the long-dead (or near-dead) cardboard star is alive and smiling, right next to you. For Warhol, the erasure of the edges of the frame became a confirming condition of fame. "A good reason to be famous," he wrote in *The Philosophy of Andy Warhol*, "is so that you can read all the big magazines and know everyone in the stories. Page after page it's just all people that you've met." [7]

Studio tours sell the experience of traveling into recognizable cinematic spaces as if entering the diegetic world of the film. A recent Hollywood joke toys with the boundaries between such commodified forays into fictional worlds and life in the "real" world. If you pay a pricey admission at the Universal Studio Tours, the joke goes, you can brave the heat and danger of a raging fire in *Backdraft*, see people shot at in cars in *Miami Vice*, and experience a 7.1 temblor in *Earthquake*. Or you can live in Los Angeles and get these sensations for free.

WHAT IS FAMILIAR?
WHAT IS RECOGNIZABLE?

At the end of Sunset Boulevard, *Norma Desmond descends the grand staircase of her mansion while the press cameras are rolling. Walking toward a camera in near psychotic glee, she stretches her arms outward and thanks "all those wonderful people out there in the dark." The aging star, Gloria Swanson, in loosely fictional drag as the aging star Norma Desmond, approaches that invisible windshield, claws at the edges of an imaginary signi-*

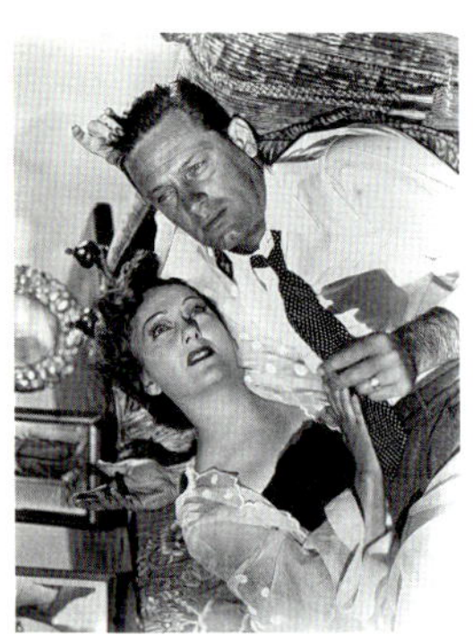

Sunset Boulevard, 1949

fier that traps her on one side of a wide and mystic hedge. She is unable to break through the frame, yet her image will remain in the memories of spectators ten thousand midnights hence.

The cinema spectator, seated in the darkened theater and caught up in this imaginary world, is a psychic repository for fictional characters and their narratives. The celebrity photograph, seen in the full light of a gallery or a magazine page, is representation at one remove. The viewer recognizes a familiar and antecedent signifier—an actor from that movie, a performer from that video, a star from that TV show. The photograph serves as a mnemonic clue, jarring memory into a surge of recognition.

As we stand outside the frame, we are both there and not there, simultaneously drawn into the virtual intimacy of the photographer's gaze and kept at bay by our real distance. The frame is that imposing metaphoric hedge separating us from a powerful imaginary realm full of recognizable yet intangible images.

ANNE FRIEDBERG teaches in the Film Studies Program at the University of California at Irvine. Her book, *Window Shopping: Cinema and the Postmodern*, published by the University of California Press, will be available in early 1993.

NOTES

[1] Roland Barthes describes the photograph's virtual record as an "illogical conjunction" of spatial immediacy ("here-now") and temporal anteriority ("having-been there"). See Barthes, "Rhetoric of the Image," in *Image, Music Text*, translated by Stephen Heath (New York: Hill and Wang, 1977): 44-45.

[2] Otto Fenichel, "The Scoptophilic Instinct and Identification," in *Collected Papers of Otto Fenichel, First Series,* (New York: W.W. Norton & Company, Inc., 1953): 373-397.

[3] See Jacques Lacan, "The Mirror Stage as Formative of the Function of the I," in *Ecrits*, translated by Alan Sheridan (New York: Tavistock Publications, W.W. Norton & Company, Inc.,1977): 1-7.

[4] Christian Metz, *The Imaginary Signifier*, translated by Ben Brewster (Bloomington: Indiana University Press, 1982).

[5] In psychoanalytic terminology, fetishism is an object-relation used to disavow the site of sexual difference. To Freud, the discovery of difference is a scenario of the visible where the sight of female genitalia—genitals without a penis—evokes the anxiety of castration for the male. In response to his sight, any form of visual distraction or disguise becomes an eroticized displacement, a fetish. A fetishist object-relation is that of acknowledgment and disavowal (of castration) in constant oscillation. [See Sigmund Freud, "Fetishism (1927)," *Collected Papers*, Volume 5, edited by James Strachey (New York: Basic Books, 1959): 198-204.]

Fetishism is more frequently used in its metaphoric capacity, without literal reference to castration. [See Jean Baudrillard, "Fetishism and Ideology: The Semiological Reduction," in *For a Critique of the Political Economy of the Sign*, translated by Charles Levin (St. Louis, MO: Telos Press, 1981).] To Marx, the commodity was also a fetish, its value transformed from a product of labor with a use value to an object in a system of capital with an exchange value. The commodity took on the mystical qualities of a fetish. [See Karl Marx, "The Fetish of the Commodity and its Secret," in *Capital*.] The film star fits these models exactly. As a commodity fetish, the film star is an object with a value beyond its use, and in psychological terms, the star is simultaneously recognized (acknowledged) as other and misrecognized (disavowed) as self.

[6] Andy Warhol, *The Philosophy of Andy Warhol (From A to B and Back Again),* (New York: Harcourt Brace Jovanovich, 1975): 78.

[7] Ibid.

SAVING FACE(s)
or: I con, you con, we all con those icons

BY MICHAEL LASSELL

"No," says the harried editor-in-chief, dismissing the name of a well-known celebrity photographer with the flick of a wrist, "he only shoots icons."

"Well," says the photo editor, having run out of names from the short list (the same names he runs out of every month at this time—two days before the magazine is supposed to be at the printer in Minneapolis), "tell him to make her an icon."

"Who the hell cares about David Cassidy, anyway?" asks the assistant editor in charge of musical artists (a champion of reggae/rap groups of the South African townships and hip-hopping neo-psychedelics from Amsterdam—both the country and the Avenue).

"Get Stephen Meisel to shoot it and they'll care," says the senior editor in charge of getting copy onto the music pages each month.

"Because the photograph is so good or because Meisel's name is on it?" inquires the younger man, not quite as ingenuously as he might have a year or two earlier.

"Both," snaps the veteran of the fame wars. "Both."

WHAT'S A MAGAZINE PROFESSIONAL TO DO?

Once upon a time you (a) cared about a subject enough to invest time, money, energy, and pages in him, her, it, or them; (b) assigned a writer and photographer you thought would respond to the subject; and (c) turned the result over to the art department for a nifty little layout.

That was then. Now celebrities have lists of photographers they are willing to sit for, and the shutterbugs themselves have agents who don't return phone calls because the clients are booked until Twelfth Night and will be back from the bathing suit shoot in Machu Picchu just long enough for Madonna's birthday party before heading to Paris for the collections, to which they will fly on the Concorde and then be limousined to the Plaza Athenée for the duration.

Oh, and by the way, you can't shoot Madonna in color unless you've got a six-figure retouching budget. Her face is hairy as a boxer's bottom, and in color it shows.

Nowadays in the world of "entertainment" rags, image is all—in more ways than one. Oh, writers are assigned to do stories and interviews, and some of them even achieve a modicum of renown, but without that all-important photo—a New Picture, one that might win the art director an award from other art directors—the article won't even run. And the way you get Madonna, Al Pacino, the Rolling Stones, or even David Hockney to sit still in front of a lens is to entice the would-be subject with a photographic offer he, she, it, or they can't refuse, someone who may be the Hurrell or Penn of the next century, in whose frame the visages of the present gaze into history, posterity, even into immortality. Then, of course, the photographer has got to get the subject to do something he, she, it, or they do/does not particularly want to do, like stripping and diving into a vat of maple syrup in the shadow of Ayres Rock.

Whew. Heady stuff. Or a crock. Depending on where you happen to sit. I have been sitting in various editorial offices in L.A. and New York for ten years or so, and I am not making up any of this. Okay. It's slightly fictionalized, partly to protect myself from future unemployment, partly because the urge to embellish is the hallmark of the contemporary journalist. But I have not strayed too far afield—just ask Annie Leibovitz how much of her editorial magazine work is art and how much is diplomacy, cajoling the sublimely and habitually reluctant into the photogenically and commercially viable ridiculous.

From the very beginning, photographers turned their glass-plate, bellows-focusing, large-format cameras on the famous—writers, at first, royals and politicians, artists and even the occasional Sarah Bernhardt. And it is to these images that we look some 150 years later to glean what spark of life may be captured in black and white (or, in many cases, various tones of sepia). You know, "the eyes are the mirror of the soul," that sort of thing. Mechanical reproduction, of course—and what gadget of the industrial revolution better exemplifies reproduction (in both its significant meanings) than the camera—made images available, widely and cheaply, and in a very real sense rendered the sitters as disposable as their photographs (which is a better reason for refusing to have your picture snapped than any primitive's fear of soul-snatching, most souls having been spirited away long, long ago).

In the age of the motion picture ("truth at 24 frames per second," to wit: 24 nearly identical images per second), photographers who understood the persuasive and seductive power of "painting with light" (a kind of celluloid neo-chiaroscuro) recorded for the ages (and profit, their own and their employers') the faces of the stars who had faces then (cf. Gloria Swanson, *Sunset Boulevard*). People like George Hurrell and Laszlo Willinger were in the service, tellingly, of publicity departments, and were charged—along with hair, makeup, and wardrobe—with creating images, not in the sense of two-dimensional aesthetic artifacts, but in the sense of public personae.

It was the job of the studio photographer to let the public know who Bette Davis, Joan Crawford, and Barbara Stanwyck were, to guide and reinforce this perception, but at all times to differentiate among them: the image of the personality *was* the personality, and the personality was the employers' product. "Strong woman" was not enough. The photographers had to be as specific as their subjects. Thus, Crawford was a strong woman grasping toward the top, Stanwyck the strong woman who could take it like a man, and Davis the strong woman with the vulnerable heart.

Tellingly, there has always been an extremely close relationship between the motion picture studios, which were in the business of making icons, and the magazines that create celebrity by assigning icons a perch in the cultural pecking order. Even the personnel sometimes overlapped. George Hoyningen-Huene, for example, was a well-known Hollywood portraitist as well as a production designer for film. Cecil Beaton, who shot the British aristocracy in a flattering light before being swept away on a tide of adoration for film stars, turned his creativity, too, to fashion and editorial photography as well as stage and film design (not to mention photojournalism).

And in this cozy arrangement, one magazine led the pack: *Vogue*. The *ne plus ultra* of the rag mag biz once ran photographs of socialites as

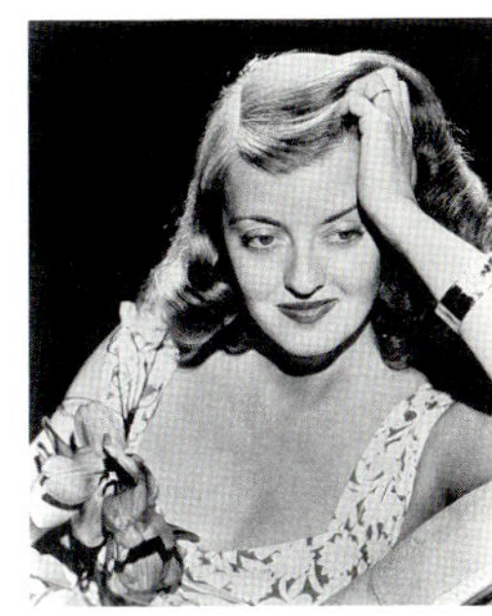

BETTE DAVIS

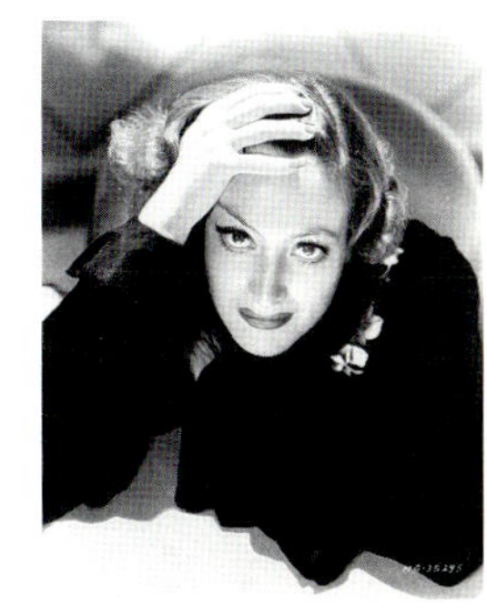

JOAN CRAWFORD

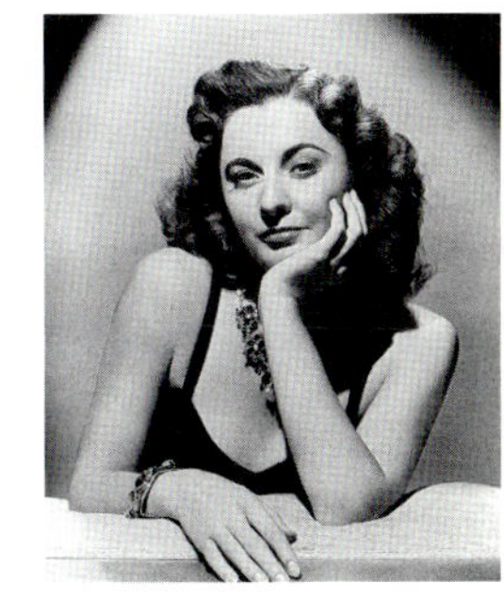

BARBARA STANWYCK

dramatically luminous as any MGM starlet who batted her eyelashes at Louis B. Mayer; but *Vogue* achieved its niche in the history of American culture by offering its pages to collaborative geniuses who could unite clothing (the product), glamour (the means of expression by which clothing becomes fashion, product becomes lifestyle), and the high-toned dialect of fame (the sales pitch by which fashion, by borrowing the credibility widely afforded to aesthetic excellence, becomes passion).

The history of *Vogue*, as its own recent exhibition in the New York Public Library (and coffee-table tome) shows, is the history of celebrity—not only because the magazine ran portraits of the famous (originally such arcane eccentrics as Dorothy Parker, later of nearly anyone momentarily "in vogue"), but because the people at *Vogue* perfected the formula by which fashion and celebrity became virtually interchangeable, the clothes as famous as the models who wore them, the clothes and the models presented as equivalent to the stars whose photos ran alongside them (look at Beaton's loving, lush photographs of Charles James's couture dresses, for example). And in the process, they enlisted every serious talent in the history of the medium, from Steichen and Man Ray to Horst, Avedon, Penn, and both Newtons (Arnold and Helmut). As times grew grim, they added visionary news photography, often by the same fashion and celebrity photographers.

Most extraordinary of all, perhaps—and germane to this show—is the relationship, both in the pages of *Vogue* and its numerous competitors, imitators, and descendants, as well as in movie-studio publicity portraiture, between commercial photography and art (a relationship that has taken some bizarre turns of late). If Beaton's photos of Charles James's dresses were fashion photographs, they were also homages to Lartigue (whose art status derives from the kind of journalistic eye that now exists only outside the world of commercial journalism). They were, additionally, elaborations of John Singer Sargent's group portraits of the *haute monde*, paintings that now hang proudly in the best art museums of the world. Beaton's fashion shots in the twenties and thirties were quoting the work of Dali, Cocteau, De Chirico, and Tanguy, for example, who would find later expression in Hollywood films of the forties and fifties (the abstract, surrealistic sets in the dance sequences of *Oklahoma* and *An American in Paris*, for example).

Lately the once-distinct worlds of fine art and commercial, or popular, art have collided, if not merged. Never really as separate as some artists, critics, and chroniclers would have us believe, they have frequently become identical. Editorial portrait and fashion photographers like Matthew Rolston, Greg Gorman, and the omnipresent Herb Ritts, among others, produce "art book" compendiums of their work. Bruce Weber is included in the 1987 Whitney Biennial. The prestigious photo journal *Aperture* devotes an issue to the art of fashion photography, and Annie Leibovitz is offered a career retrospective that travels the golden road from the National Gallery of Art in Washington, D.C., to the International Center for Photography in New York City.

Always relevant to discussions of this sort, of course, is the late Andy Warhol, an artist who not only used photography in his work but who also reveled in celebrity, incorporating media icons—Marilyn Monroe, Elizabeth Taylor, Jackie Kennedy Onassis, Mao Tse-tung—into his silkscreen paintings. Warhol's magazine *Interview* was a forum in which the celebrated could wallow in the fact of their celebrity, right-wing dictators from Middle Eastern and Central American totalitarian countries chatting amiably with the latest vacuous supermodel or drugged-out rock 'n' roll freak. "Andy Warhol," says hip scenester Fran Lebowitz, a latter-day Dorothy Parker, "made fame famous."

This interplay of movies and magazines, of art and media, has become, of course, rich material from which a whole new generation of the most serious artists—painters, photographers, conceptualists—takes its energy. Robert Heinecken manipulates the ways in which advertising images manipulate and subvert perception, as well as the ways in which the abutting images in magazines inform one another. Cindy Sherman, plucking images from films, memories of films, and fantasies of films, manipulates the way she is seen from one obsessive self-portrait to the next and by so doing calls into question not only the ways in which femininity is packaged and sold, but the ways in which identity itself is now a question of one's relationship to media images. In an even more sophisticated realm, John Baldessari, a shrewd critic of the uses of imagery and a man of great, dry wit, manipulates images from film, television, and magazines, creating whole new vectors of perception in the juxtaposition of images, their size, and shape.

But Heinecken, Sherman, and Baldessari, for all their insightful work, are still working with the same images we see in editorial portraits, advertising, fashion photography, in music videos, films, and TV series. The distinction between "photographers" and "artists" (including some, but not all, photographers) is not their say-so, or number of their books, or the amount of money their pictures fetch in galleries or major magazine markets, but the ways they manipulate these basic narrative images, as if they were simply colors on a palette, in order to manipulate viewers into critical flights of imagination beyond the celebrity/image/sales-gimmick loop.

What we in the magazine business have both created and inherited is the notion that image is all… not necessarily the public persona of an individual, but the appearance of a public persona that is visited upon an individual by an excellent photograph. We have come to publish and even commission the image of an image, and this is a telling distinction.

"He takes the same picture every time," said my editor-in-chief one day about a well-known L.A. photographer, which she meant as a put-down of some kind but which, in fact, seems exactly the point. The photograph is no longer about the subject at all but about (a) the photograph, (b) the photographer, and (c) the business. It is glamour (and it is always glamour of one sort or another) no longer in the service of fantasy, but glamour in the service of itself: it is the facade of facade, the record of a construct (in the same manner that a photograph of an installation or a performance comes to stand for, and be sold perpetually in lieu of, the transient event itself), and this is one of the reasons today's celebrities seem indistinguishable one from the other. The enormously expensive shoots of the most in-demand f-stoppers are calculated to render the sitter moot. And so all celebrity photographs these days are photographs of celebrity itself, i.e. "image advertising," offering not a product, not even a talented property, but a hieroglyph for the notion of notoriety. And if the photograph is the window to anyone's soul these days, it is the photographer's.

Consequently, the recent "all-Bruce Weber" issue of *Interview* magazine (February 1992) may be the quintessential celebrity magazine of our era, since the subjects of the photographs are not only largely indistinguishable one from the other (their icon potential having eclipsed their identities), but the editorial photographs are themselves indistinguishable from the advertisements on facing and interlacing pages. This is no accident, of course, since Weber, whose fame derives primarily from his underwear and Obsession advertising photos for Calvin Klein, is in large measure responsible for the trend in image advertising, in which it is not the product but the glamorous (i.e. sexual) evocation of the advertising process itself that is on sale.

Add to this confusion the now-courant mania among art directors for "narrative" in multi-spread layouts, in which the photographs are made to tell some kind of story, even though the photographer has had no such intention (more often the photographers, being hipper than next year's disco diva, are in on the process). The same is going on in advertising, of course, where Benetton has appropriated images of plague, social upheaval, and natural disaster to peddle its pedal-pushers and puddle-jumpers. The advertising page, like the editorial page, becomes a two-dimensional surface in the same way that an abstract painting does: splotch equals splotch equals whatever you want it to equal.

Now, this all sounds terribly pejorative, but that ain't necessarily so. It is, however, a phenomenon. Weber and his colleagues, imitators, and even some of his detractors, have created a world in which ambiguity has replaced possibility, even in the area of sexuality (as in "sex sells"—and it does). If everything—even the man dying of AIDS in his family's arms—is subject to the voyeuristic gaze of the photographer/art director/ad man's hardcore push, then everything becomes eroticized, including the act of buying and selling.

Because our whole top crop of celebrity photographers overemphasizes the surface of their pictures (developing unique finishes, textures, lighting methods), we create a universe in which the ante continues to be upped on the erotic nature of the artifact itself, while, in effect, neutering the subject, whether it is Richard Gere, Axl Rose, Cindy Crawford, or Magic Johnson. Hollywood hey-day portraits are artificial, too, and entice with sometimes far-from-subtle innuendo ("You, too, might possess this woman or man"), but the artifice is in the subject, not the artifact.

Nowadays photographs are manipulated not only by getting the subject into some bizarre situation, but by actually retouching—by hand and by computer. This change is also a matter of degree and intention rather than of fact. Studio portraits were, of course, retouched to the stratosphere—by hand. Herb Ritts, whose photos seem to have the sun-baked quality of a shot snapped casually against a blazing adobe background, often submits photos to magazines with overlays that look like complex weather charts full of elaborate instructions. These are offered not necessarily to improve the appearance of his sitters (although he does do this) but to create a "more perfect" picture—removing shadows, textures, anything that spoils the surface of the experience.

Sometimes, of course, this makes for memorable imagery, or at least for pictures that call broad social issues into question. When Ritts poses Pee-wee Herman on a horse in full (albeit faux) cowboy regalia, he not only recalls Western kitsch of the kind Pee-wee himself evokes in his own aesthetic, the photographer also calls into question the whole notion of masculinity, contemporary and historical. And when Whoopi Goldberg submerges herself in a tub of milk for Annie Leibovitz, the overtones are more American (and Hollywood) racism than Cleopatra. But do Pee-wee and Whoopi escape being the brunts of these pictures as well as their subjects?

Imposition of the photographer's vision on subject matter (while reducing the integrity of the subject) is dangerous. It is this attitude that, for example, has raised charges of racism by gay black men against the late Robert Mapplethorpe, who no doubt believed himself to be reveling in a cloud of erotic power in his now-infamous photos, particularly those of African-American male nudes—or at least selected body parts. However, by imposing his own sexuality onto his models, Mapplethorpe may well have depersonalized them, reducing the men in his pictures to well-lit stereotypes, luminous organs in the stead of individuals. Often, content expands beyond intention.

As an editor, I have constantly come up against "strong pictures" that have nothing whatever to do with the subject or with the content of stories the photos are meant to illustrate. It is a best-of-worlds scenario when subject, photo, and article/interview are of a piece—or when they abut one another to create interesting tensions. More often the story (often as manipulated by publicists and others as the photo) must be amended to work with the photograph rather than the other way around. This is partly because photography is now more expensive (sometimes many thousands of dollars per day in expenses alone) and more difficult to arrange, but also because we live in a world that communicates much more directly visually than linguistically.

Part of what I am saying (and seeing in the course of my work) is that magazines are simply becoming agents of a widely credited alteration in perception: the increasing supremacy of communication by image rather than word. And this catering to computer facility (manual dexterity as well as "literacy") and to the cutting speed of a 30-second TV commercial spot not only reinforces the process, it also midwifes in stop-frame time this new relationship between object and its representation, in which the object ceases to exist at all.

Magazines are not simply in the business of running pictures of celebrities these days but in running a "Herb Ritts Madonna," which is neither Madonna herself nor Madonna's public persona (however much Ritts may have helped shape it) but an entity all itself, which younger photographers will ape for its style rather than its content. Herb Ritts's pictures of Madonna are not only part of who she is perceived to be but of who she is.

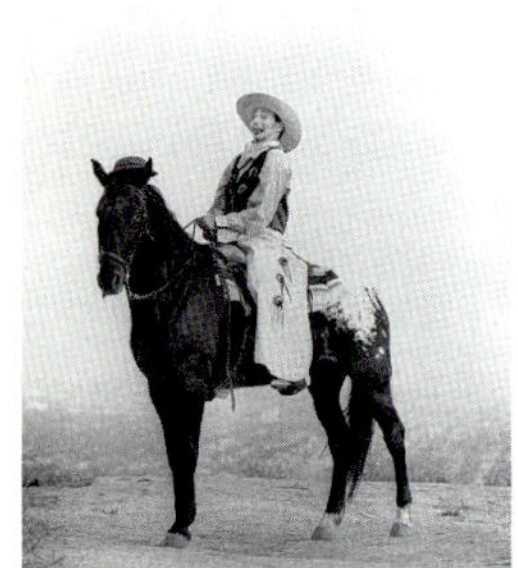

HERB RITTS
Pee-wee Herman, 1987

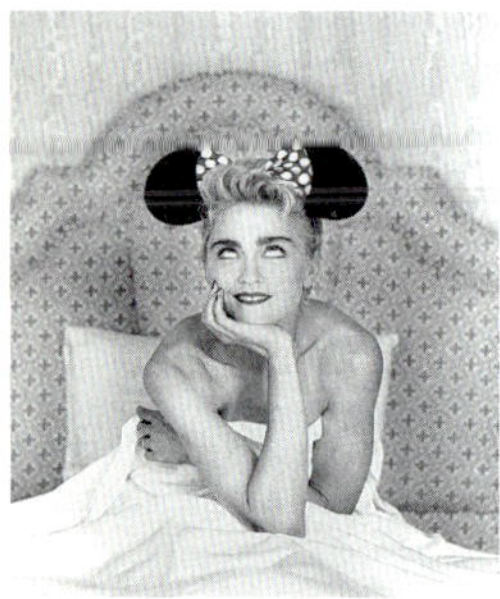

HERB RITTS
Madonna, Tokyo, 1987

The danger, as I see it, is not that we are becoming more visual than literary but that individual images are ceasing to have meaning. Music videos, which more than anything shape the speed of modern perception (since longer film formats follow their lead), are notable more for the incongruity, the surreality of their images, than for the speed at which they race by. And, if "Man dying of AIDS" comes to signify "Benetton sweaters," we are voluntarily sacrificing the image as a means of communication, and with it the power of logic and the joy of the surreptitiously or serendipitously illogical, magical, mystical, or supernatural.

This is not by any means to suggest that we do not live in surreal times. But words are symbols related to meaning. Images, which were once restricted to religious images (icons), are meant to have meaning, as well, and the notion that image, in the abstract, is its own meaning is dangerous (as is the concept that words are their own meaning), given the power of media to manipulate. Calvin Klein underwear, after all, is not appreciably better than J.C. Penney's brand. It exists because of the power of the images used to create a demand for it and because those images have no meaning beyond themselves (a kind of cowardly and undifferentiated homo- or hetero- or ambi-sexuality that is as remote from the viewer as the model is close to the photographer, or at least to his lens).

Now, the word "con," of course, means to dupe, to defraud, particularly to sell somebody something he or she may not want, to sell somebody a bill of goods, to extract money from someone against his or her better judgment. It also means to know, as in to recognize, from a root meaning "to learn by reading." Both meanings are therefore appropriate to advertising, and to magazine publishing, which, remind yourself, sells information in order to make a profit. Icon is etymologically related to both meanings of the word con. It is an object that is both mystical and familiar, a touchstone of something larger than itself. We recognize it and are taught to desire it.

Iconic images, a part of Western society since the cave paintings of France, joined popular culture (or vice versa) in the 19th century and became commonplace with the invention of movie cameras. Fanzines flourished because they provided pictures of out-of-reach celebrities and brought at least an image within the ordinary grasp. For better or worse, those images have now passed into another realm and have taken on a life of their own. The photographs themselves are creating rather than recording celebrity (just as the television news creates events by the collaborating presence of its minicams).

By abandoning its journalistic function (recording) in order to take up a function of advocacy—taking a specific point of view in order to sell magazines (often with no regard whatsoever for the integrity of the photograph with respect to the person it depicts)—the magazine puts itself in a position of discrimination and censorship. If the goal is to (a) sell magazines and (b) provide memorable imagery (and it is always in that order), then the images chosen become attempts to control not only what is received by the public but how the public itself is meant to receive it; and the frame around the faces—with full cooperation of the sitters and their agents—becomes more important than the faces themselves, just as the gilt and bejeweled icons of the crucified Christ or the weeping Virgin become more important than the personages they are meant to invoke, not to supplant.

"Ah," says the crone-like Meg Ryan sometime in the 21st century, drowning an aged Kiefer Sutherland in her pool and casting a jaded look back at the 1990s, "we had photographers then."

MICHAEL LASSELL is a writer, editor, poet, and photographer living in New York City. He has interviewed scores of celebrities for such magazines as *Interview*, *L.A. Style*, and *The Advocate*. His published works include *Poems for Lost and Un-lost Boys*, Amelia, 1985, and *Decade Dance*, Alyson Publications, 1990.

On the Confidence Game as a Model for Culture, or the Applause Sign in My Mind Is Always Flashing

BY DAVID ROBBINS

TRUST ME, it makes no difference whether you frame the folks out there as audience or as electorate: Sooner or later they'll demand a darn good reason why you deserve to be kept on the public nipple. When that delicate moment arises, I handle it the same way whether I'm performing at Madison Square Garden, MOCA, or some haunted grange hall out on the prairie, because consistency is the key to training the public. Consistency and, of course, ruthlessness. I let the assembled know that so far as yours truly is concerned their needs aren't even under consideration; that I'm unashamedly a media creation and, as such, an official of the shadow government, not only unelected but unimpeachable; that cutting off my access to public space'll violate my Constitutional rights; and that if they do try it I'll simply write up the experience in my memoirs, which'll only make the thing thicker and even more expensive. "Go ahead," I say, "spend your children's money." Then, as the *pièce de résistance*, I whip out a knife and slice my right pants leg open from crotch to knee, exposing the pursuit of happiness clause I've had branded into my upper thigh so near the delectables. It's gratuitous nonsense, of course, because by that point the crowd's begging me to say anything I like, anything at all: There's nothing like the threat of litigation—so personal! so endless!—to get a crowd lapping up every word as if it were mother's milk. Sometimes, if the audience has recovered its composure before I've left the stage, one of the bolder men may ask how I developed such uncompromising passion for public life, and then I tell them. I always begin my story in the same way, and this is how I begin:

For many years, I never dreamed. At least, such was the evidence; if dreams there were, no traces remained in the morning. Then, one Sunday morning following a marathon of Saturday TV (an experiment in dosage and tolerance)—after cartoons and wrestling, sports and sports bloopers, film reviews and interviews with celebrity offspring, after the week in rock, infomercials and edutainment, after news and commentary, cheesy prime-time sitcoms and queasy horror flicks and easy stand-up comedy, all of it laced with hundreds of commercials—I awakened certain that, yes, indeed, I had dreamed. Recalling specific plots or specific images remained outside my capacity, naturally, because of the drug years, but I did have a distinct impression of the dreams' structure—their sequencing and duration, pacing and editing.

Here's what I remembered: Some kind of narrative, perhaps fifteen minutes in length, though whether in real time or a proportional "dream time" I couldn't determine. Then, an interruption: four or five shorter dreams, clustered together, each one a burst perhaps a minute in length, or what seemed a minute. Echoing commercial breaks, these shorter dreams weren't, however, surreal parodies of television commercials. *They were commercials for other dreams.* These were followed in turn by another long narrative, conceivably but not necessarily a resumption of the first. This basic pattern, alternating between rambling narratives and clumps of rapid-fire promo spots, had repeated itself, with variations, throughout the night.

Okay. Then came the part of the story where I lay sprawled under the bedcovers in a happy daze, drunk with the knowledge of something unnameable, blissed out on the vanilla glow suffusing the window shade, savoring the rich results of an experiment in self-programming.... Television had penetrated all the way to my unconscious mind's organization of its response to conscious experience.

Move over, Columbus, I'd discovered America. On that glorious morning, at long last, I saw through myself, saw that the excruciating psychosexual 3-D chess tourney-without-end I'd called my interior life was really just another, slightly more complex video game, programmed and programmable. Finally I understood what was meant by the phrase "let yourself go," and I did just that. From that day forward, the permanent out-of-body experience became my preferred means of transport. Simply put, I took myself public.

I also took action:

Dialed my analyst—at *home*, on a *weekend*—and fired him.

Fair is fair, so called my family—on Christmas—and fired them.

Stopped being an artist, and dammit, started acting like one: Why struggle to add to the great sea of images when I'd my own to maintain?

Right away, things began looking up. Acquired an agent—the notorious Faxine de Montage, from Third Person Management, way, way, way out on Wilshire. Inked a lifetime contract with a deep-pockets sponsor, General Pronouns. Endorsed the output of the right stars and was endorsed in turn. It worked like a charm; within what seemed like minutes, I knew everybody who was anybody.

A very special someone helped me land a position with the Feds after the White House re-located to Hollywood. Not just any post, either. A culture job, cooked up by the back room cigarheads in response to mounting pressure to support the arts. Naturally, the Feds had opted for the route of least commitment, choosing to fashion a role for a national artist which fell somewhere between artist laureate and house band. Responsibility for inventing the artist's work fell to the Secretary of Media, and though initially jittery about the danger of generating any sort of content which, later on, might have thrown a wrench into the President's re-election machine, the Secretary'd eventually found a clever way 'round the horn: The national artist wouldn't actually produce any physical work at all. No, the artist's work would consist solely and entirely of convincing top gallerists, roving curators, and museum heavies to include his name on exhibition announcement cards and in magazine ads. *Et voilà*: the first totally mag-lev career. Just smoke and mylar stuff? Perhaps—but perhaps an oeuvre of "merciless purity" (Clementine Standish, *The New York Times*), with "the artist's only real product his participation in the official version of art history" (Sugar Ray Kerwin, *ArtMoment*).

The Secretary had auditioned dozens of hungry unknowns eager to take on the long-term responsibilities of an artist's public life before I came along and grabbed the brass ring—with a little help from my friends, granted, though Mr. Secretary also admired my genuinely hard-won lack of depth. He certainly made the right choice, because I was totally believable—poll anybody you like. In fact, during my years as national artist I not only pulled off every aspect of the career my superiors had envisioned, I actually upped the ante, managing to convince several prestigious auction houses to include my name occasionally in their catalogues!

So began my career in the public eye. Okay, I may have been just a speck, but even so those heady, social days and nights taught me a lot.

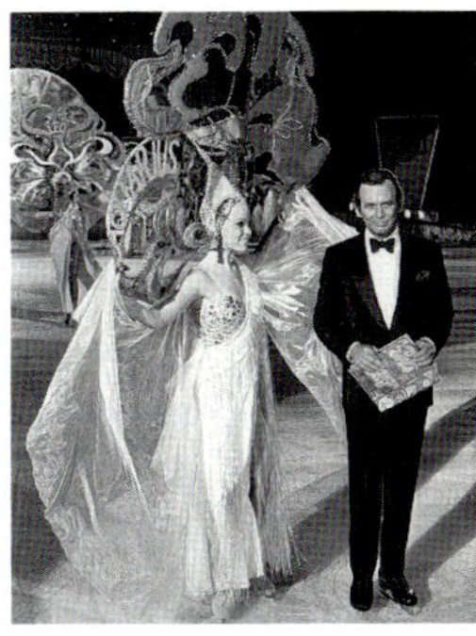

DAVID JANSSEN
*Highlights of the 1971
Ice Capades*, 1971

So many functions to attend, so many appearances to make, not just at the mandatory vernissage, but at film premieres, beauty contests, embassy dinners, PAC fundraisers, pansexual orgies.... Those evenings taught me much of what I needed to know about appearances—how to spot them, why they count, how to keep them up. *God*, it was great to be young and artificial! Of course, I still carry the scars; sometimes, around four A.M., if I've had enough Punt e Mes, I'll scrub away a layer of pancake to reveal some of the less off-putting. If I'm feeling really generous, I might even confess to that evening's companion the really dark knowledge I'd acquired from that period—how truth is only truth according to whom it is revealed. Truth must be *recognized* as truth in order to be truth, which means that truth'll only rise as high as the audience'll let it. Scary thought.

Where was I? Oh yeah: at me. Well, the government takes care of its own, rewarding by promotion, so up the ladder I went, out of High Culture into Popular. Named chief of Cancelled TV Family Services, working out of the Office of Retouching and Airbrush. That was some stretch, believe me, because actually showing an interest in other people was not, customarily, my strong suit. But still I wanted to serve. Dear old Faxine, agent, best friend, pubic hair stylist without peer, saved the day by putting me through a crash course in acknowledging the reality of others. Not a few tears were shed out at the beach house that weekend.

The position was a mean red challenge. Cancelled TV Family Syndrome had just been identified, and not a lot was known about it, but it was having devastating effects on the entertainment industry's morale. When movies and plays were the principal dramatic fare, actors had pretended to be families for relatively short periods—the weeks it commonly took to complete a movie, the months of a hit play's successful run. But television required actors to continue for years to imagine themselves related to a group of people with whom they shared no real blood kinship. Had those genealogical pretenses continued for a lifetime, the television actor's ability to draw from two separate sources of familial care and affection would have been enviable. Unfortunately, the ruthless commercial realities of the broadcasting marketplace propelled every televised family toward another, less sanguine fate; sooner or later, declining ratings, executive caprice, or attacks by vicious, roving packs of self-righteous consumers resulted in the cancellation of every TV show. When cancellation struck prime time soaps and sitcoms, nationally broadcast "homes" were broken overnight, and the actors who'd been part of them were forced to re-adjust to dimly remembered uni-family lives with meddlesome biological kin. Suddenly cut off from professional portrayals of nurturing support, many actors faced fragile, confusing and unhappy life-episodes upon rejoining the often harrowing Freudian circus of the nuclear family.

Well, one does what one can do. I did plenty. Placed a guilt lien on TV network corporate earnings. With that dough, bought twelve acres adjacent to the Angeles National Forest and built the Jack and Connie Brooks Center for the Treatment of Cancelled TV Family Syndrome, named for the realtors who sold us the land. In six months, the Center was ready. The rest was up to the afflicted actors.

Did it work? I had to hire extra staff to handle the influx of autographed headshots.

After that kind of success, what choice had I but to resign and join the private sector? Together with a bunch of Ivy League smart alecks who'd been unnaturally influenced by early issues of the National Lampoon and, consequently, had been unable to kick the habit of generating ideas for the full spectrum of entertainment media, I founded CultCo, the first entertainment thinktank. We produced rock bands, books, TV shows, movies, art exhibitions, computer games, toys, senatorial candidates—anything that we felt might serve as a vehicle for our ideas.

CultCo held that there were no bad ideas; when people referred to a "bad" idea, they really meant an idea that had been either poorly tailored for, or improperly assigned to, an inappropriate medium or context. All any idea required was the right lighting. My main contribution was to reposition this attitude as evidence of the commodification of thought itself—the more information contexts there existed to serve as vehicles for ideas, the

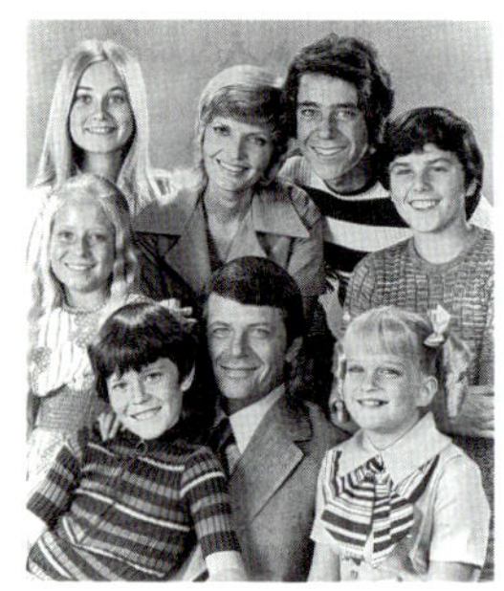

THE BRADY BUNCH

more the very activity of thinking came to equal capital—and then to systematize and professionalize this resoundingly Media Age habit of mind. Pointing to a new condition of mind is half the battle, every time.

CultCo absolutely cleaned up: Served the audience in every way imaginable, formulated new extremes of profitable selflessness, defined the cutting edge of the service economy. One, two, three. Brilliant stuff. People stood in line to stand in awe. Even the genius grant people phoned, but I wasn't able to name the song playing on the radio at the time, so they passed me over.

Pas de problème, because I'd spun enough lucre out of CultCo to buy lifelong independence, and I knew just what to do with it—pursue the golden fleece of the Media Age: Unaffiliated Celebrity. Attained by a handful—Warhol definitely, John and Yoko, Madonna, Michael Jackson (though he had nothing to report), and possibly Jeff Koons (though it was much too early to tell)—unaffiliated celebrity (specifically: unhampered access to public life, and the dispassionate exploitation of its plastic nature for conceptual ends, that is, for ends other than one's own glory) was the closest that Media Man could come to pure citizenship, the nearest he was going to get to the glory days of the stars of the Enlightenment, Jefferson and Franklin and the old boys who'd had the good fortune to have vats full of raw steaming nation as their medium. In media-soaked America, only unaffiliated celebrity approximated the old guys' ambition and scope, their chart-busting, best-selling combination of genuine intellectual independence and coast-to-coast, house-by-house, *tête*-by-*tête* headbanging effectiveness. Unalloyed with any one medium or production context, and therefore free from any single set of institutional controls—a condition which amounted, in effect, to the absence of control—unaffiliated celebrity was the virus in the software of public life, the Image World maverick who might do anything, say anything, support any cause, sometimes out of nostalgia for the days when congruence of word and deed was a legible human trait, sure, but often as not for the perverse and arguably schizoid joy of probing the inhuman frontiers of the public self, that self-machine both more and less than human. Unaffiliated celebrity was wild card politics, the eroticized out-of-body experience *par excellence* and, to this reporter, the only game in town. I packed a suitcase and hit the road to stardom.

Well, that's my story. Now my time is spent criss-crossing our big juicy demographic of a country, commandeering local talk shows by day, terrorizing paying audiences in rented arenas at night and, in every venue, speaking about the issues that matter today: "Just How Important is Importance?," "Should the Bill of Rights Be Digitally Re-Mastered?," "Civil Rights: The Balkanization of America?," "On the Desirability of Minting Kennedy Half-dollars with Little Holes Drilled in Their Foreheads for Greater Historical Accuracy," whatever.... The topic varies daily, but the sublime ambition of my candidacy remains constant, toned, and hard. It has to: I'm running for deity.

One final thought before I recede from view, for now. As with almost every public life during the past century, mine's been constructed within the sanctioning gaze of the camera. Consequently, you can't know whether I'm talking straight or just performing for the Big Lens. And that, beloved friends or audience or electorate or whomever you decide you need to be this time, means you can't even be certain that I believe what I'm telling you. On the other hand, there's always the chance that some version of me—some fortunate, neatly integrated version I can point to but can never touch—actually does believe it. There's that chance. Make you a deal: I'll just dangle here before you, spinning slowly in the light, and you can try to photograph me from just the right angle. A dollar a shot.

DAVID ROBBINS is an artist and writer living in New York City. His published works include *The Camera Believes Everything*, Editions Schwartz, Stuttgart, and *Foundation Papers From the Archives of the Institute for Advanced Comedic Behavior*.

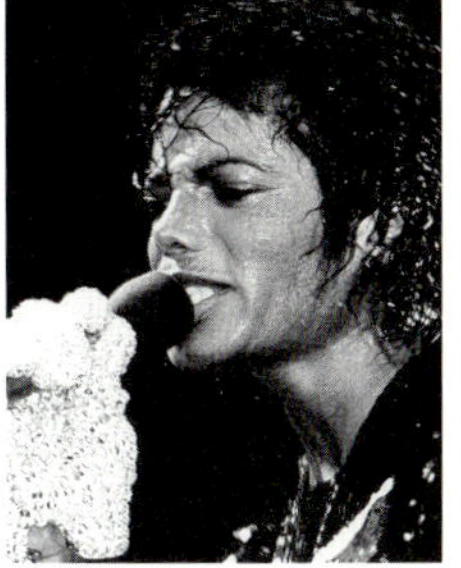

MICHAEL JACKSON

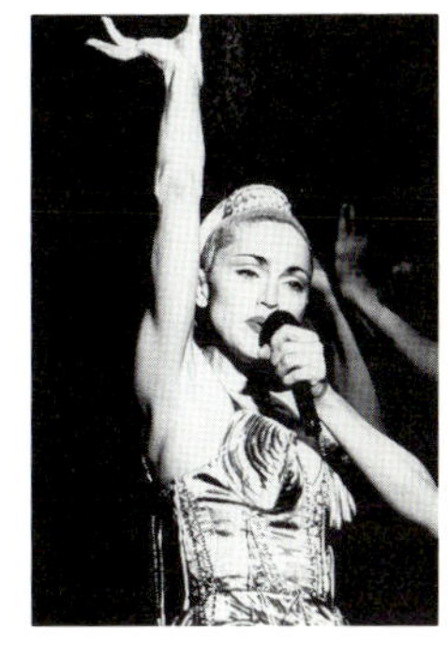

MADONNA

JAMES ABBE
Charlie Chaplin in "The Pilgrim," 1923

CHARLES ROSHER
*Mary Pickford in "Tess of the
Storm Country,"* 1922

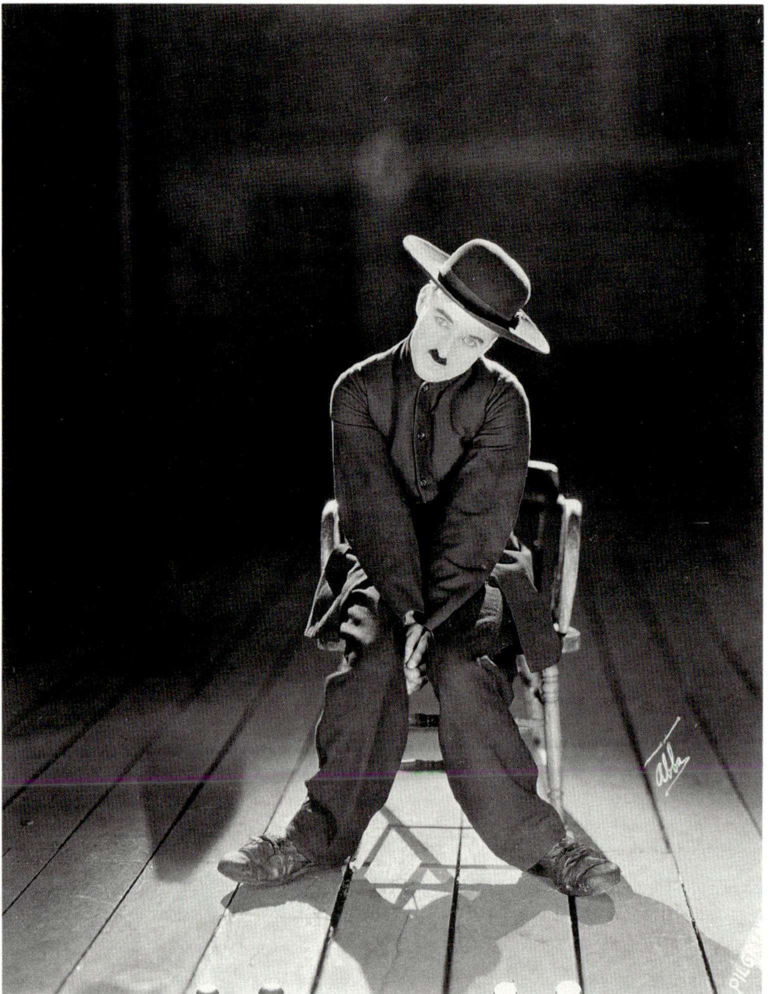

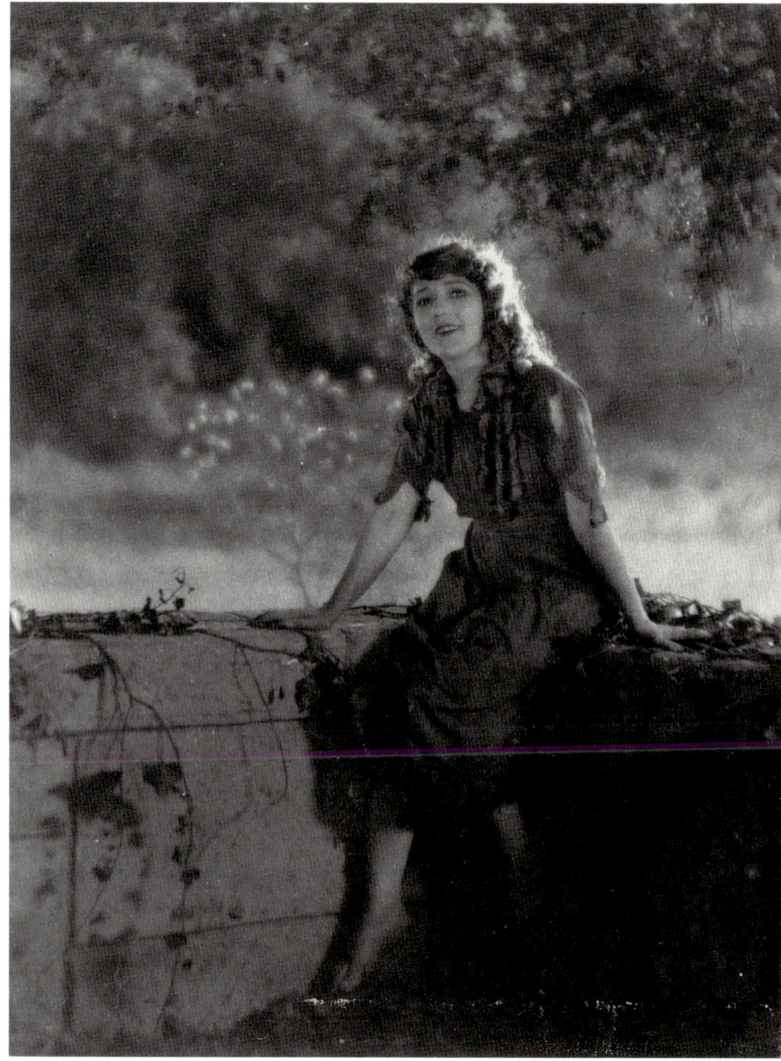

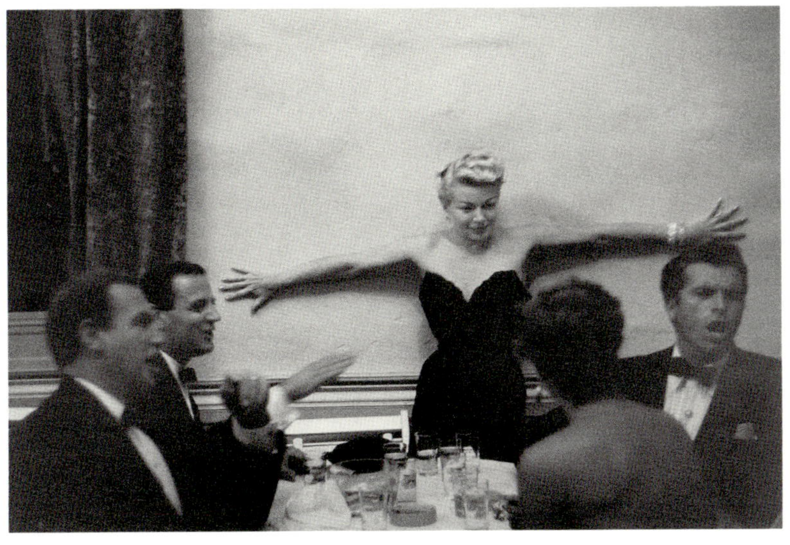

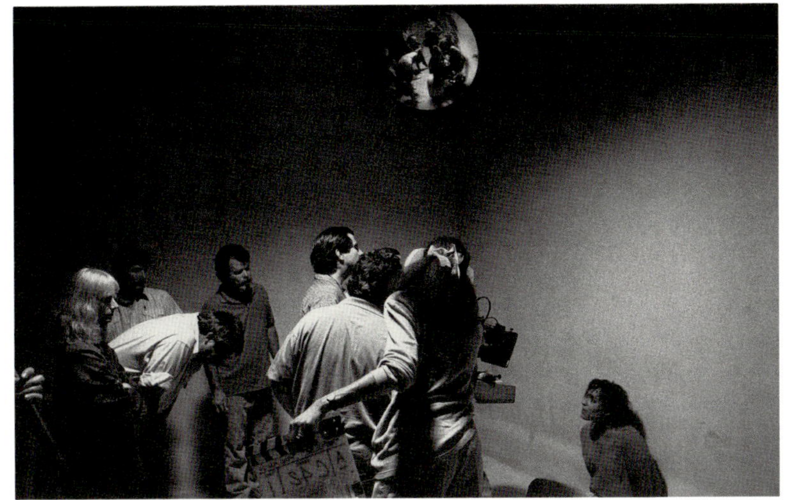

RUTH ORKIN

*Lana Turner at Famous Party Given
by Marion Davies, Esther Williams,
Fernando Lamas, and Ben Gage,* 1952

JANE O'NEAL

On the Set of "Impulse," 1989

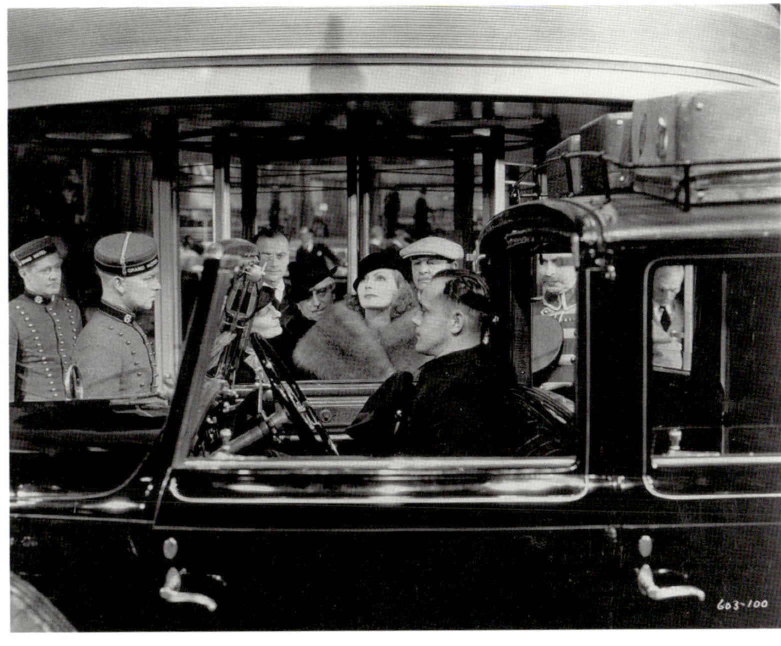

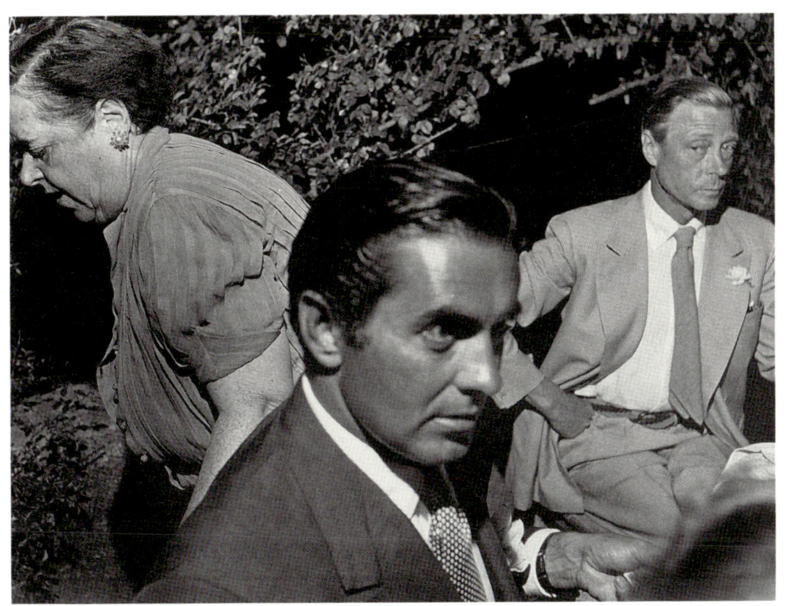

EDMUND GOULDING

Greta Garbo in "Grand Hotel," c. 1932

JOHN SWOPE

*Elsa Maxwell, Tyrone Power and the
Duke of Windsor,* 1942

MAX YAVNO

Betty Grable's Legs, n.d.

GARRY WINOGRAND

Marilyn Monroe, "Seven Year Itch"
Location, c. 1957

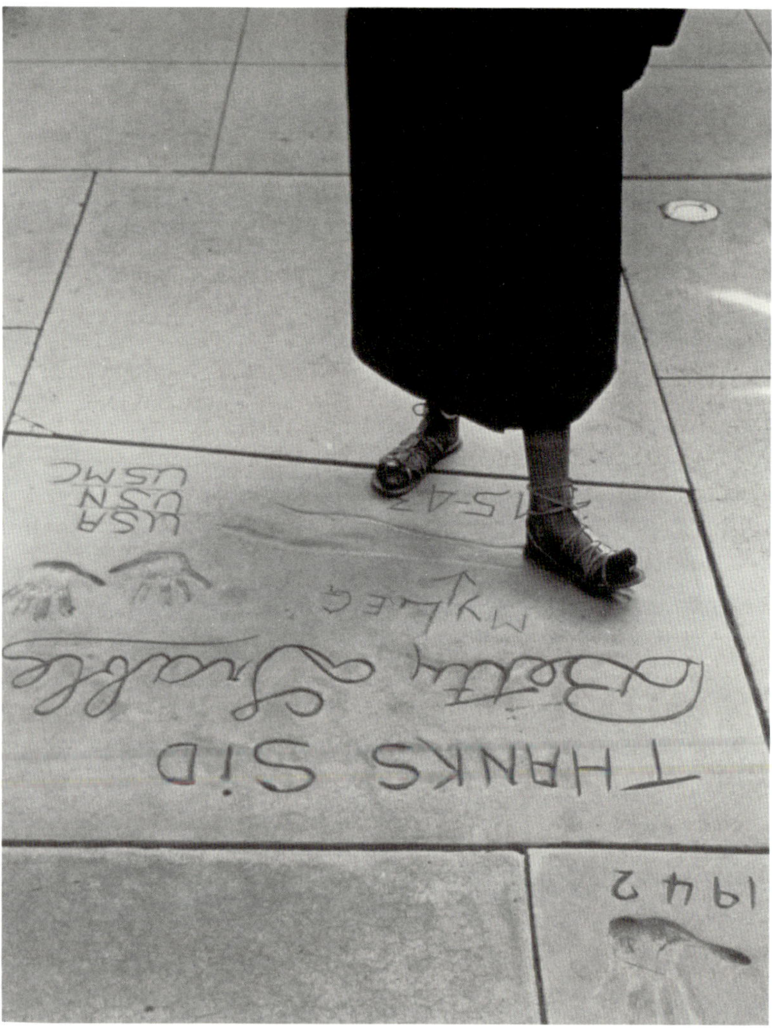

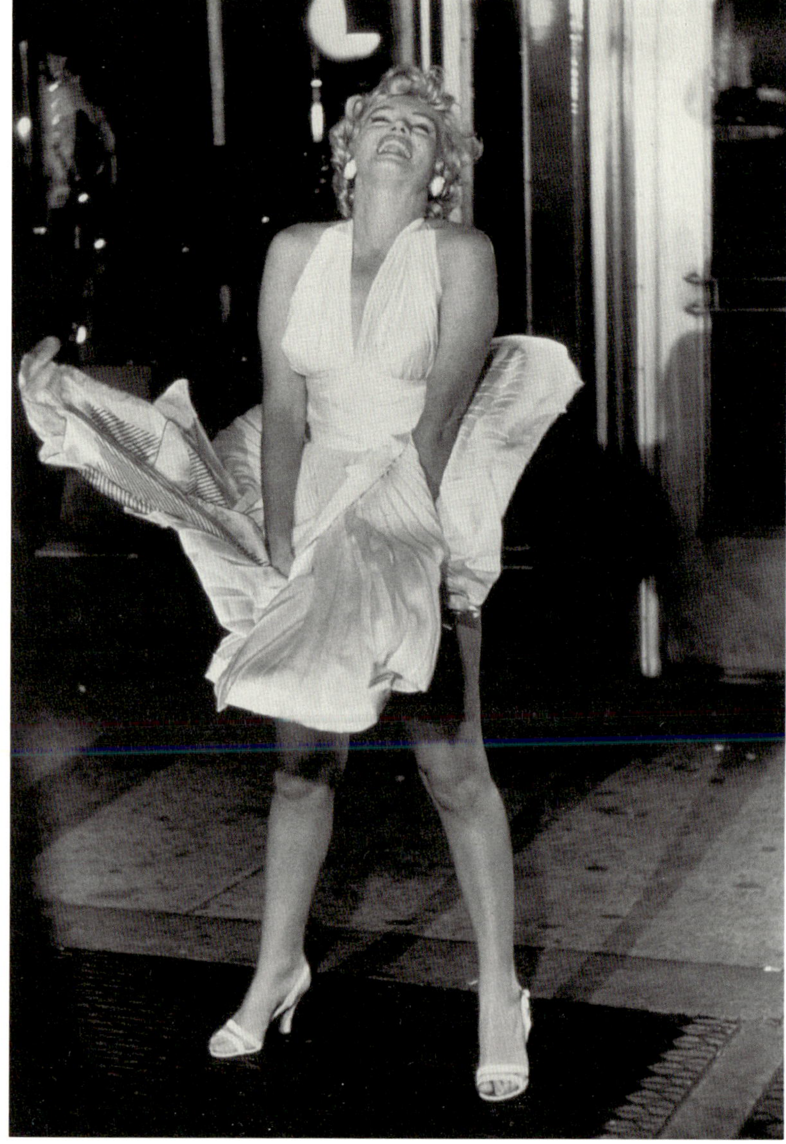

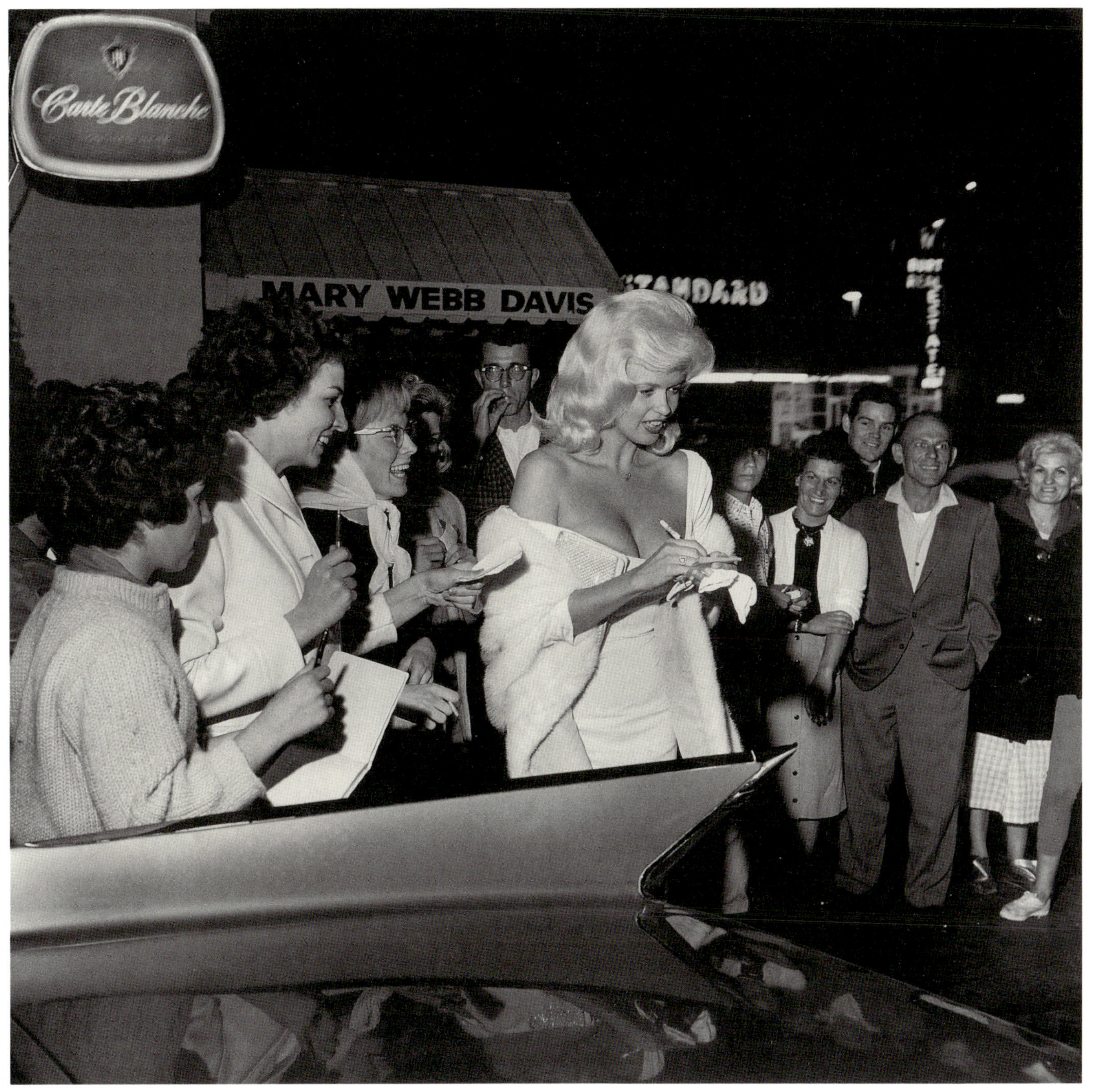

Jayne Mansfield Signing
Autographs in front of Dino's
Restaurant on the Sunset Strip
in Los Angeles, 1961

ROBERT COBURN

Rita Hayworth and Glenn Ford, c. 1946

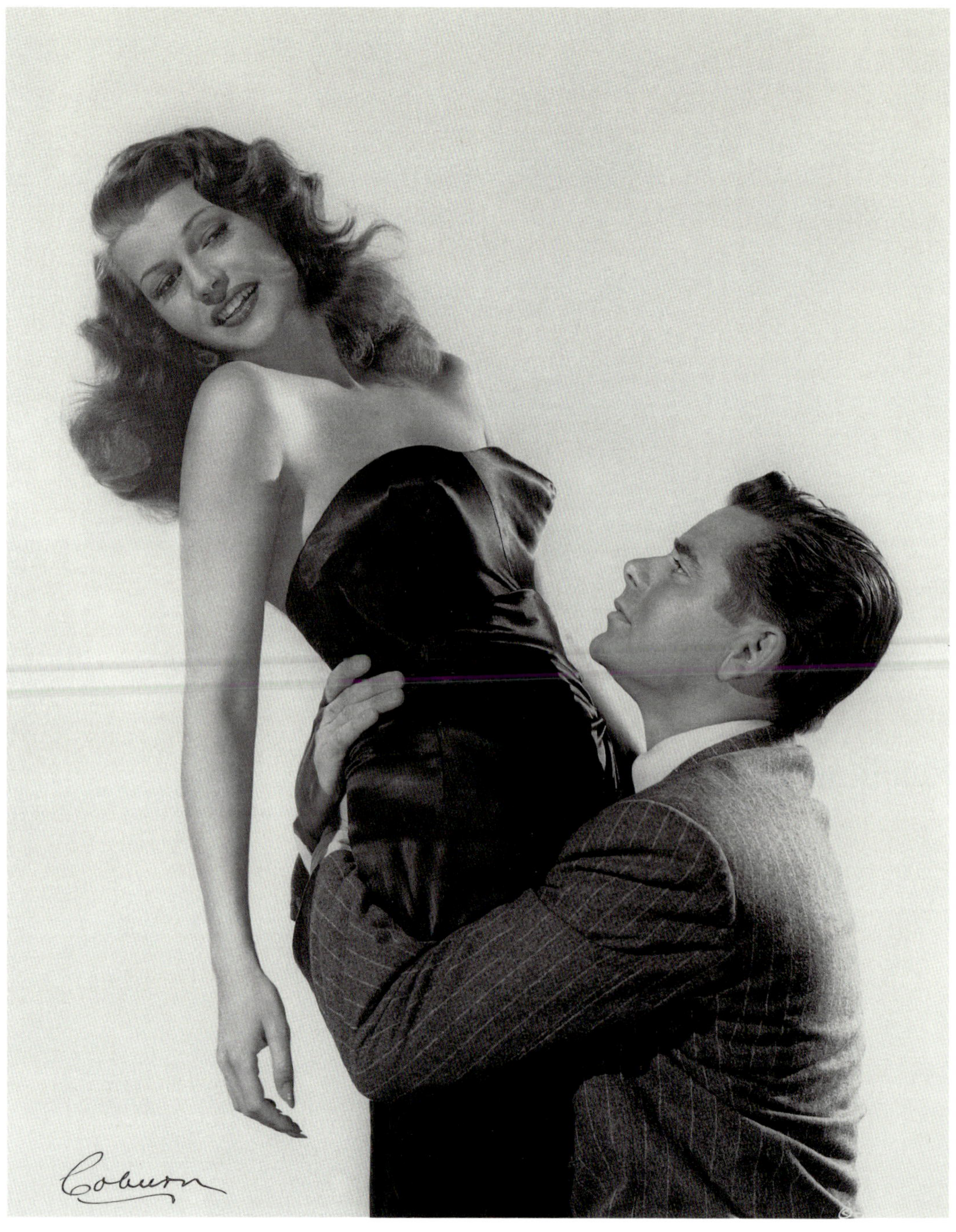

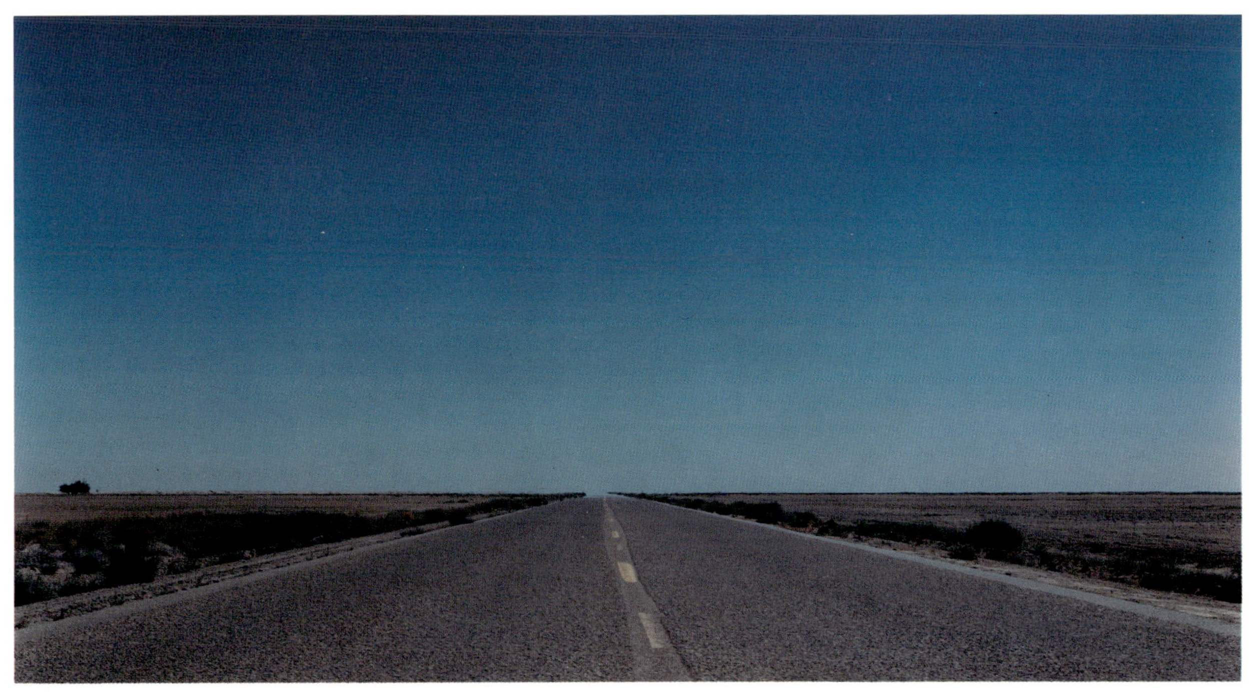

CINDY BERNARD
*Ask the Dust: North by Northwest
(1959/1990), 1990*

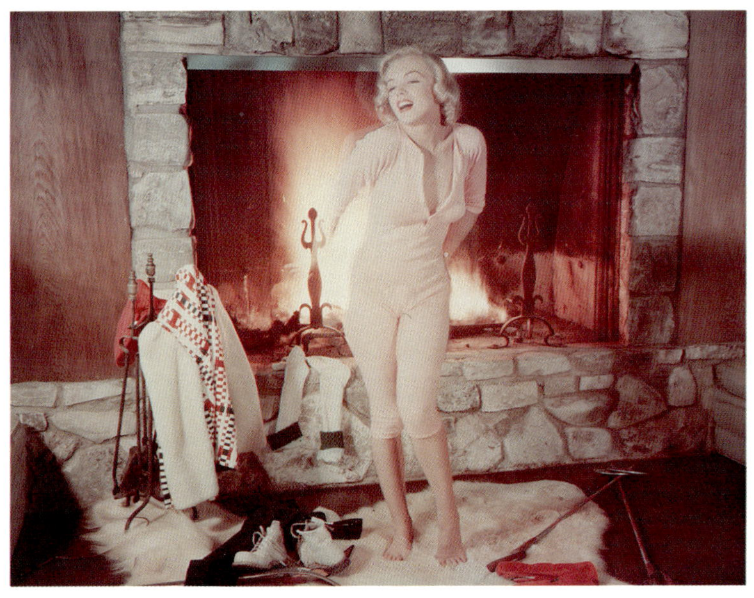

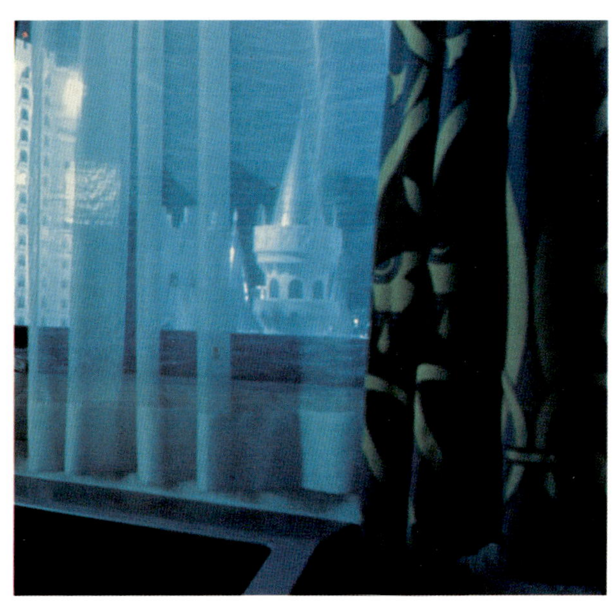

JOHN FLOREA
Marilyn Monroe, 1953

JACK PIERSON
Excalibur, 1992

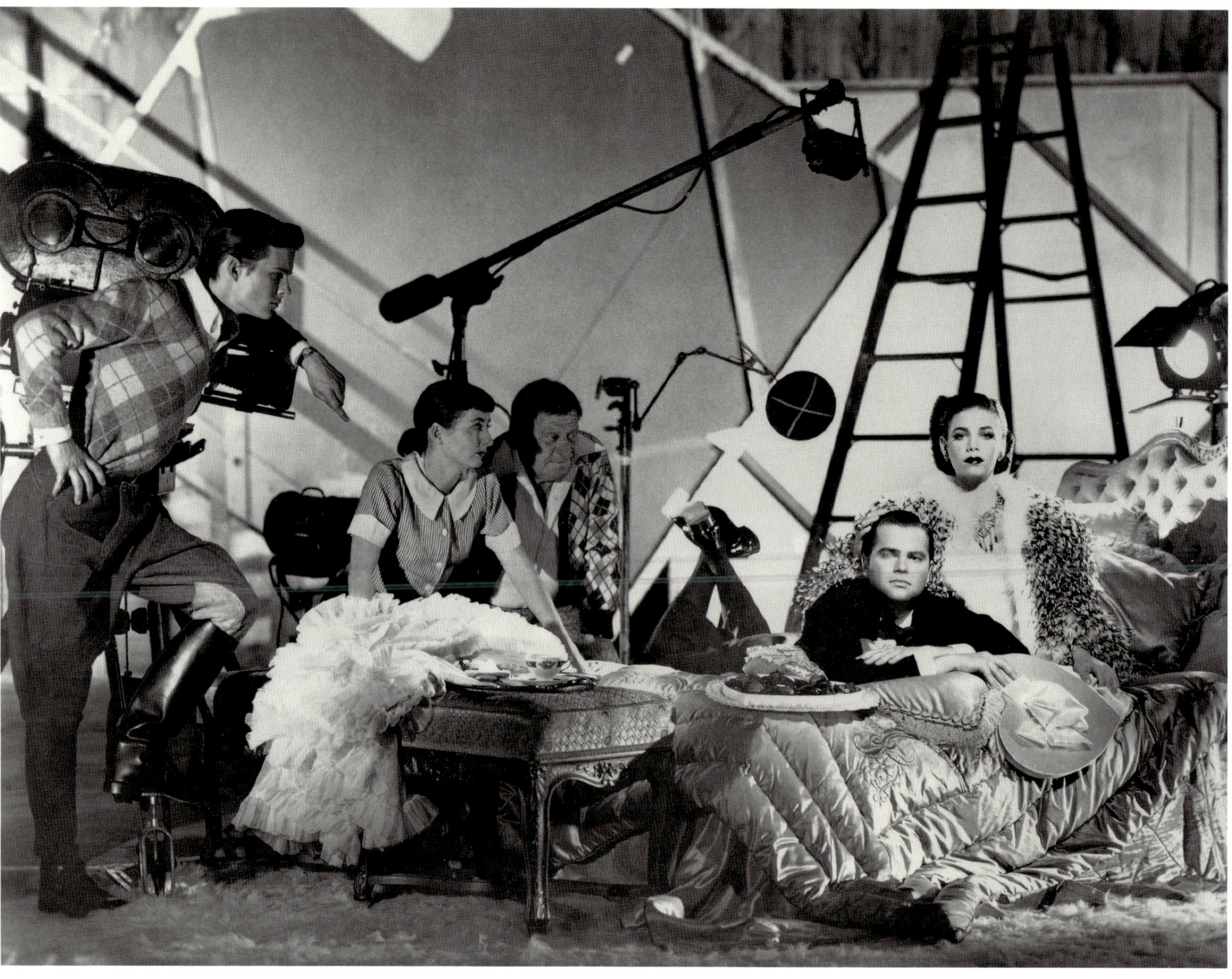

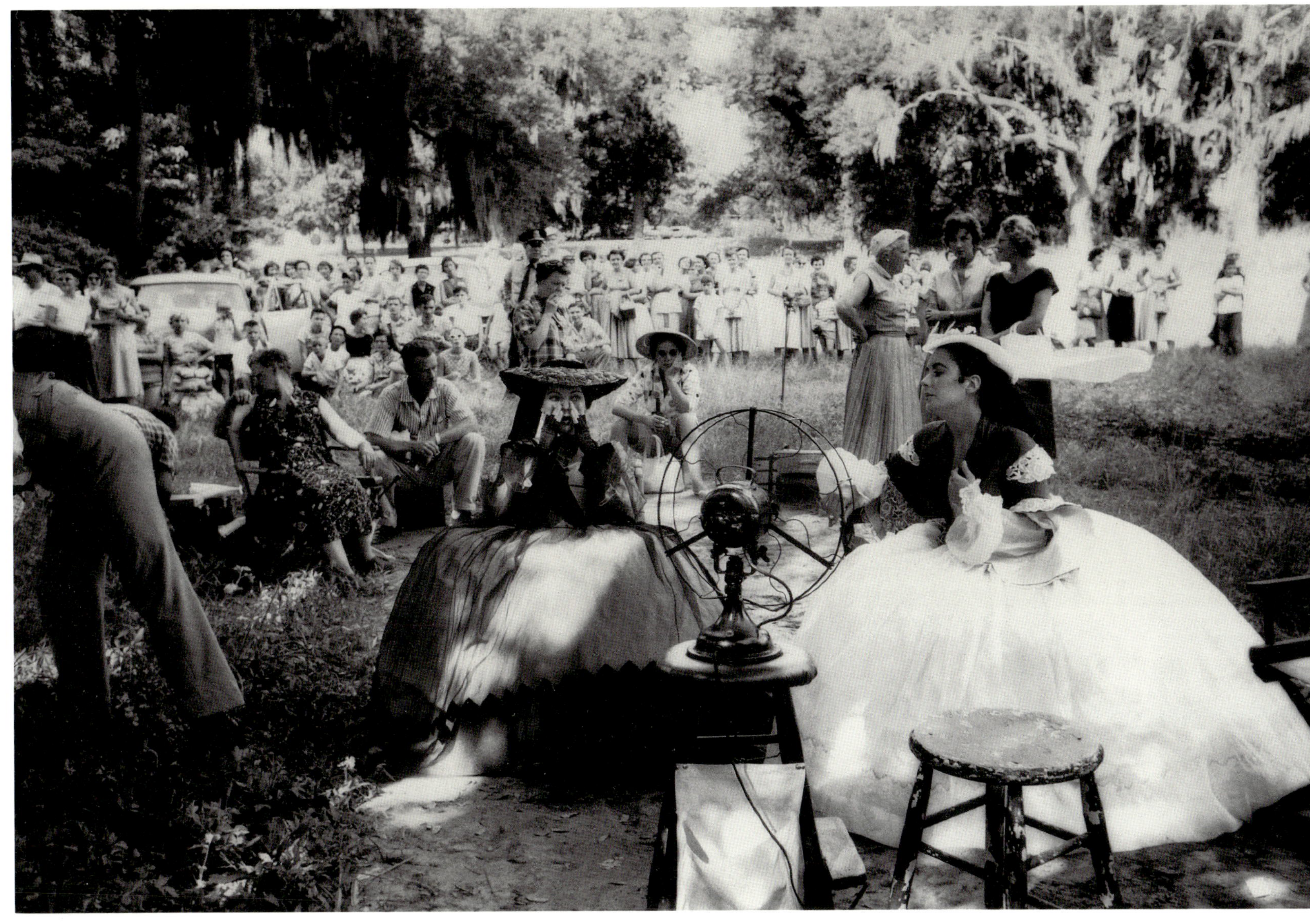

43

John Engstead
Sugar 'n' Spice (Peggy Lee), n.d.

Christian Marclay
Absolutely, 1991

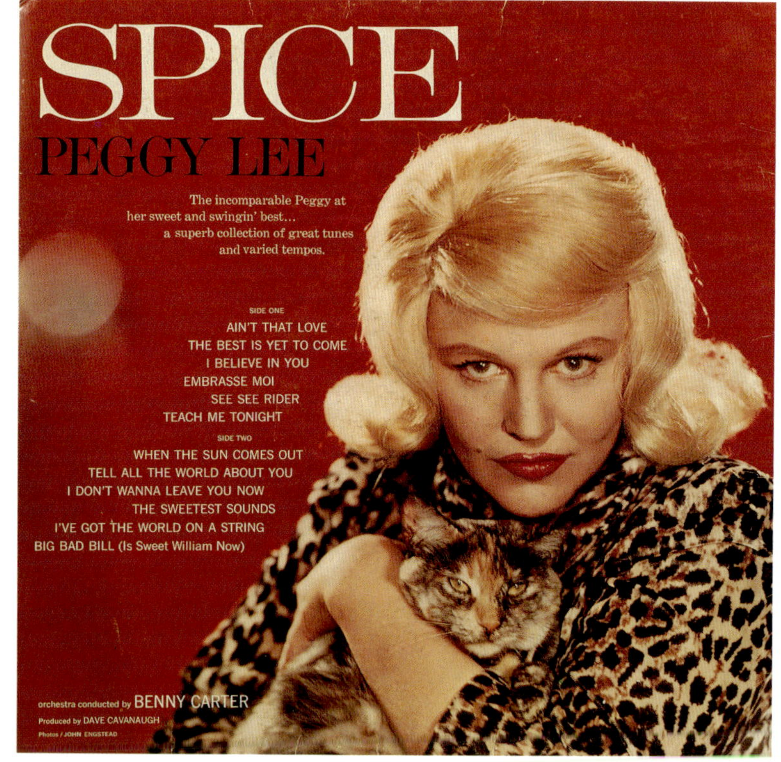

SPICE
PEGGY LEE
The incomparable Peggy at
her sweet and swingin' best...
a superb collection of great tunes
and varied tempos.

SIDE ONE
AIN'T THAT LOVE
THE BEST IS YET TO COME
I BELIEVE IN YOU
EMBRASSE MOI
SEE SEE RIDER
TEACH ME TONIGHT

SIDE TWO
WHEN THE SUN COMES OUT
TELL ALL THE WORLD ABOUT YOU
I DON'T WANNA LEAVE YOU NOW
THE SWEETEST SOUNDS
I'VE GOT THE WORLD ON A STRING
BIG BAD BILL (Is Sweet William Now)

orchestra conducted by BENNY CARTER
Produced by DAVE CAVANAUGH
Photos / JOHN ENGSTEAD

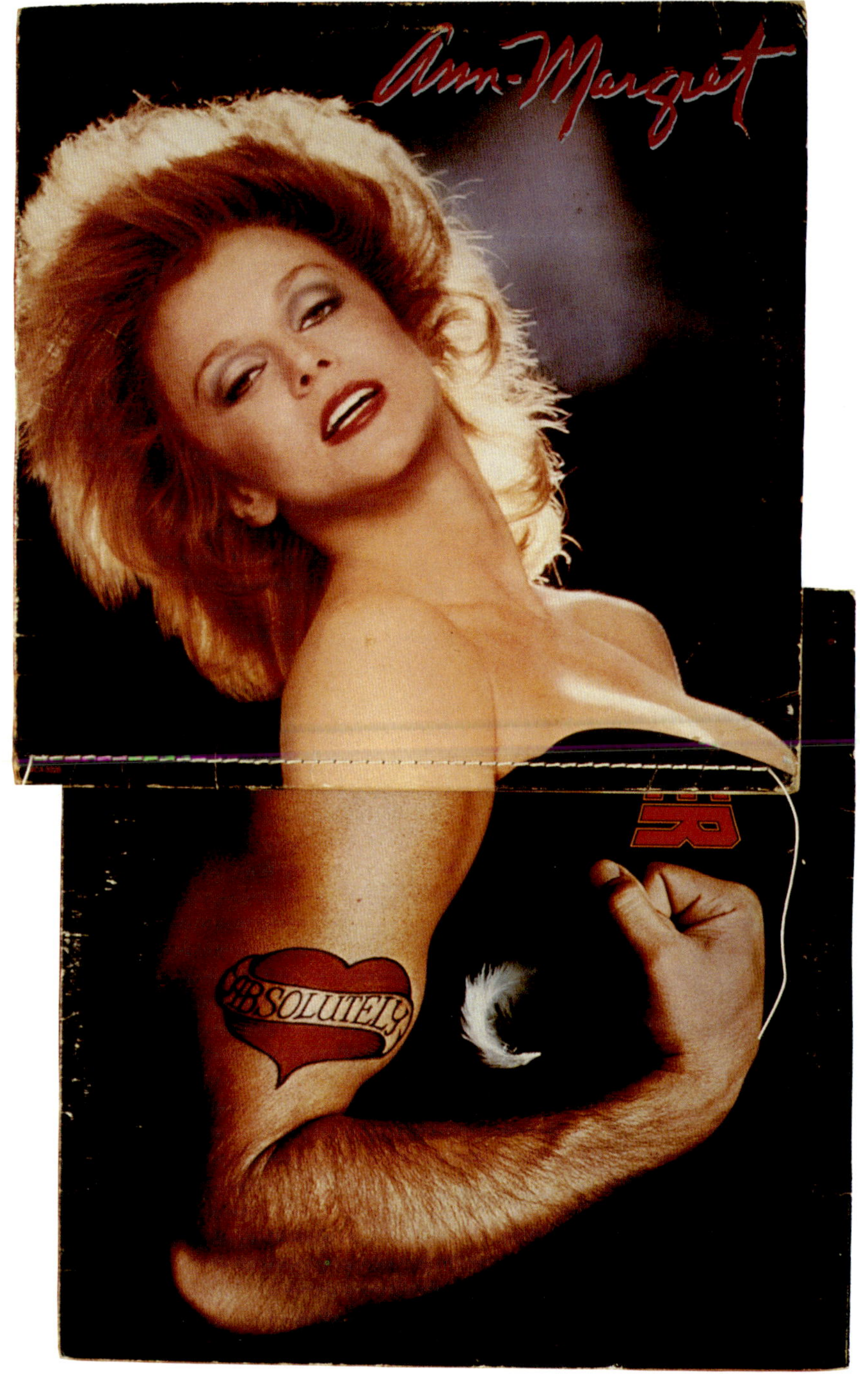

Ann-Margret
ABSOLUTELY

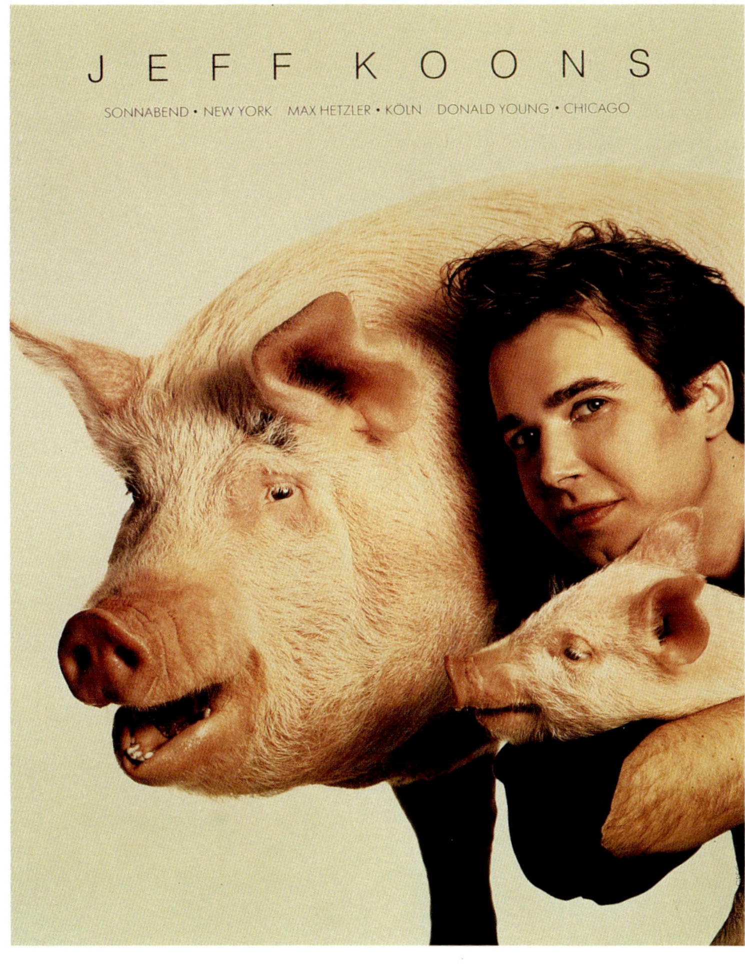

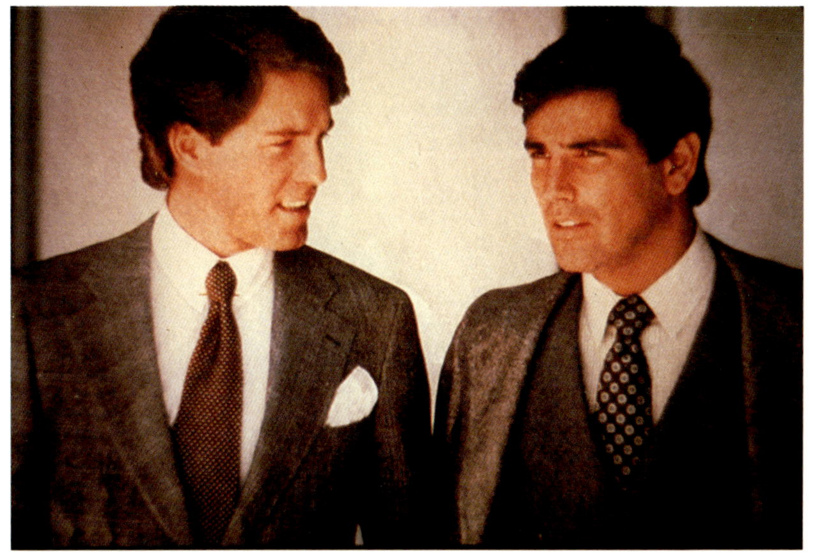

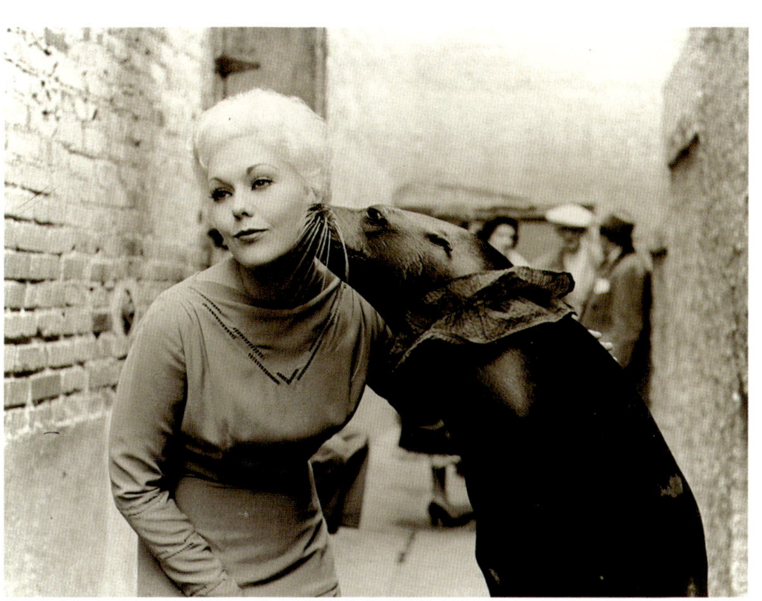

JEFF KOONS
Art Magazine Ad, 1988-89

RICHARD PRINCE
Untitled (mixed couple—men),
1977-78

ROBERT COBURN II
*Kim Novak (Columbia
Pictures)*, 1957

45

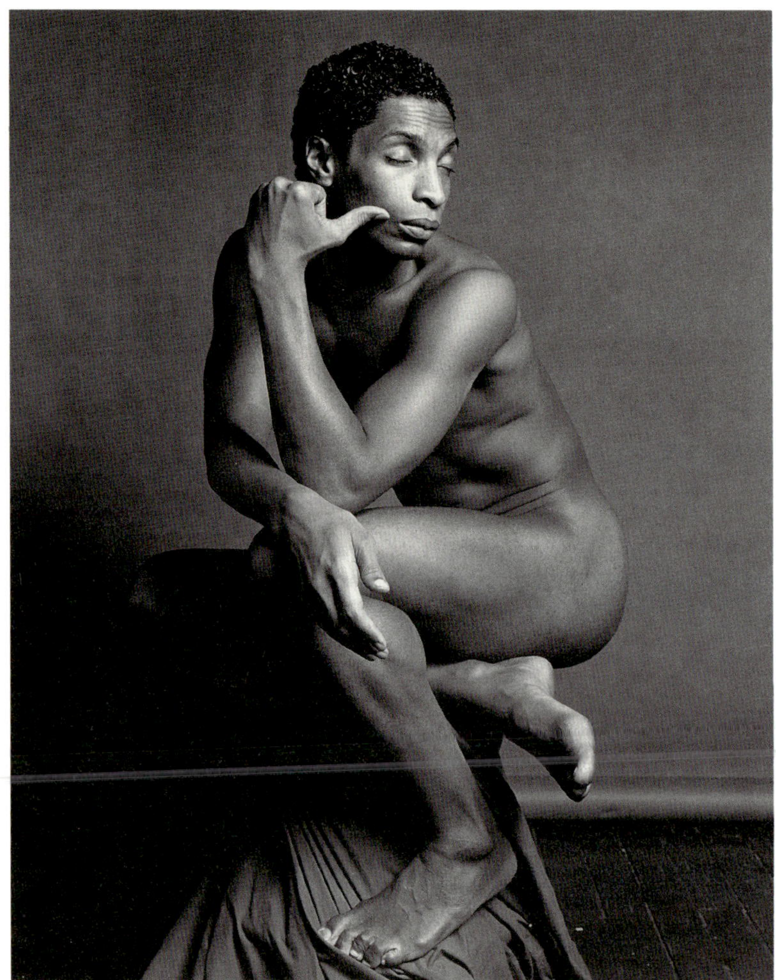

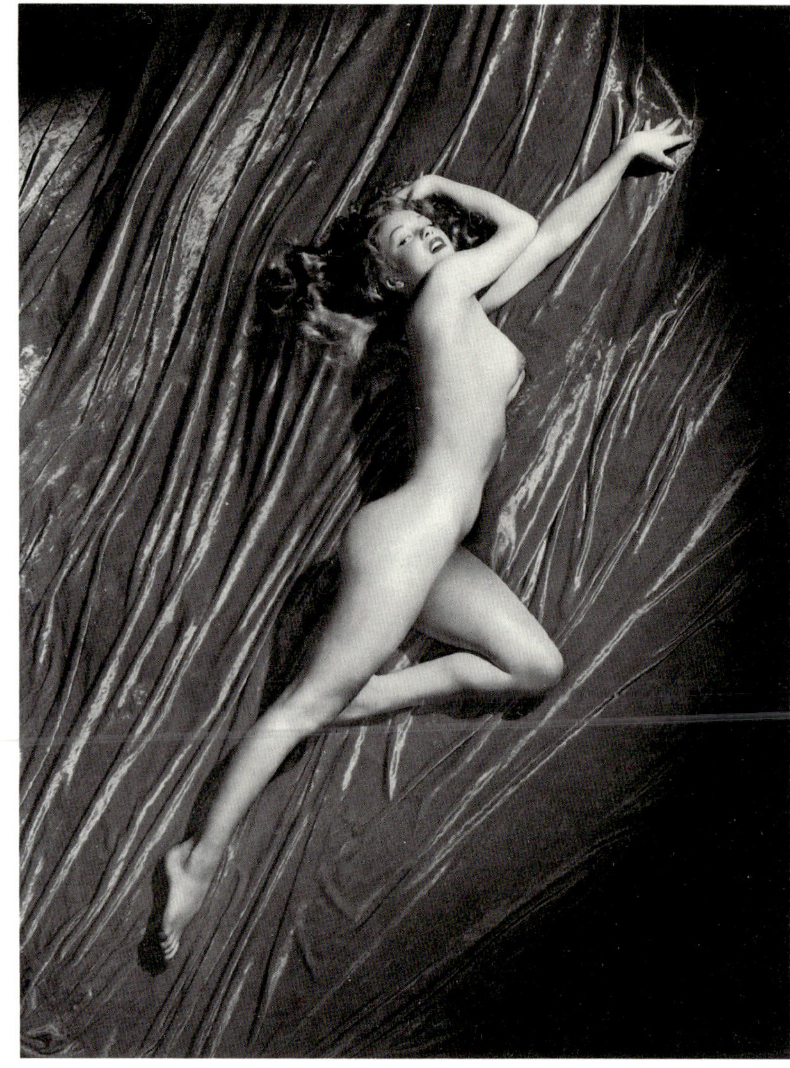

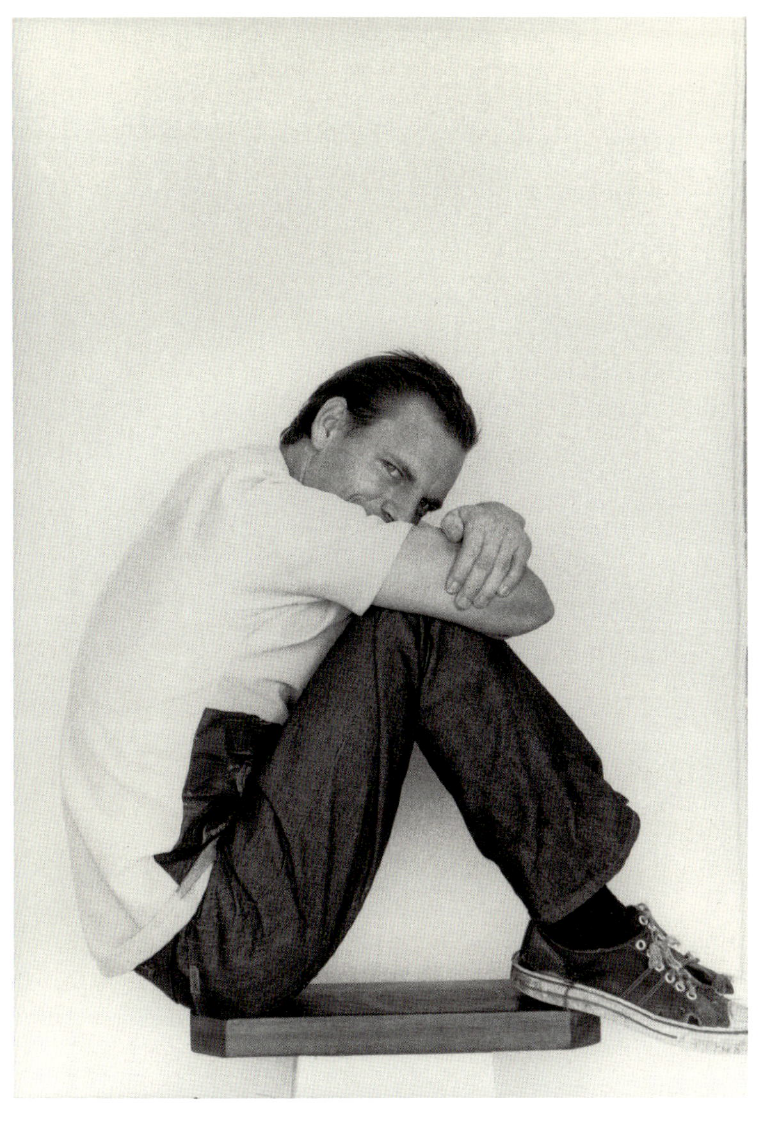

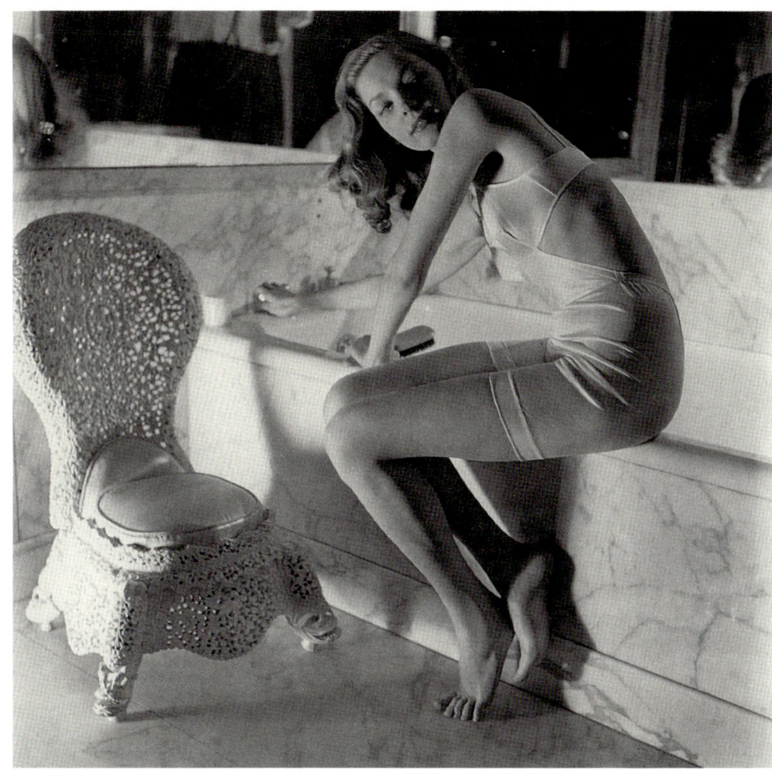

JOHN BRUMFIELD
*Robert Posing Coyly as a
Hollywood Star*, 1977

LOUISE DAHL-WOLFE
Lauren Bacall, 1943

ROCKY SCHENCK
Phranc, 1989

JIMMY DeSANA
Aluminum Foil #3, 1986

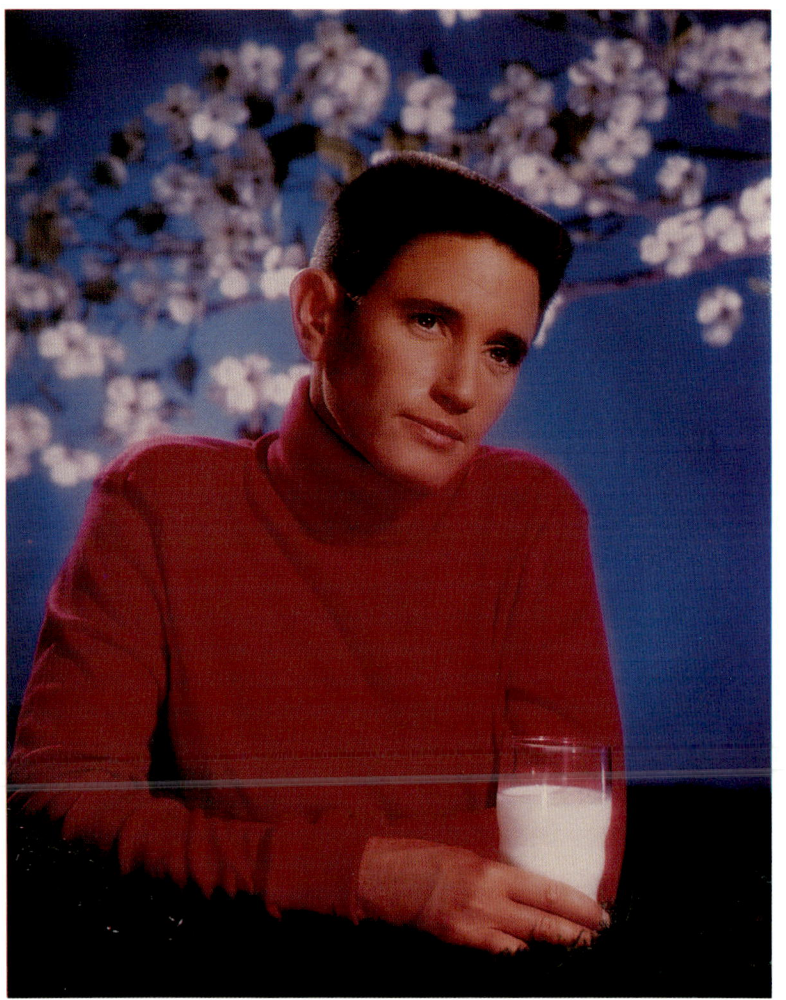

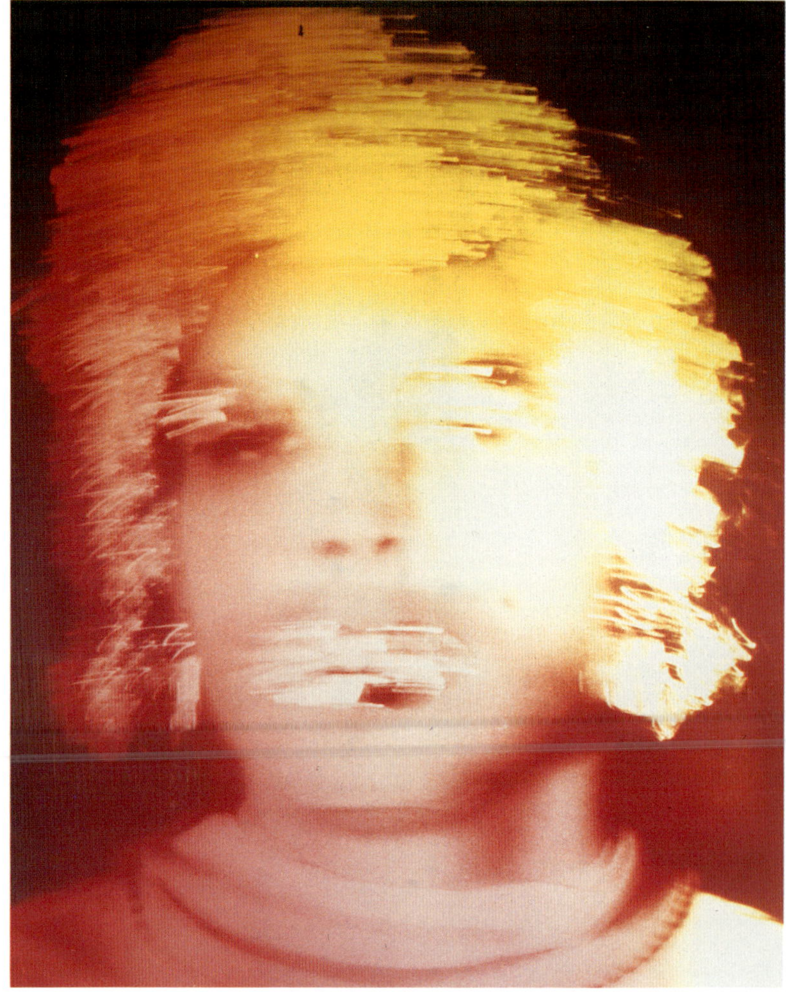

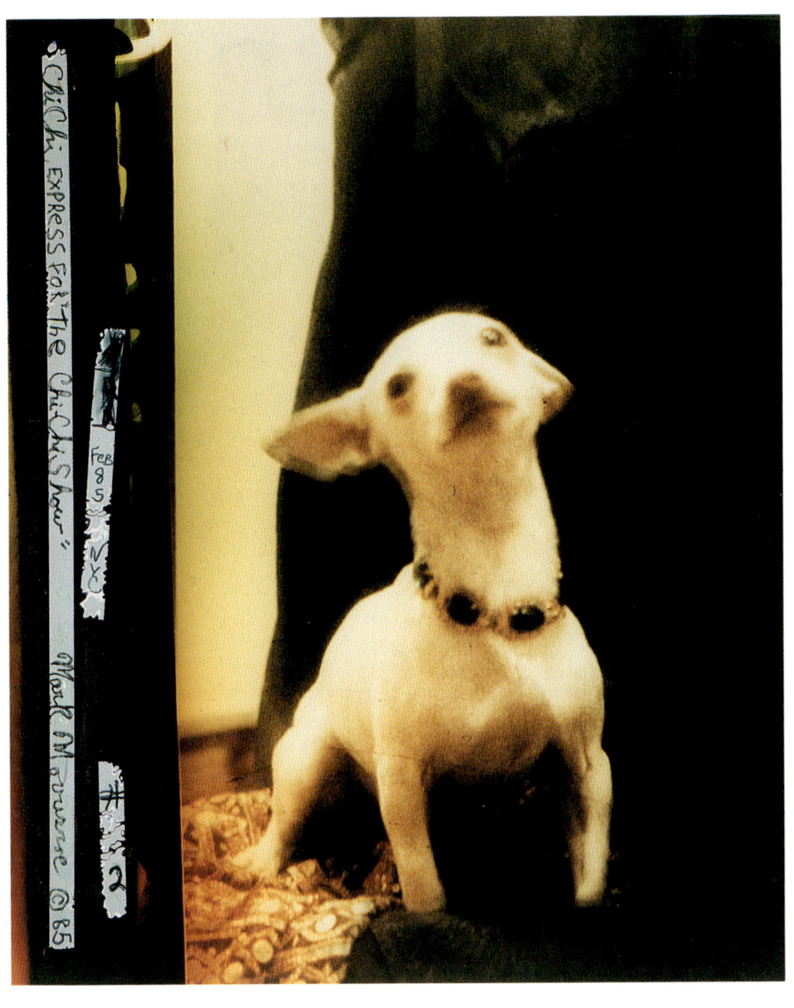

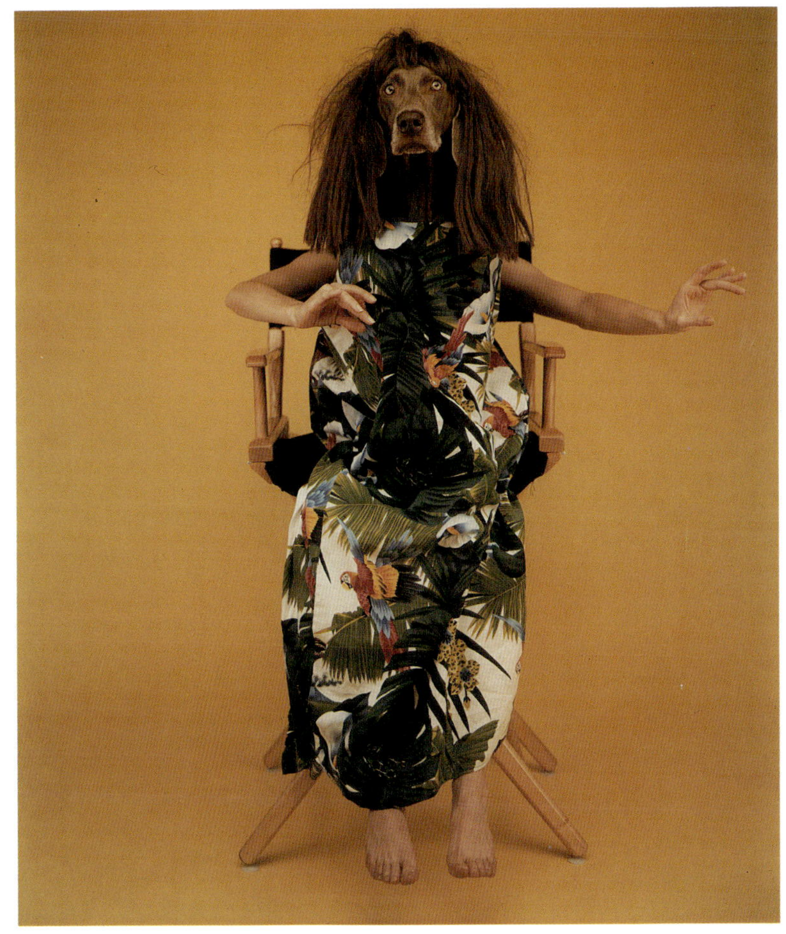

MARK MORRISROE
Portrait of Chi-Chi, 1985

WILLIAM WEGMAN
Island Way, 1990

Greg Gorman

*Divine with Bulldogs, Personal
Publicity, Los Angeles*, 1984

Paul Jasmin

Kathy, 1991

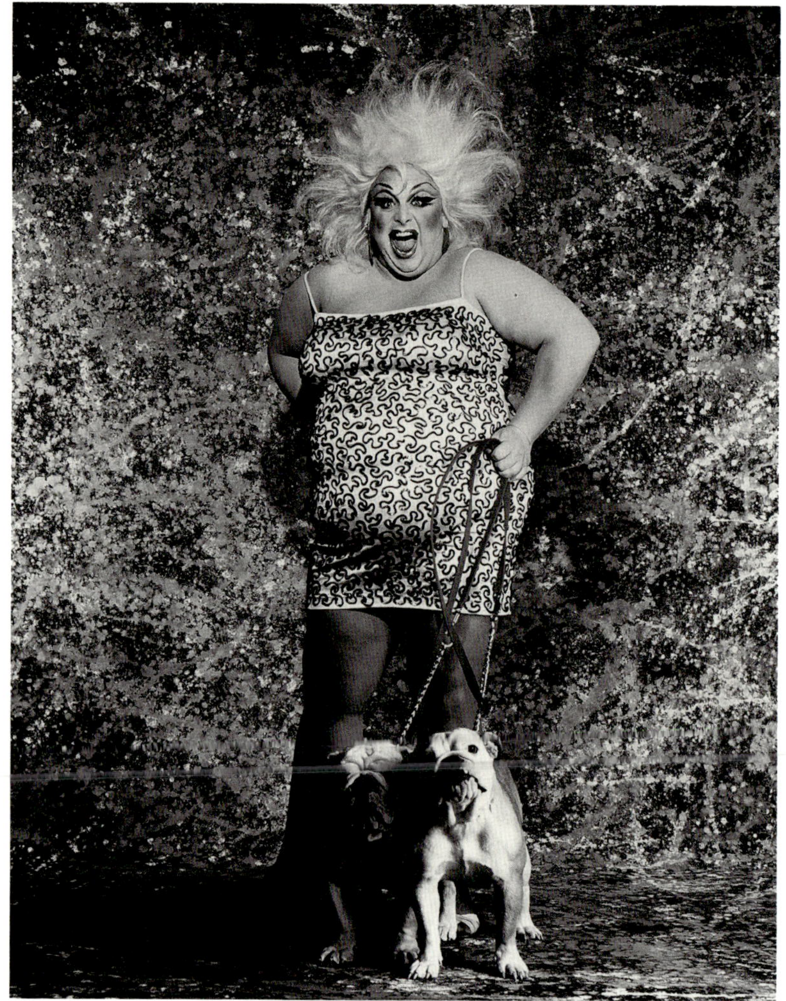

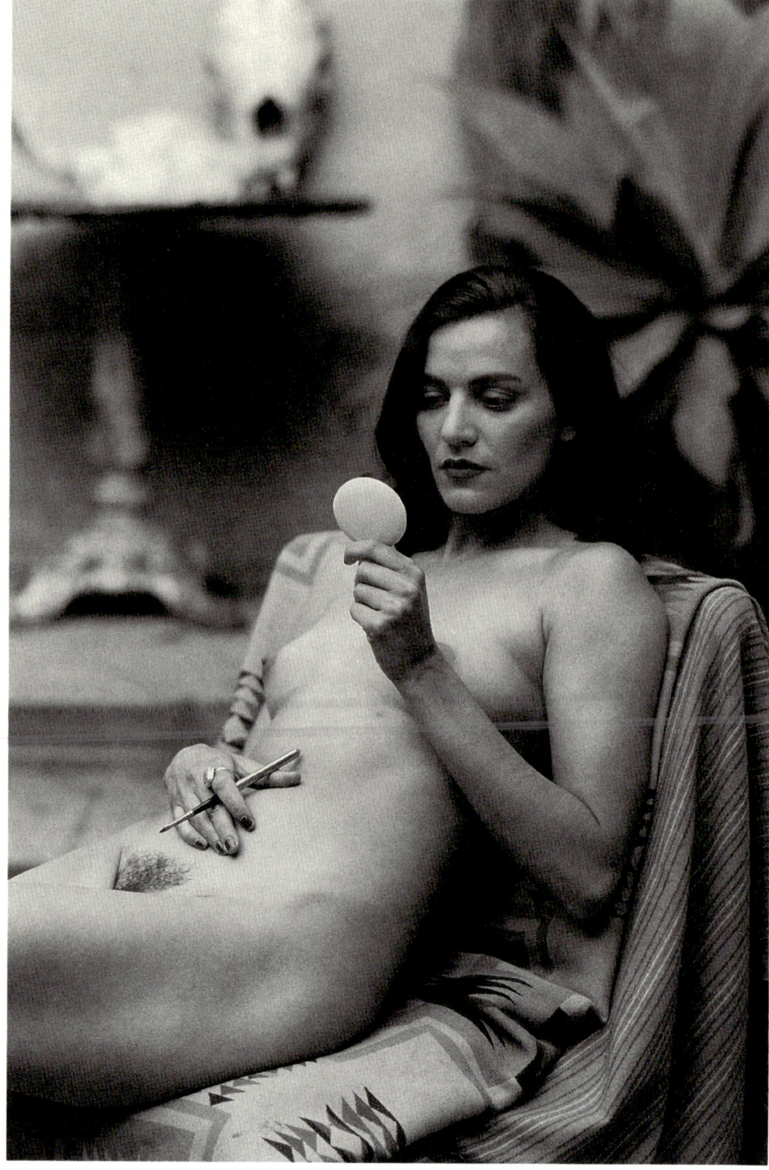

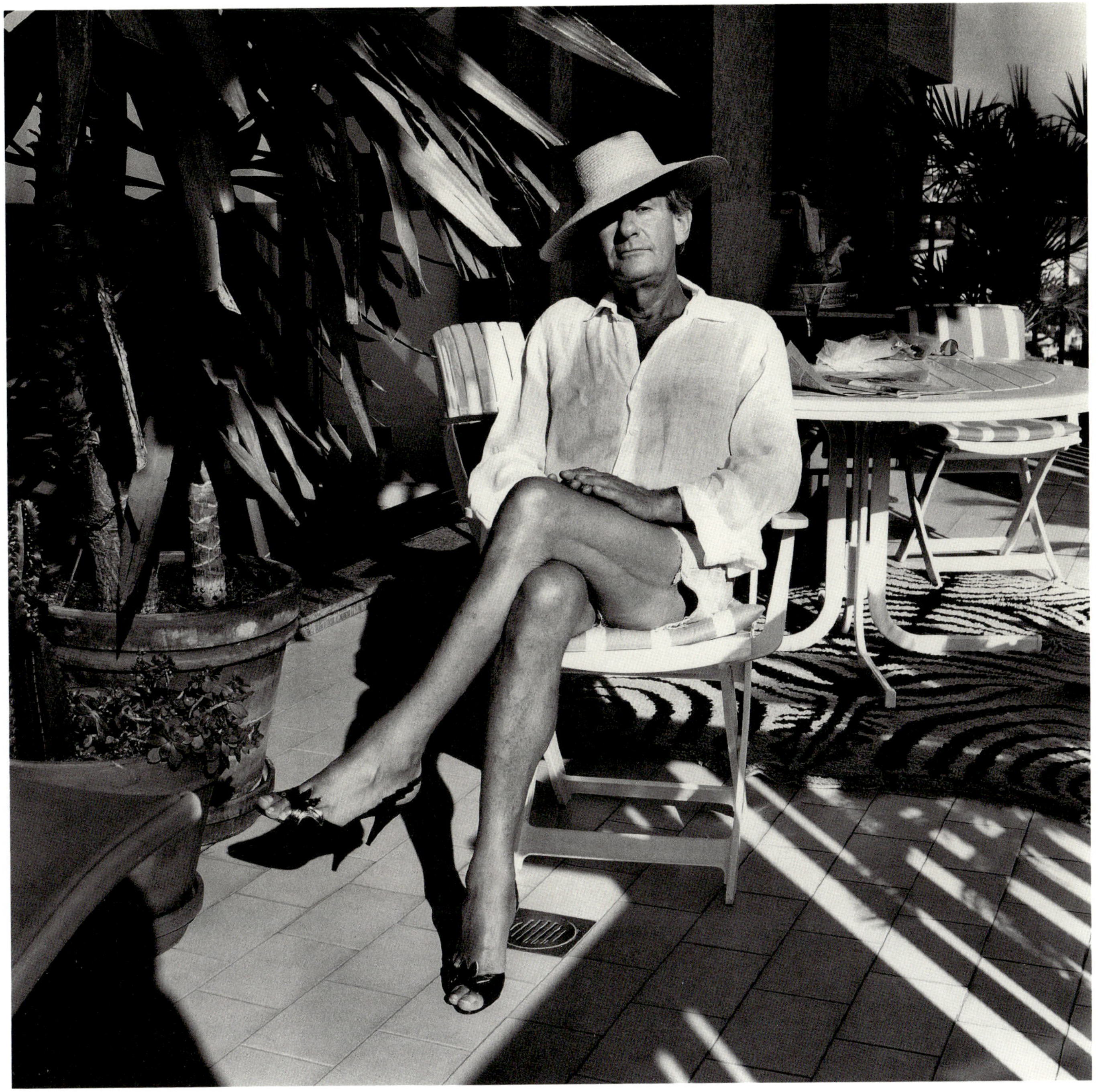

ALICE SPRINGS
My Husband (Monte Carlo), 1987

CINDY SHERMAN

*Untitled (#180–Michael Jackson
face),* 1987

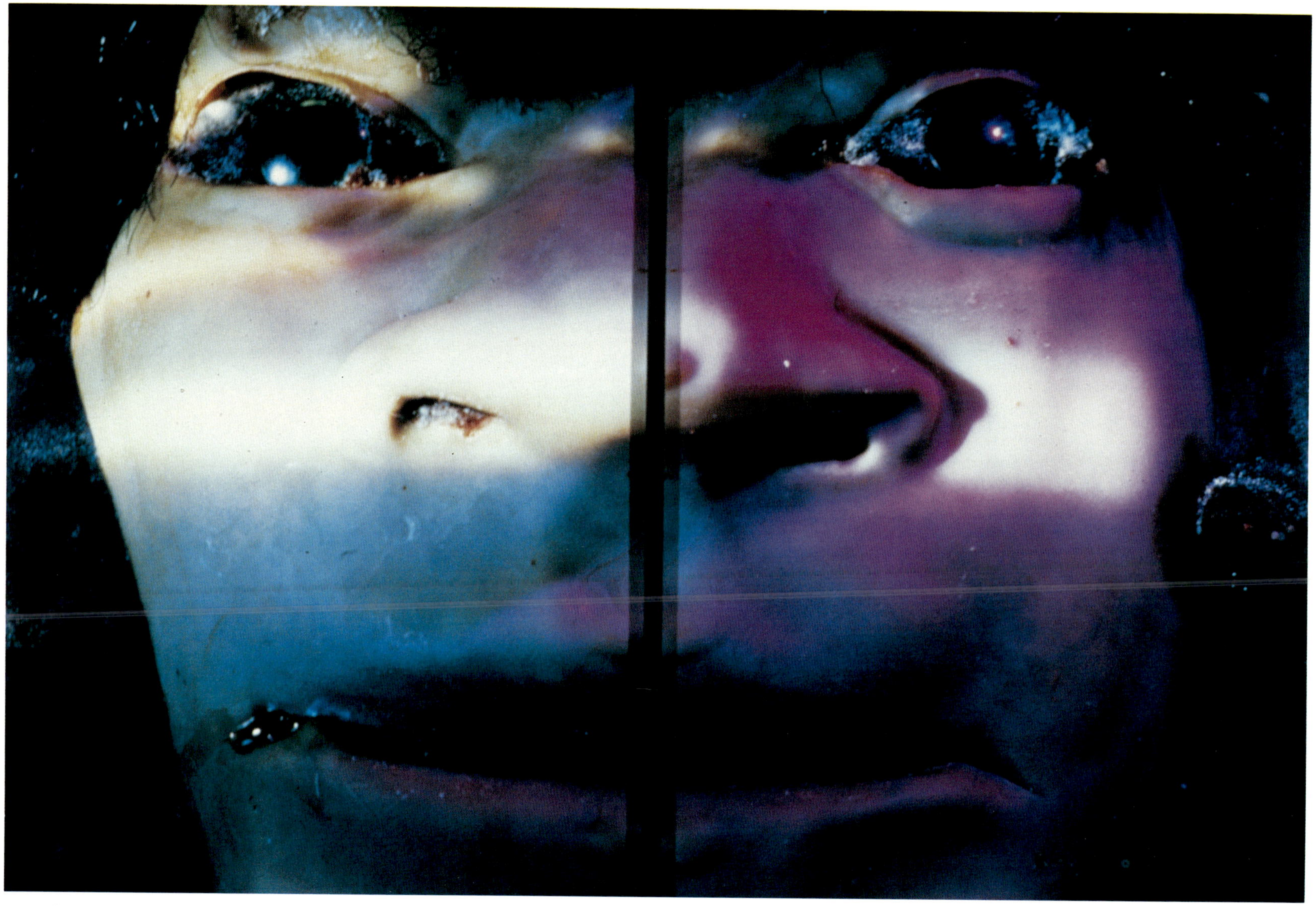

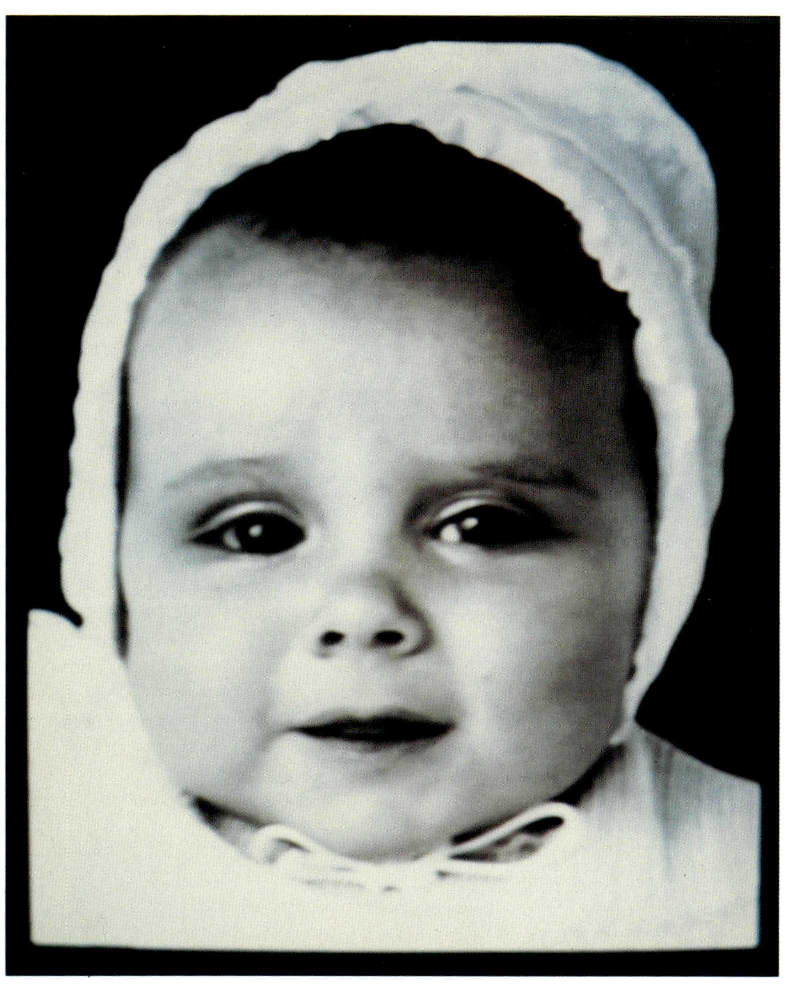

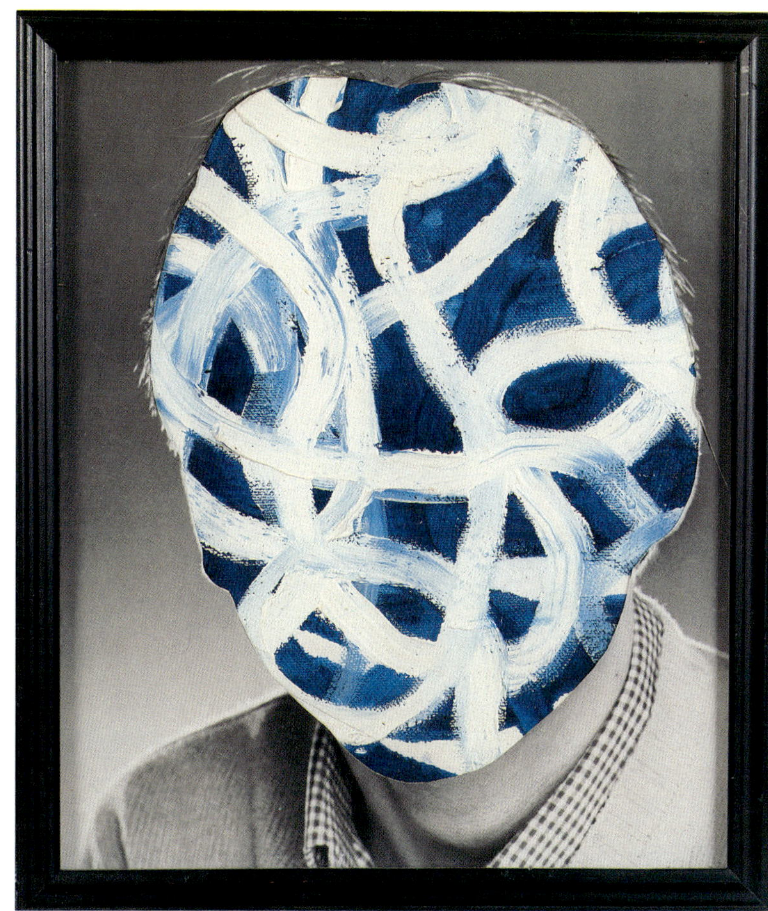

NANCY BURSON
Baby Marilyn, 1988

ANDREW MASULLO
#2249, 1989-90

CECIL BEATON
Orson Welles (with Bust of Shakespeare), 1936

EUGENE ROBERT RICHEE
Tallulah Bankhead, n.d.

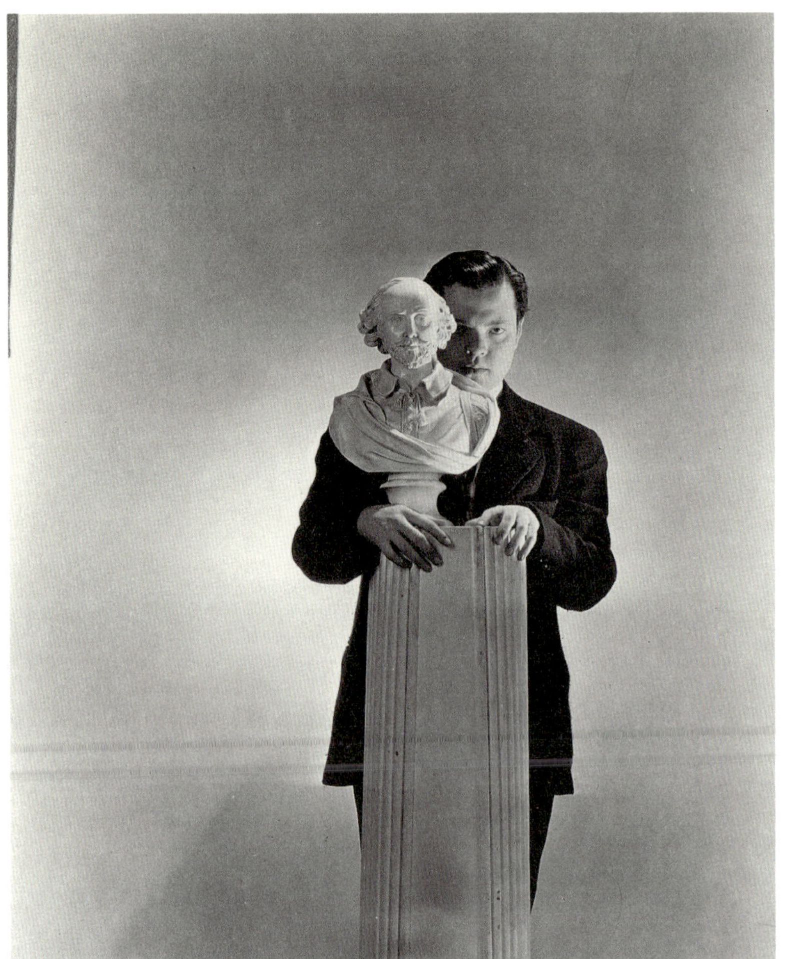

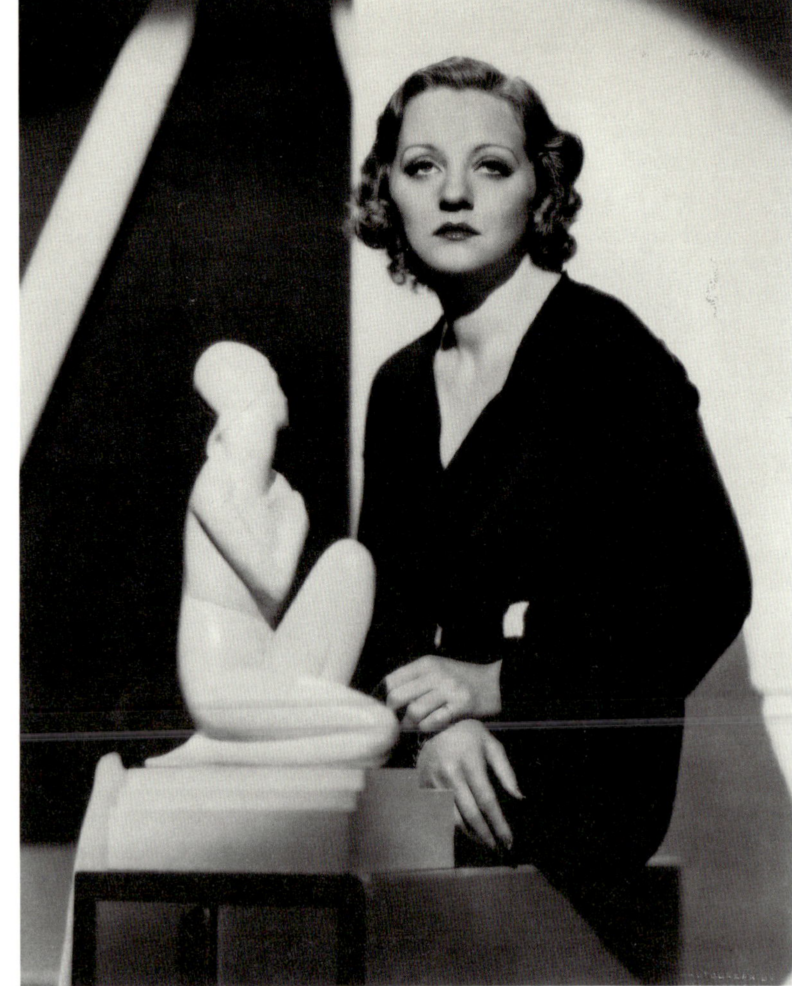

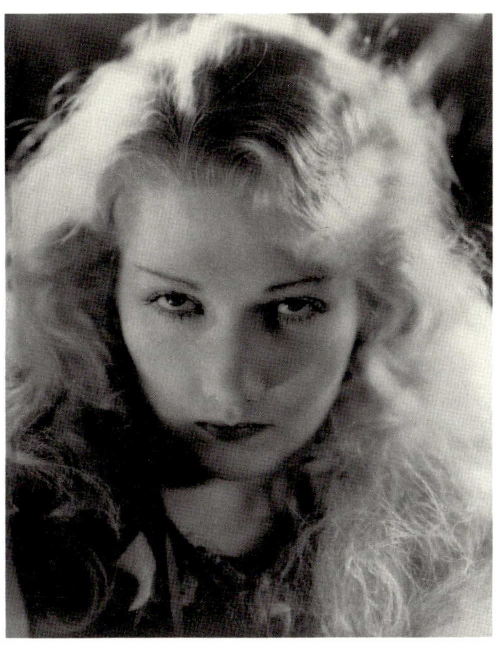

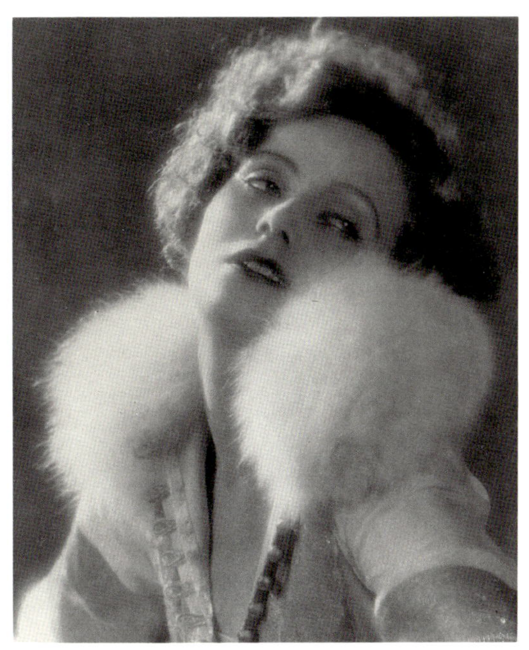

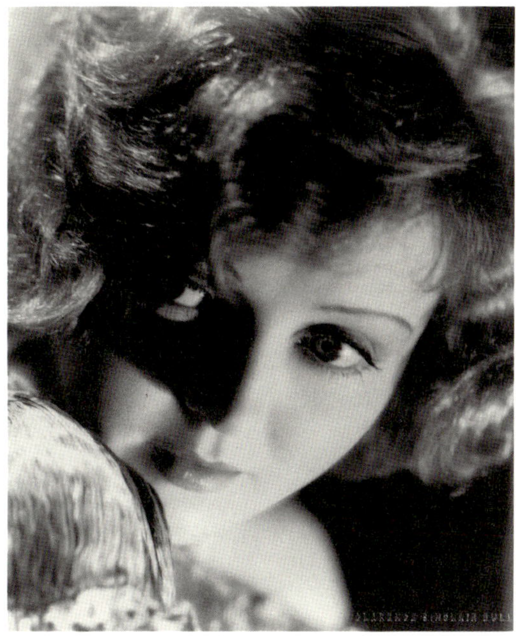

GEORGE HURRELL
Edwina Booth, 1932

RUTH HARRIET LOUISE
Greta Garbo, Metro Goldwyn, n.d.

CLARENCE SINCLAIR BULL
*Nancy Carroll in Leon Gordon's
Drama "Undesirable Lady,"* n.d.

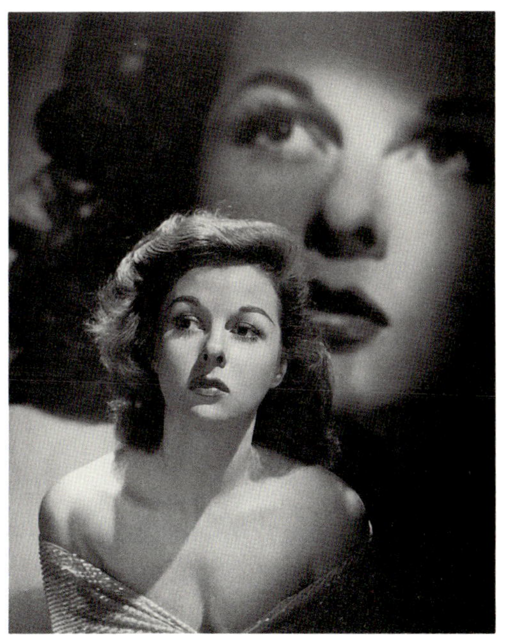

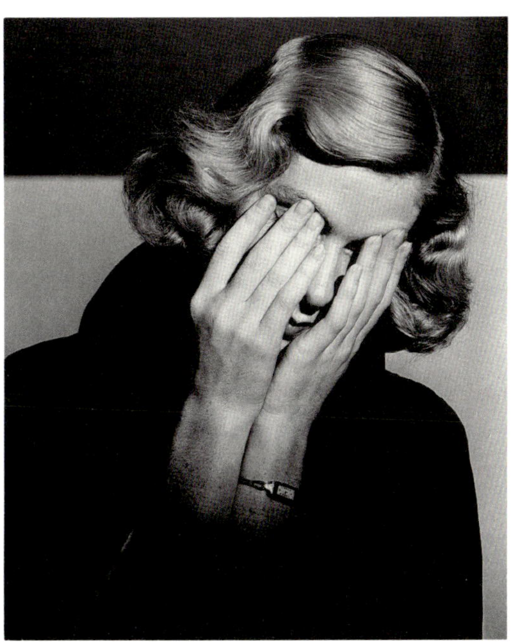

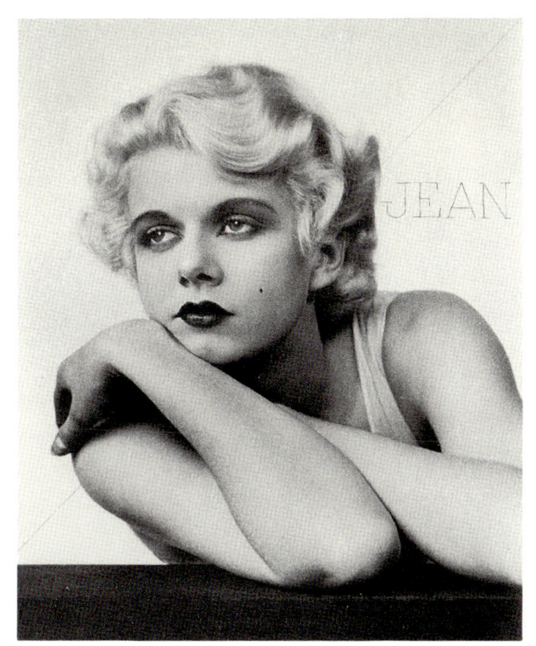

LASZLO WILLINGER
Susan Hayward, n.d.

MAX DUPAIN
Greta Garbo, 1940

WILLIAM MORTENSEN
Jean Harlow, c. 1927

CHRISTOPHER WILLIAMS
Andra Millian, Women and Roses
(detail), 1986

ANNE ROWLAND
Untitled (Frank Sinatra), 1987

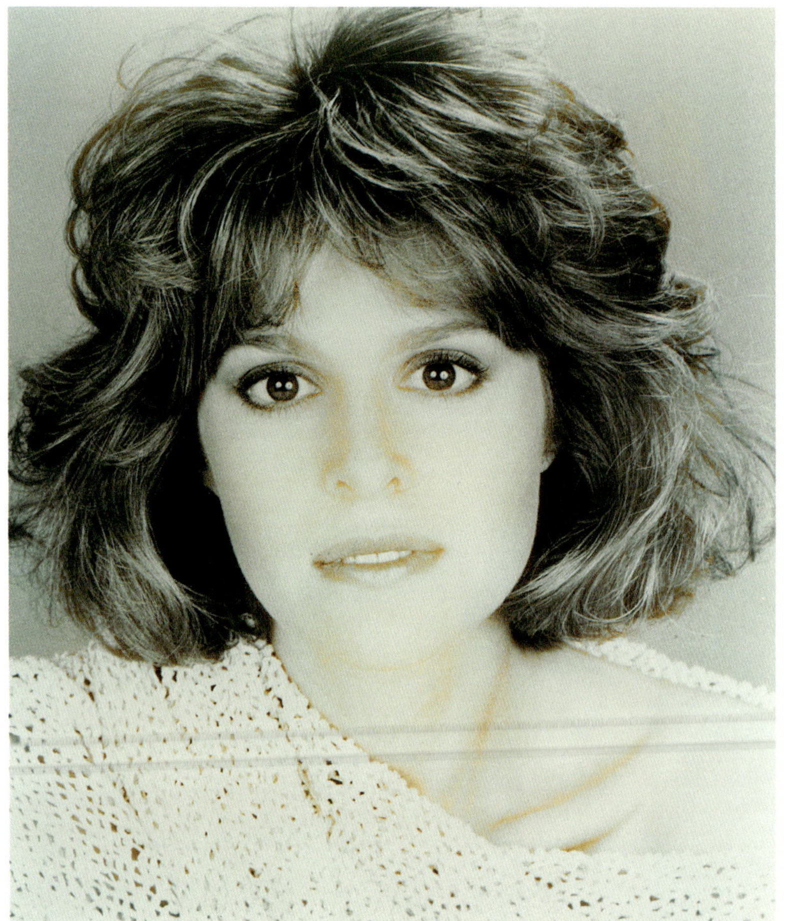

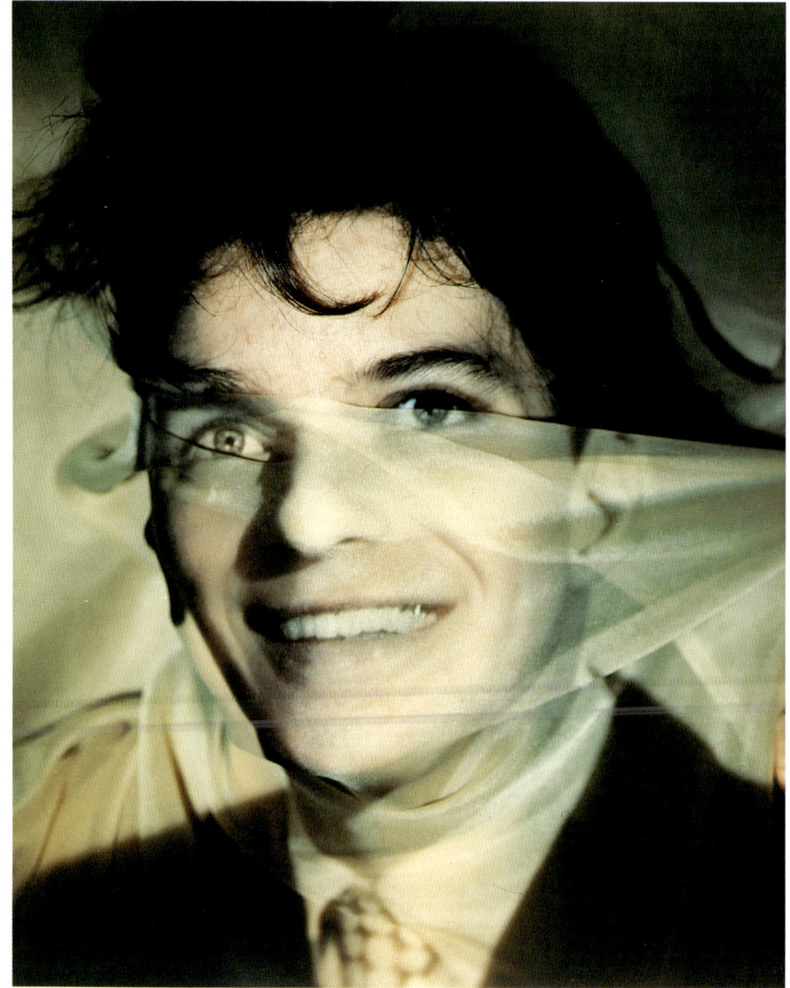

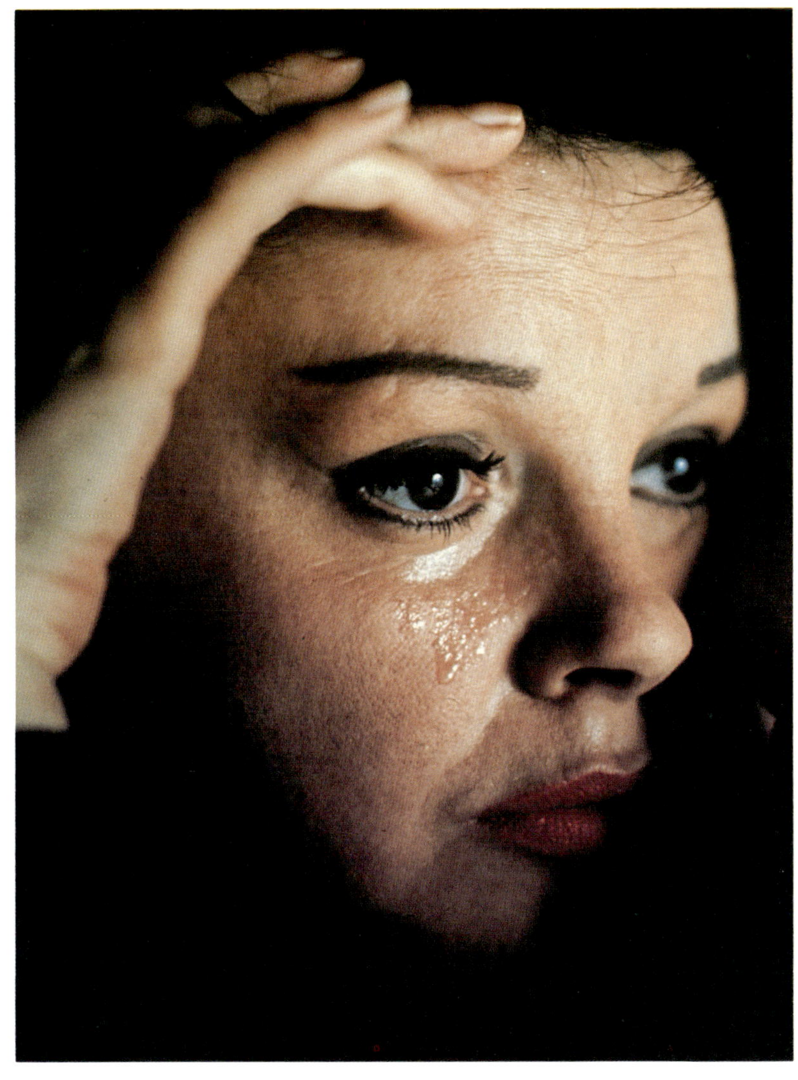

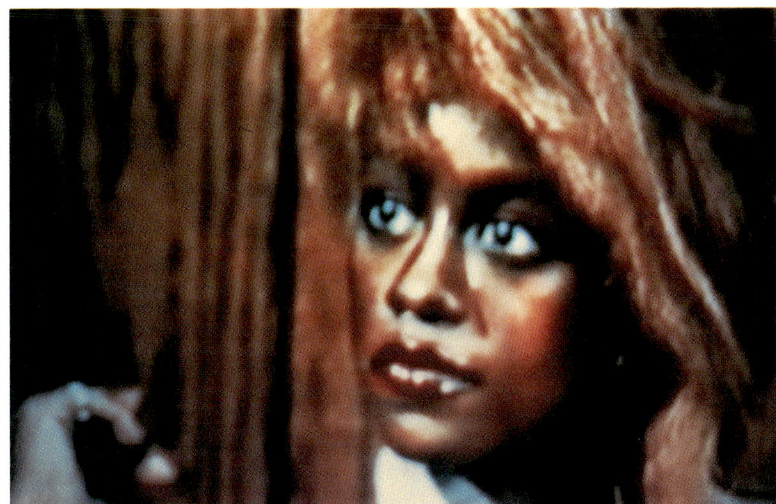

Douglas Kirkland
Judy Garland, 1961

René Santos
Untitled, 1984

MAX MUNN AUTREY

Max M. Autrey with 11 Portraits, c. 1947

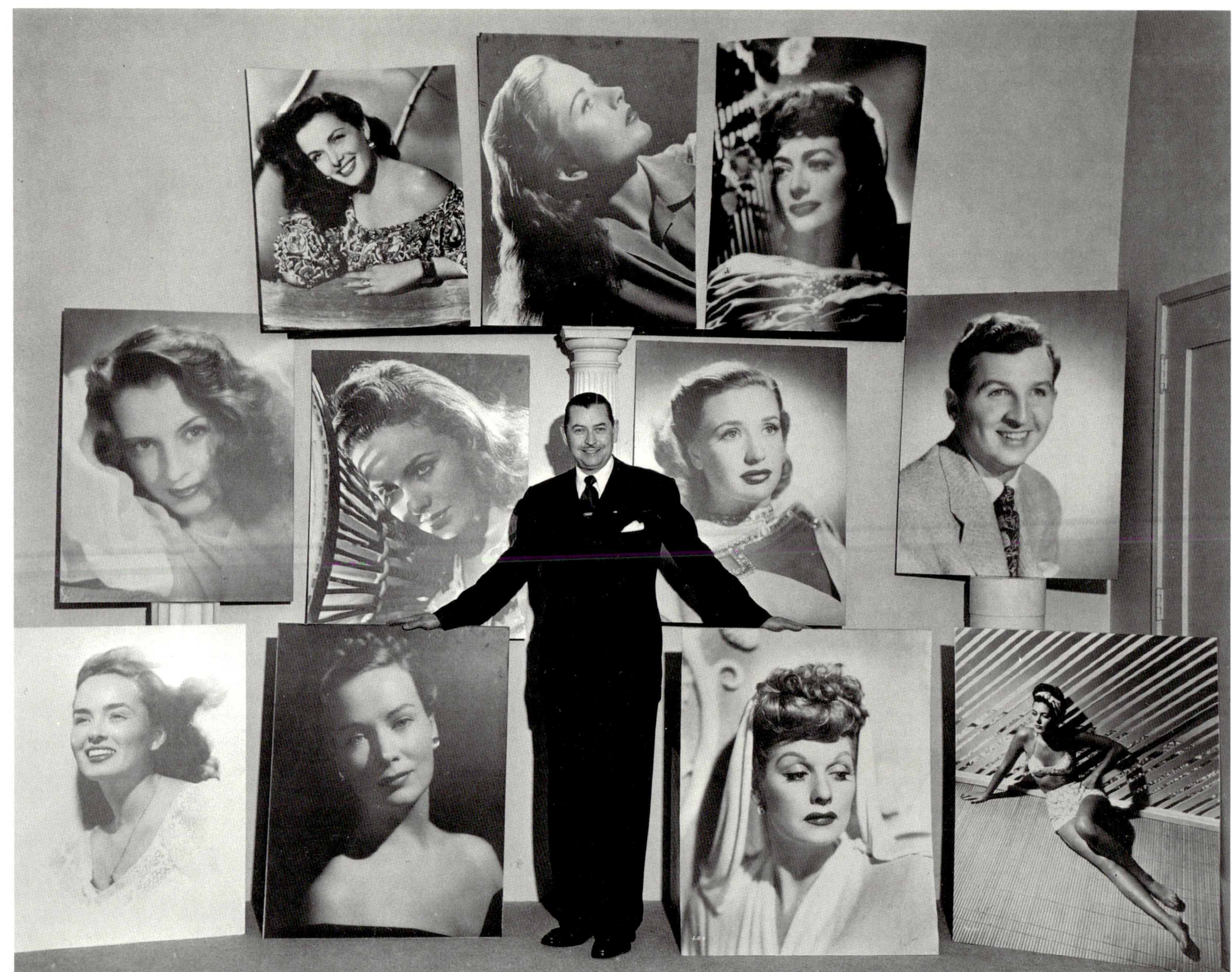

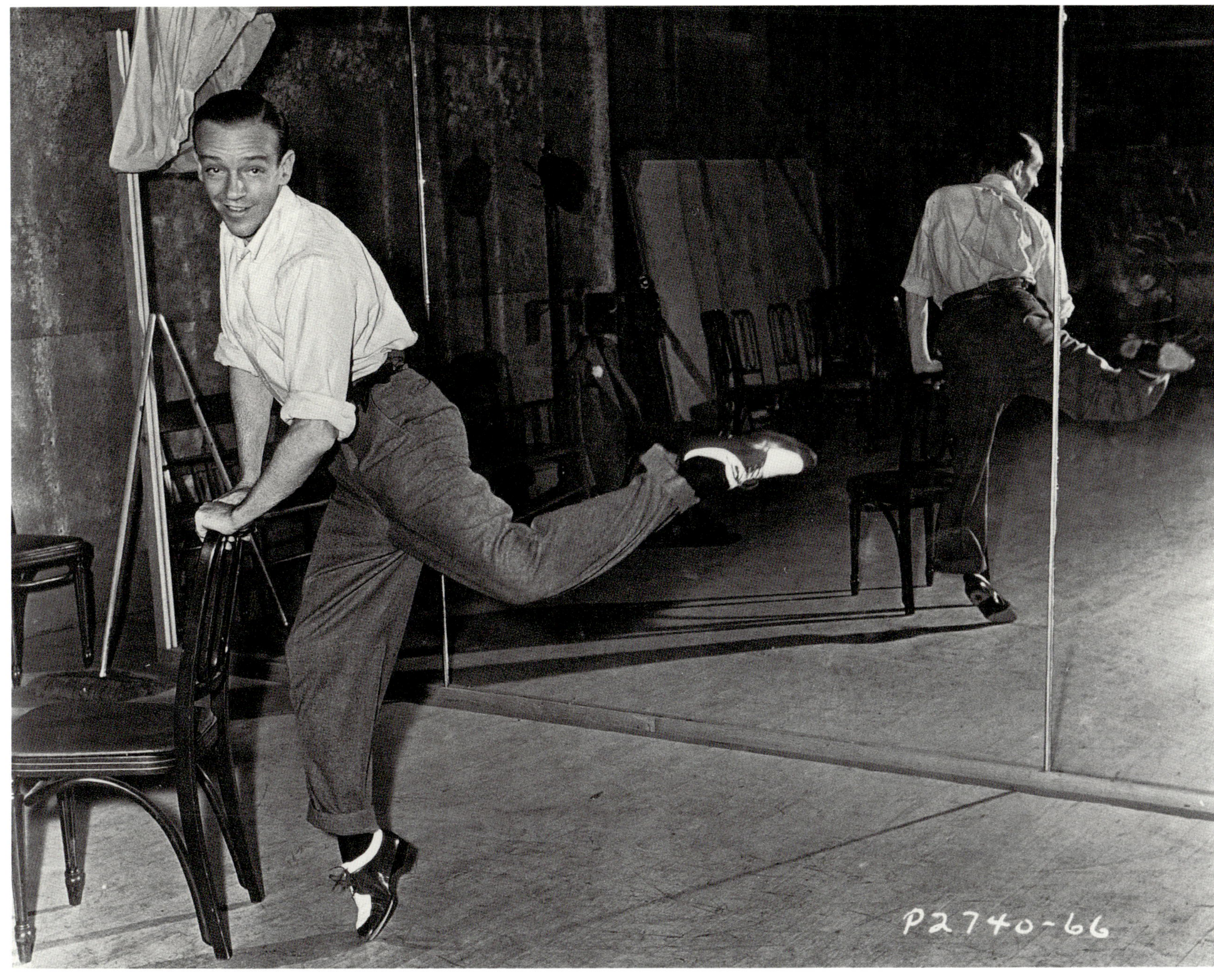

UNIDENTIFIED ARTIST
Fred Astaire, Dancing, n.d.

ALEXIS SMITH
Miss April, 1992

LAURIE SIMMONS
English Lady, 1987

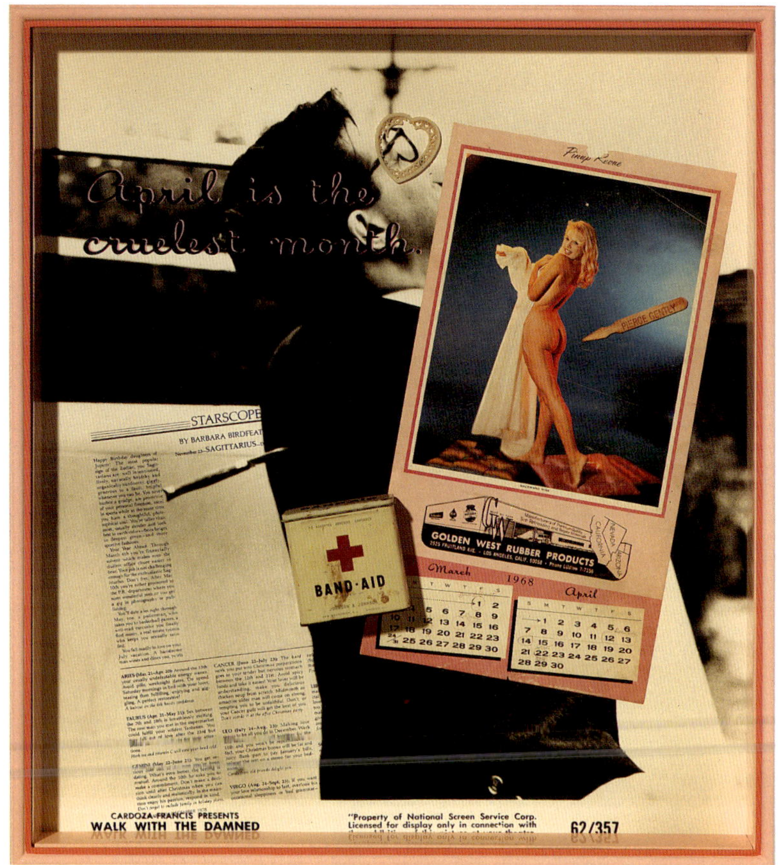

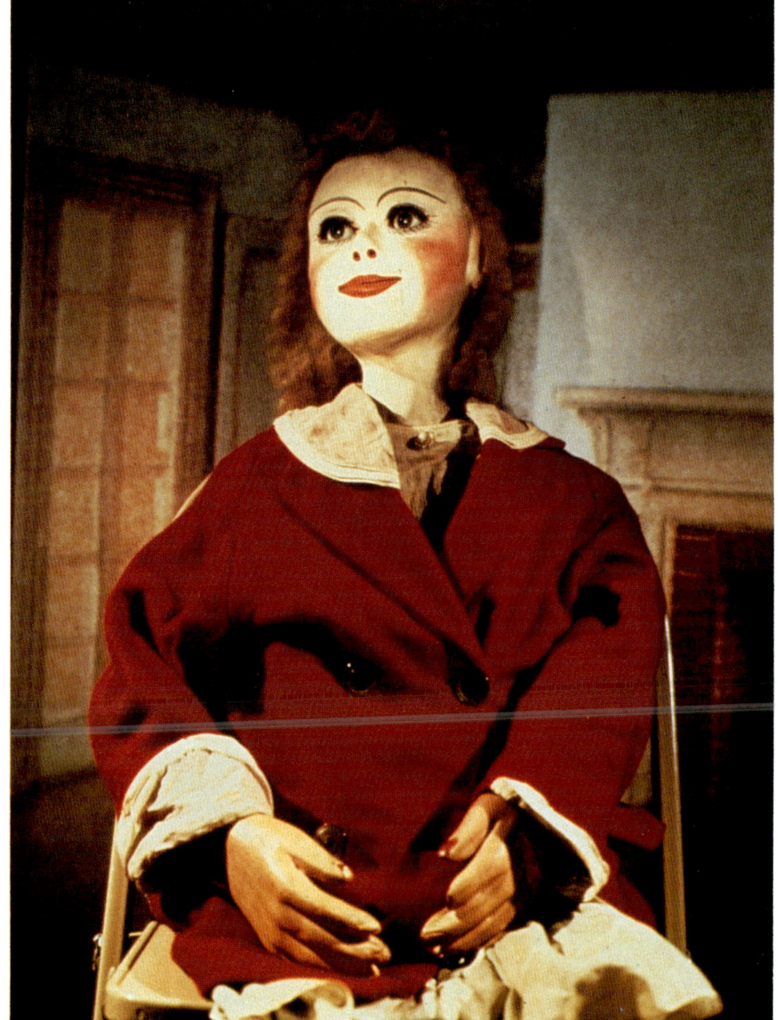

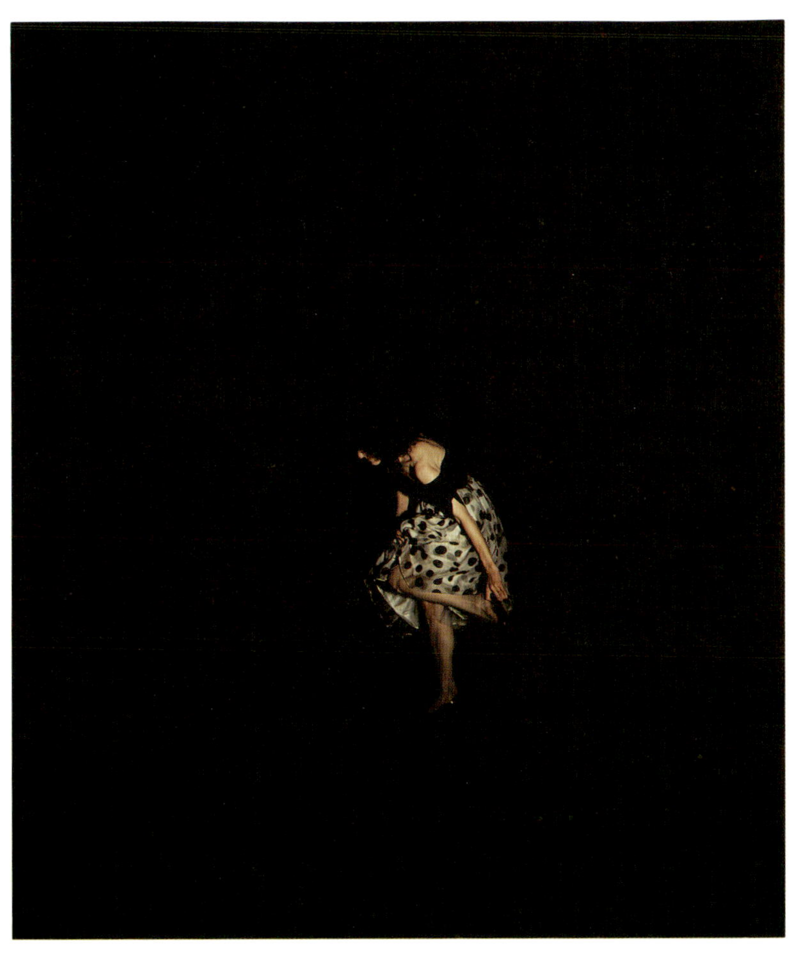

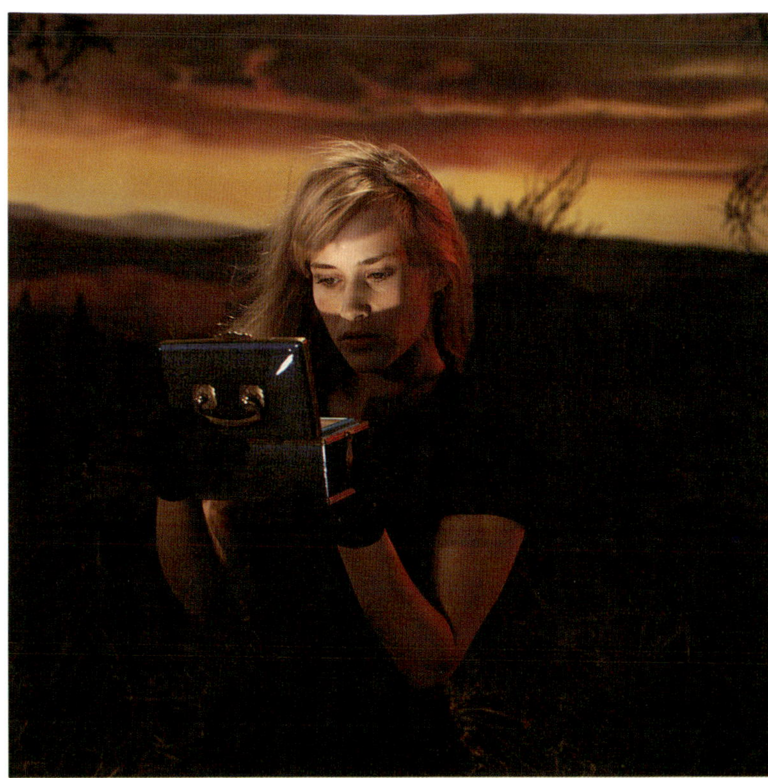

EILEEN COWIN
Untitled, 1986

BRUCE AND
NORMAN YONEMOTO
Made in Hollywood, 1989

JOHN BALDESSARI
Two Dwarfs, 1990

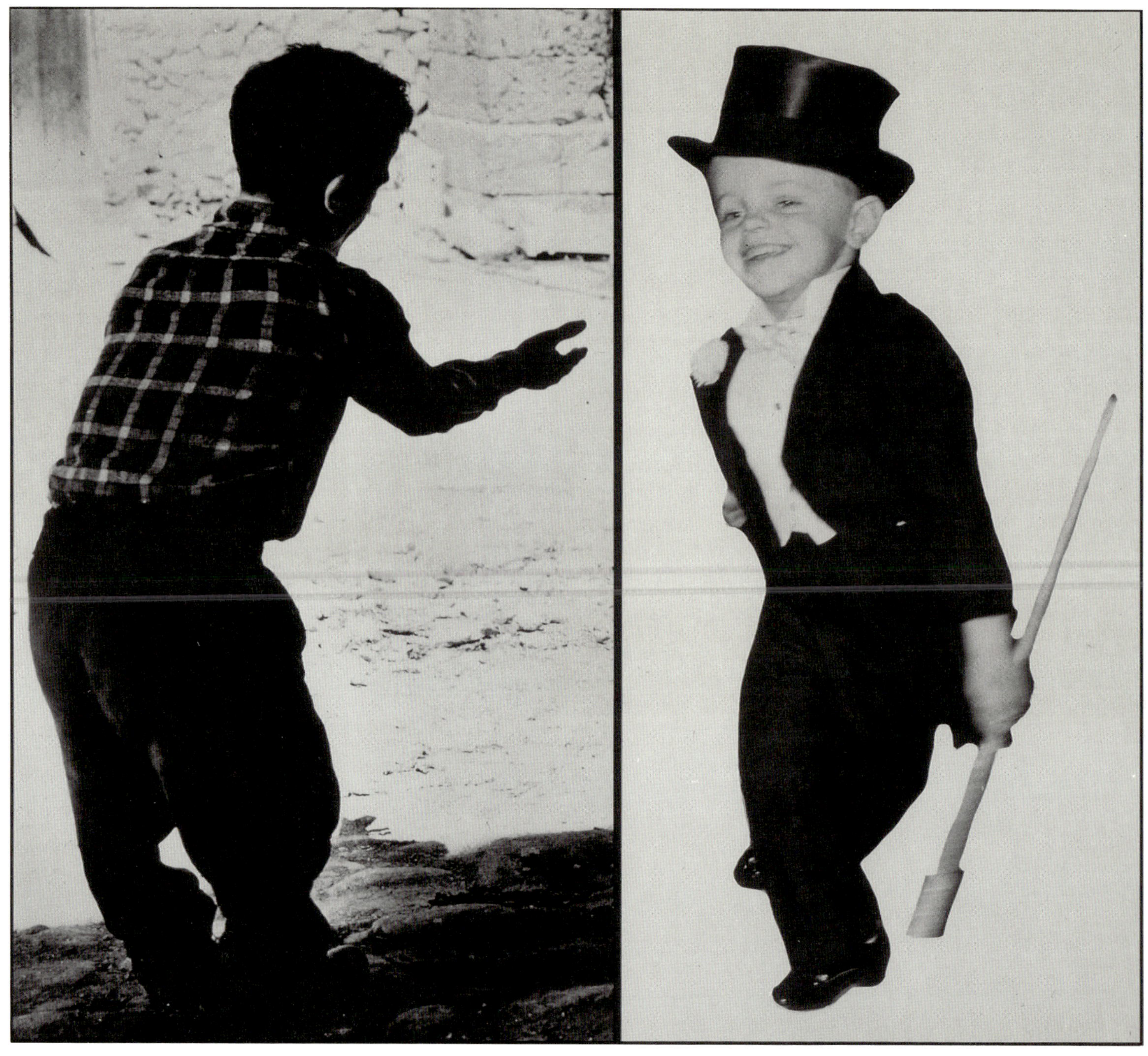

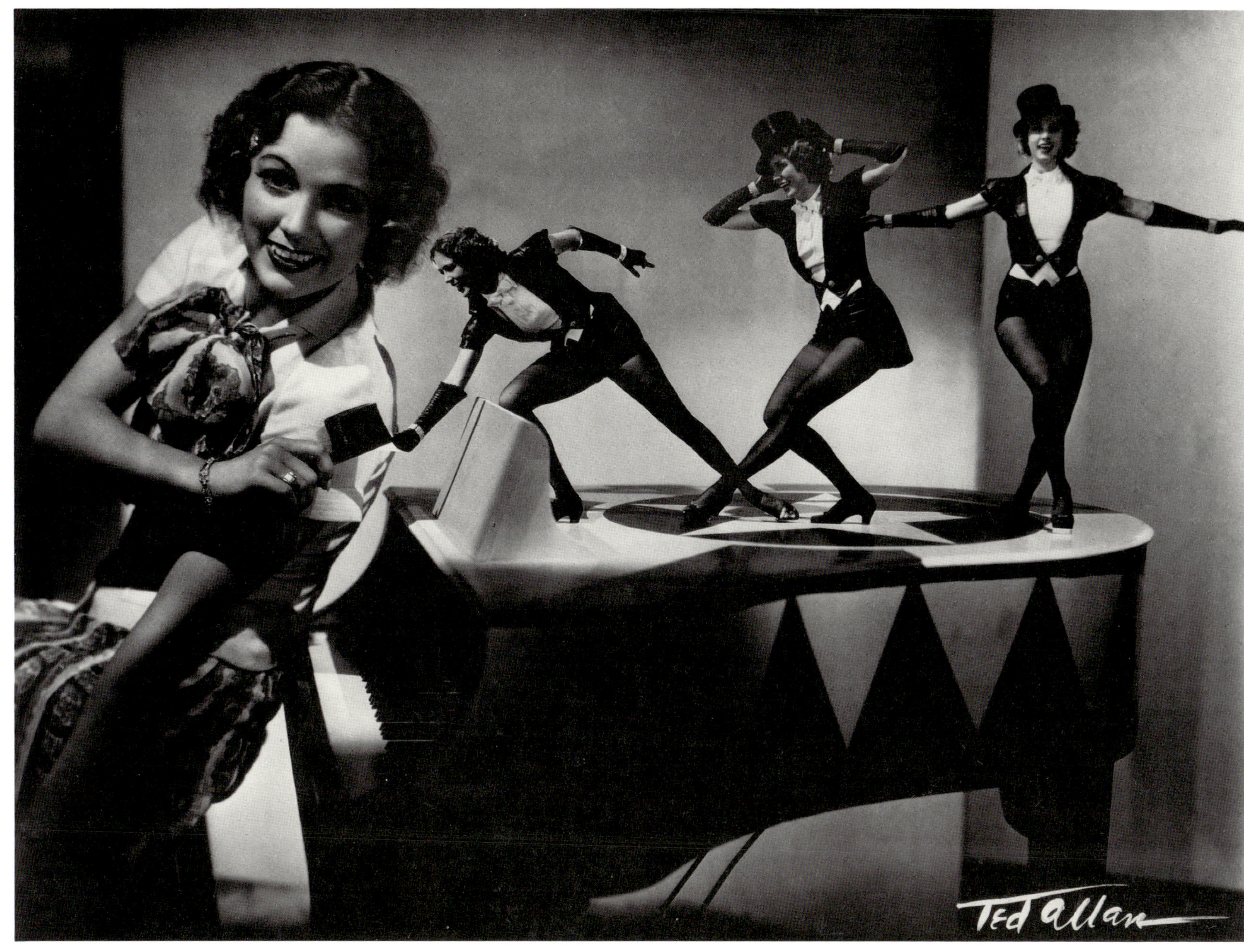

TED ALLAN

Eleanor Powell, "Broadway Melody of 1936," 1936

BONNIE SCHIFFMAN

Angelyne, 1987

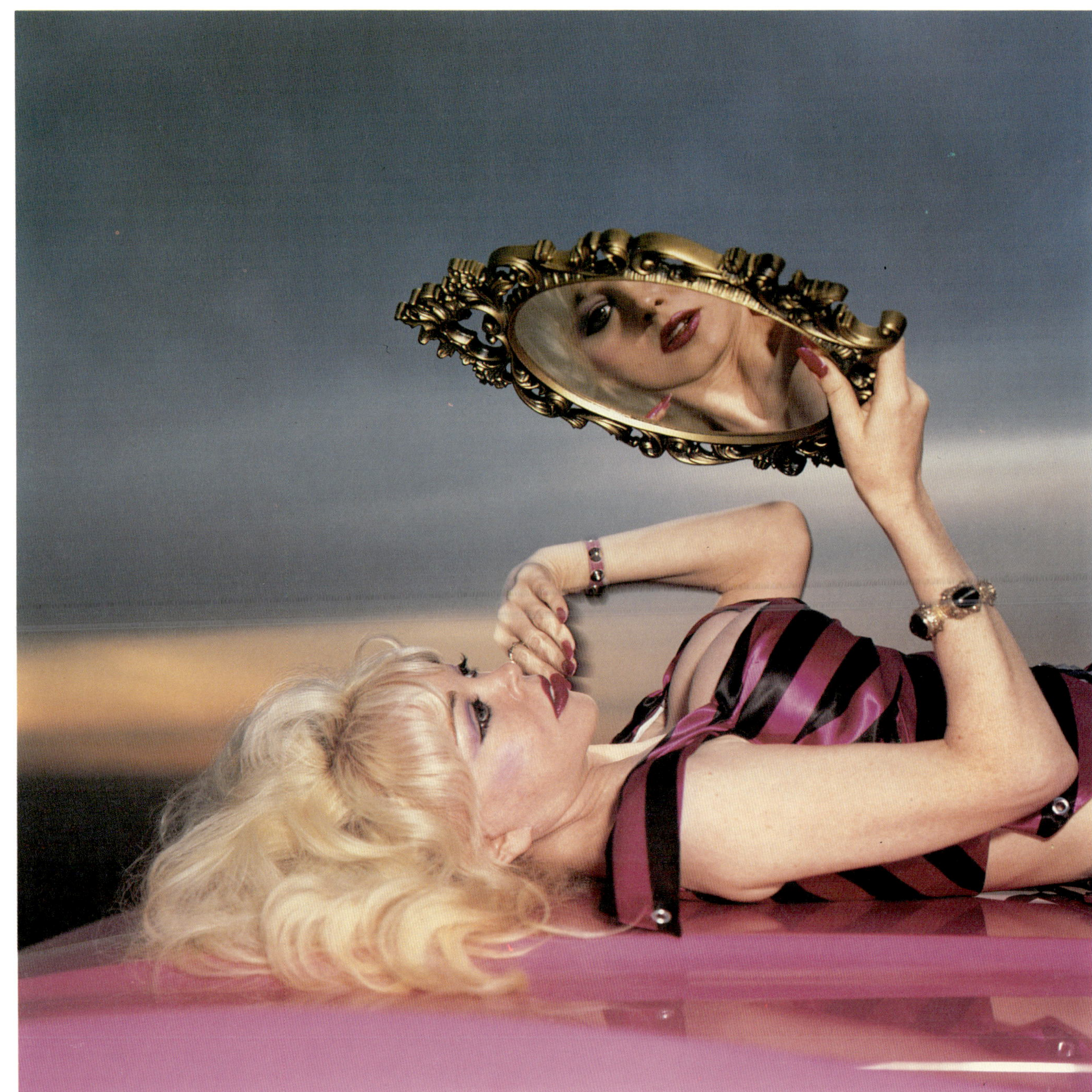

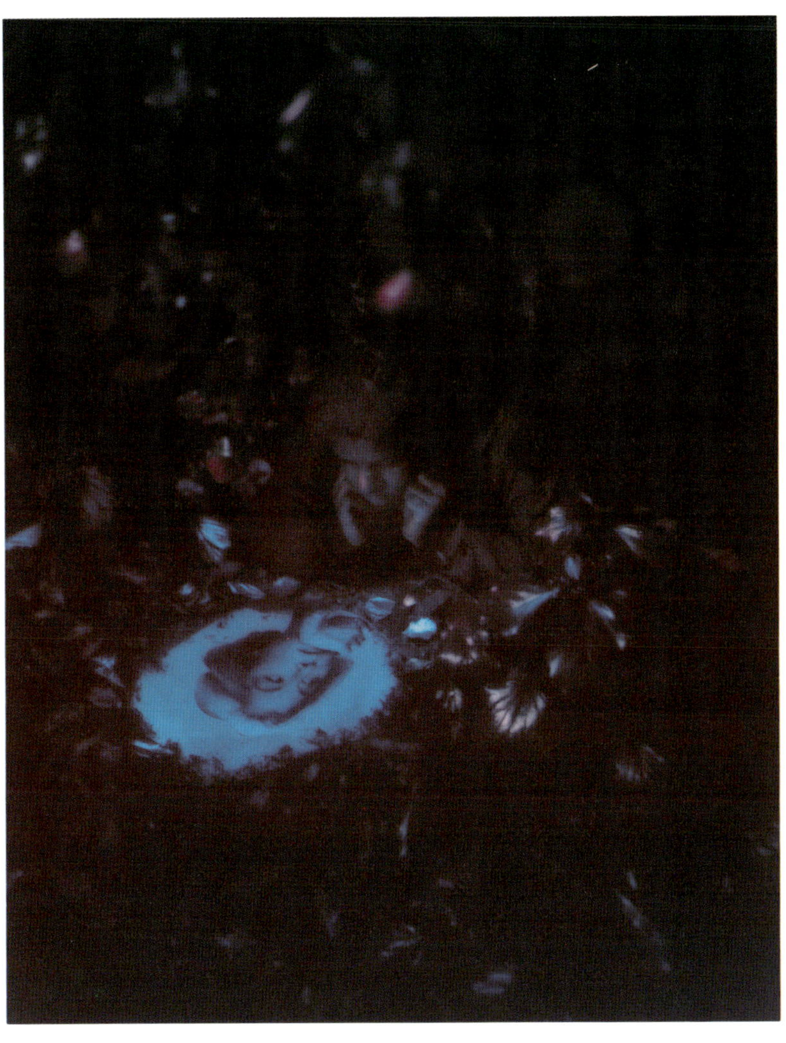

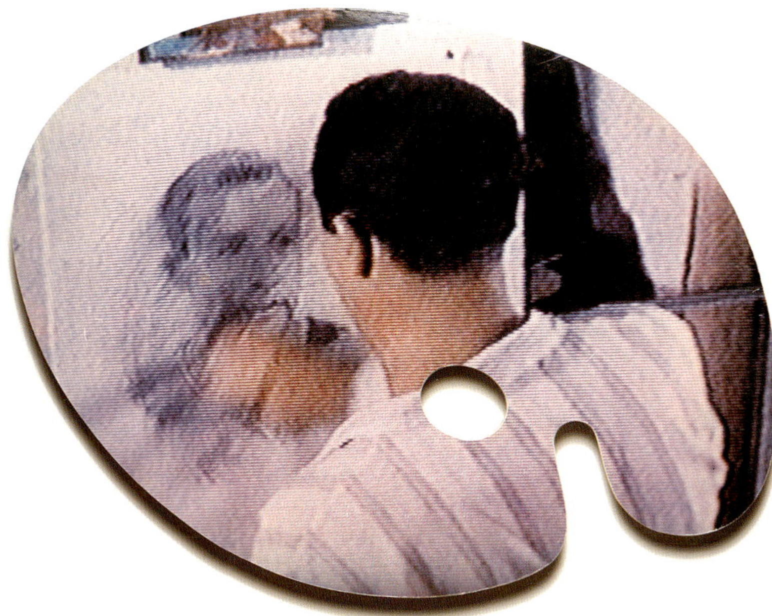

Nancy Barton
and Michael Glass
  Untitled (from the show *Butter
  Wouldn't Melt in My Mouth*), 1990

Theresa Pendlebury
  Untitled ("*An American in Paris*"), 1988

JOHN BOSKOVICH

Self-portrait, 1986-87

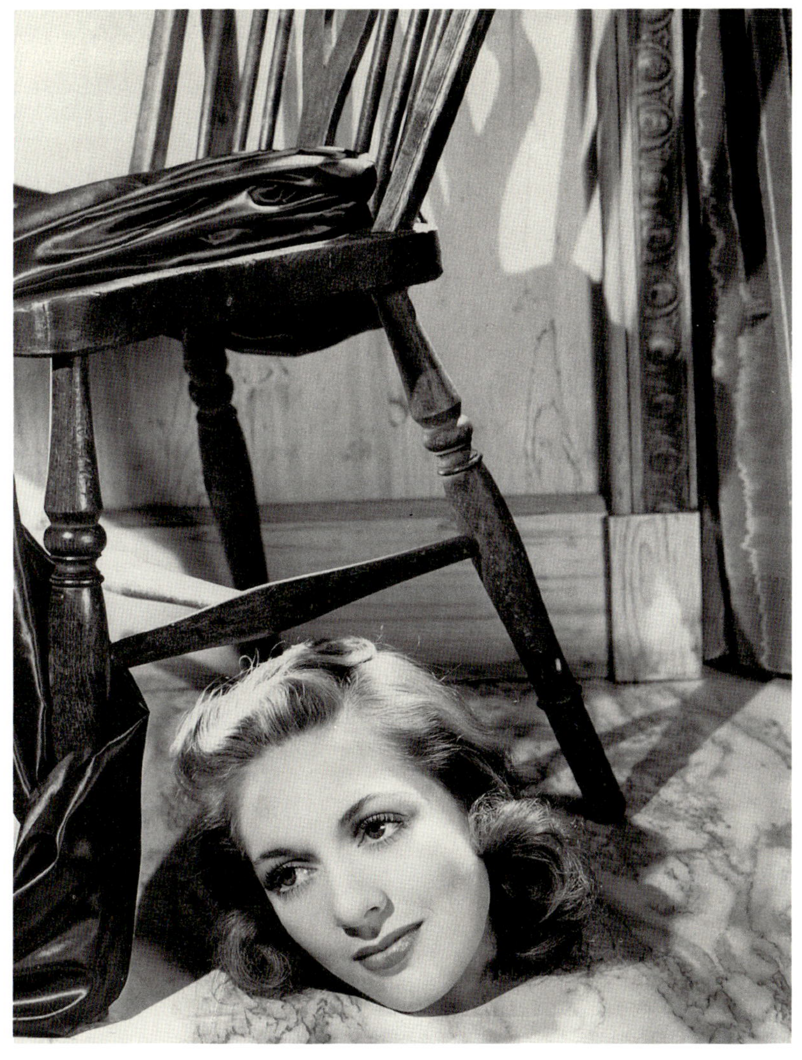

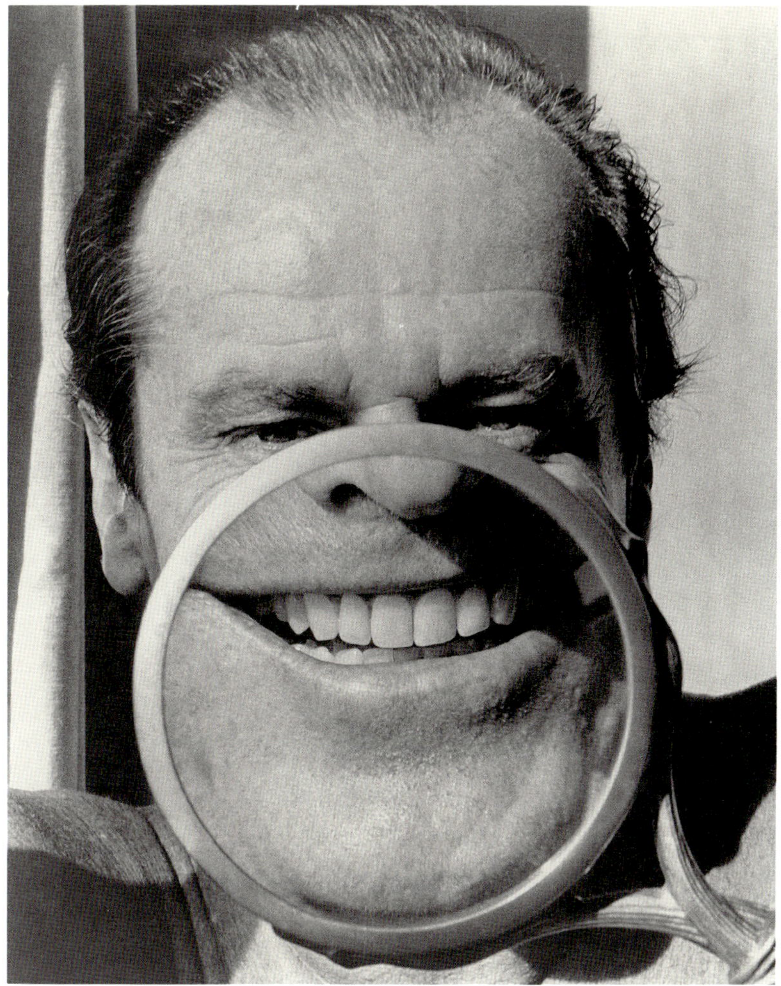

Angus McBean
Woman's Head under Chair, c. 1940

Herb Ritts
Jack Nicholson, L.A., 1986

FRANK POWOLNY

Tony Perkins, c. 1960

LOUISE LAWLER

*Recognition Maybe, May Not
Be Useful,* 1990

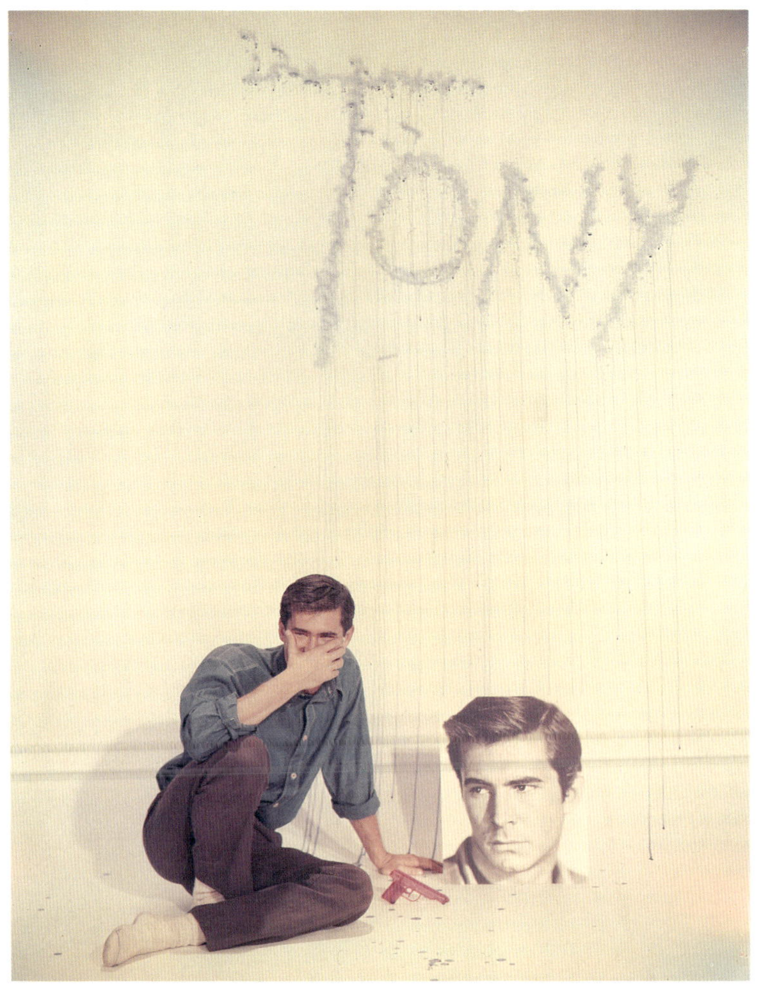

TONY

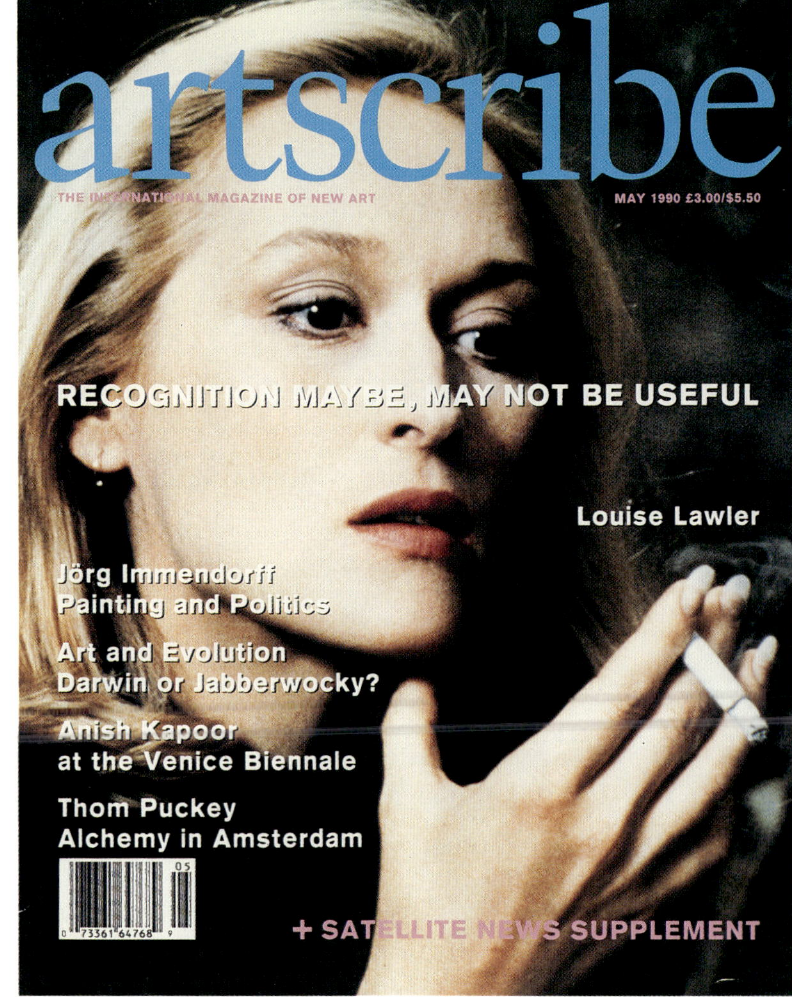

artscribe
THE INTERNATIONAL MAGAZINE OF NEW ART
MAY 1990 £3.00/$5.50

RECOGNITION MAYBE, MAY NOT BE USEFUL

Louise Lawler

Jörg Immendorff
Painting and Politics

Art and Evolution
Darwin or Jabberwocky?

Anish Kapoor
at the Venice Biennale

Thom Puckey
Alchemy in Amsterdam

+ SATELLITE NEWS SUPPLEMENT

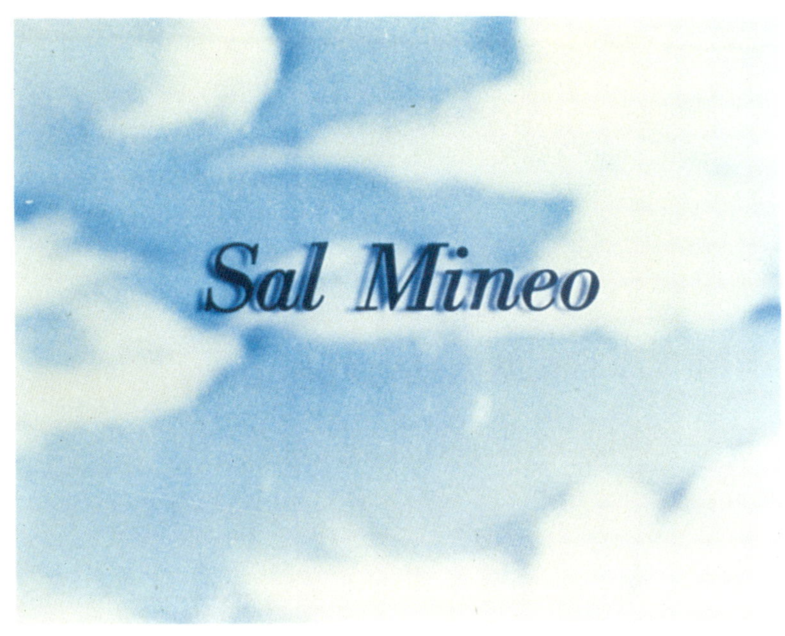

Sal Mineo

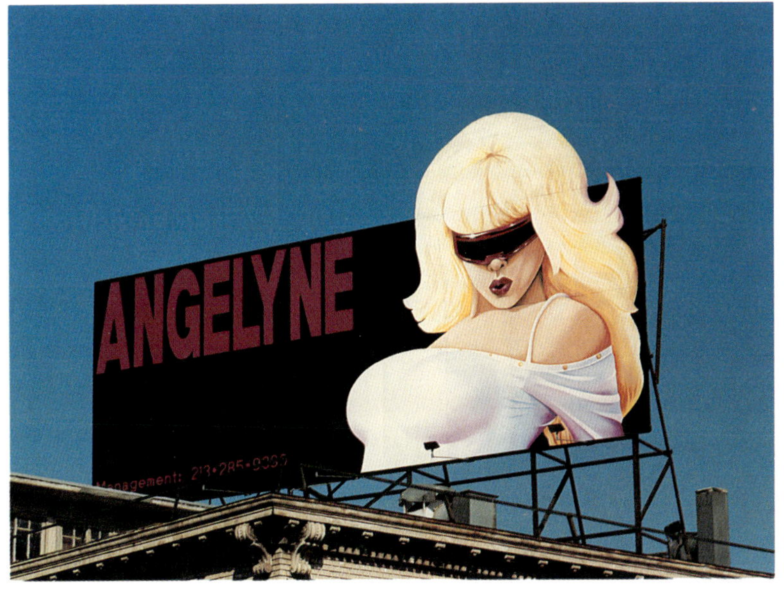

ANGELYNE
Management: 213•285•9300

KATHE BURKHART
Kathe Burkhart by
Elizabeth Taylor (from the
Elizabeth Taylor Series), 1989

LARRY JOHNSON
Untitled (Movie Stars on
Clouds—Sal Mineo) 1983

ANGELYNE
Angelyne Billboard, 1992

Jean Simmons, Laughing, 1950
Jean Simmons, Crying, 1950

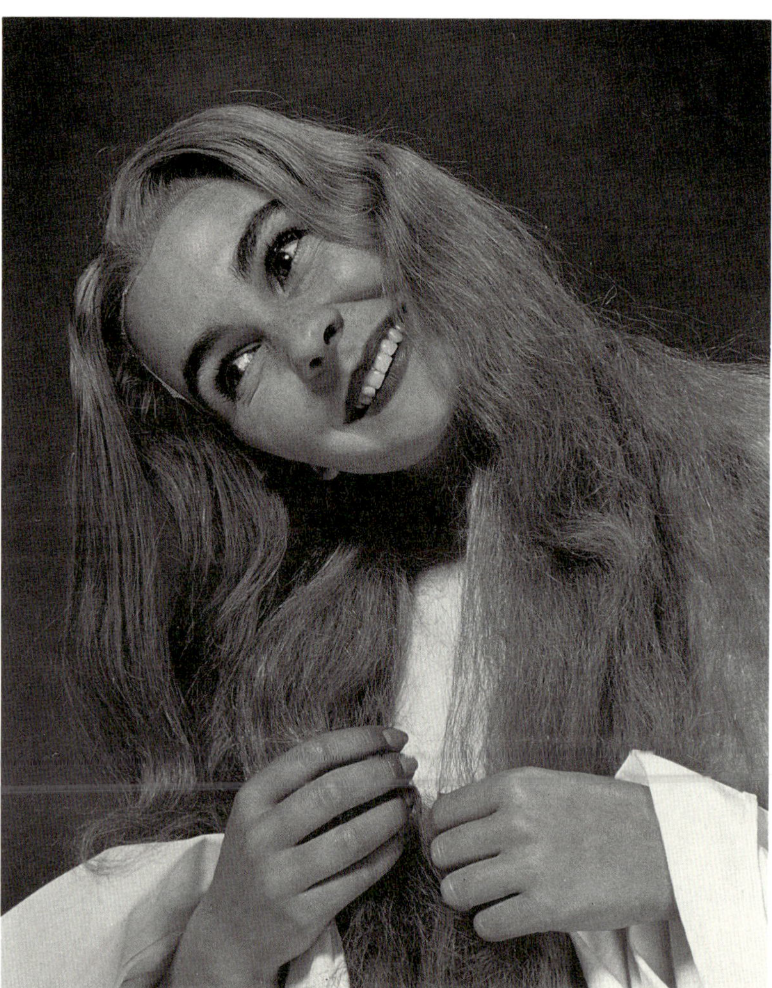
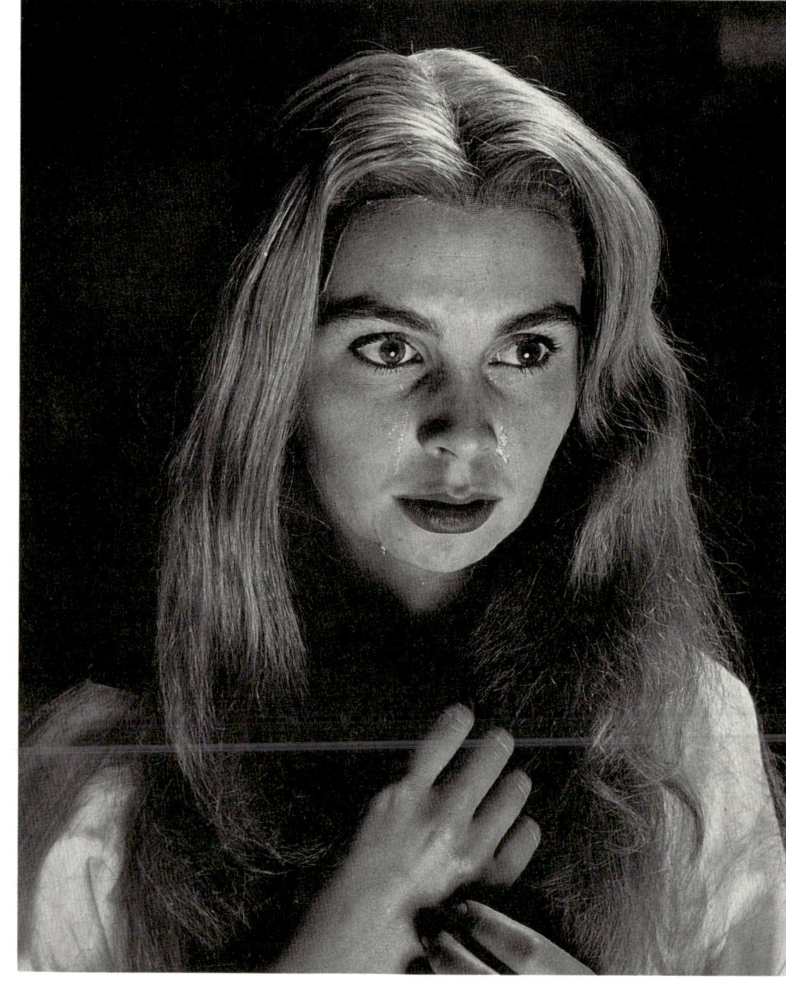

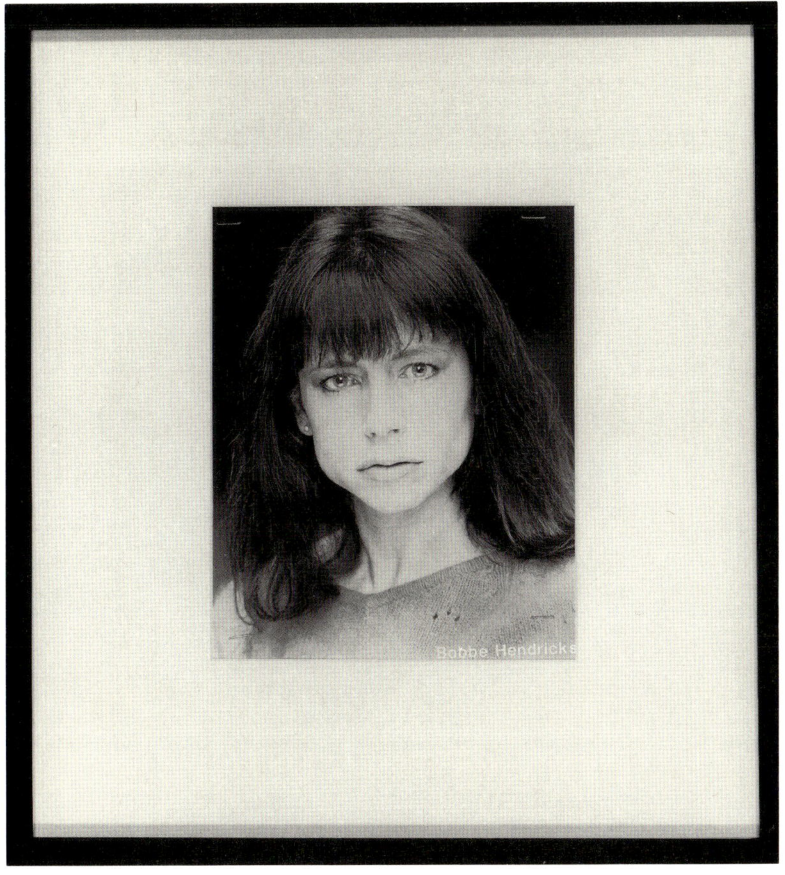

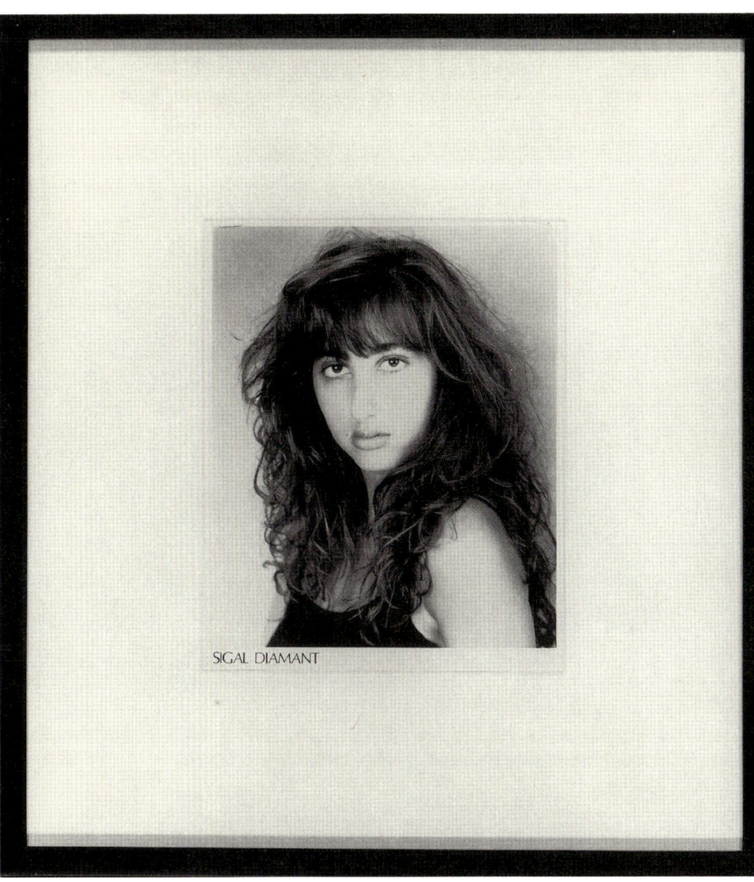

DAVID AND TIM TATTU
Self-portraits, 1992

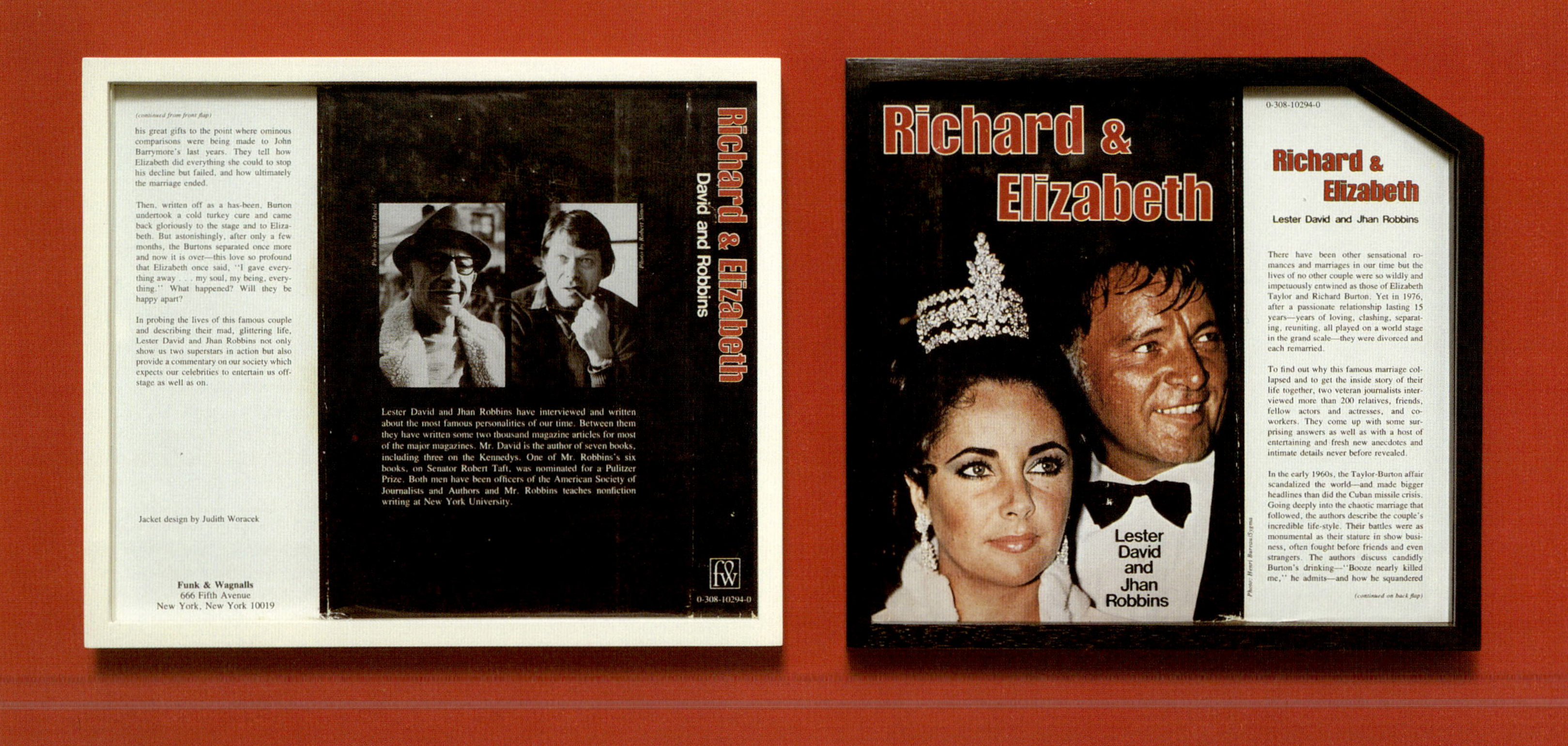

(continued from front flap)

his great gifts to the point where ominous comparisons were being made to John Barrymore's last years. They tell how Elizabeth did everything she could to stop his decline but failed, and how ultimately the marriage ended.

Then, written off as a has-been, Burton undertook a cold turkey cure and came back gloriously to the stage and to Elizabeth. But astonishingly, after only a few months, the Burtons separated once more and now it is over—this love so profound that Elizabeth once said, "I gave everything away . . . my soul, my being, everything." What happened? Will they be happy apart?

In probing the lives of this famous couple and describing their mad, glittering life, Lester David and Jhan Robbins not only show us two superstars in action but also provide a commentary on our society which expects our celebrities to entertain us off-stage as well as on.

Jacket design by Judith Woracek

Funk & Wagnalls
666 Fifth Avenue
New York, New York 10019

Lester David and Jhan Robbins have interviewed and written about the most famous personalities of our time. Between them they have written some two thousand magazine articles for most of the major magazines. Mr. David is the author of seven books, including three on the Kennedys. One of Mr. Robbins's six books, on Senator Robert Taft, was nominated for a Pulitzer Prize. Both men have been officers of the American Society of Journalists and Authors and Mr. Robbins teaches nonfiction writing at New York University.

0-308-10294-0

Richard & Elizabeth

David and Robbins

Richard & Elizabeth

Lester David and Jhan Robbins

0-308-10294-0

There have been other sensational romances and marriages in our time but the lives of no other couple were so wildly and impetuously entwined as those of Elizabeth Taylor and Richard Burton. Yet in 1976, after a passionate relationship lasting 15 years—years of loving, clashing, separating, reuniting, all played on a world stage in the grand scale—they were divorced and each remarried.

To find out why this famous marriage collapsed and to get the inside story of their life together, two veteran journalists interviewed more than 200 relatives, friends, fellow actors and actresses, and co-workers. They come up with some surprising answers as well as with a host of entertaining and fresh new anecdotes and intimate details never before revealed.

In the early 1960s, the Taylor-Burton affair scandalized the world—and made bigger headlines than did the Cuban missile crisis. Going deeply into the chaotic marriage that followed, the authors describe the couple's incredible life-style. Their battles were as monumental as their stature in show business, often fought before friends and even strangers. The authors discuss candidly Burton's drinking—"Booze nearly killed me," he admits—and how he squandered

(continued on back flap)

Lester David and Jhan Robbins

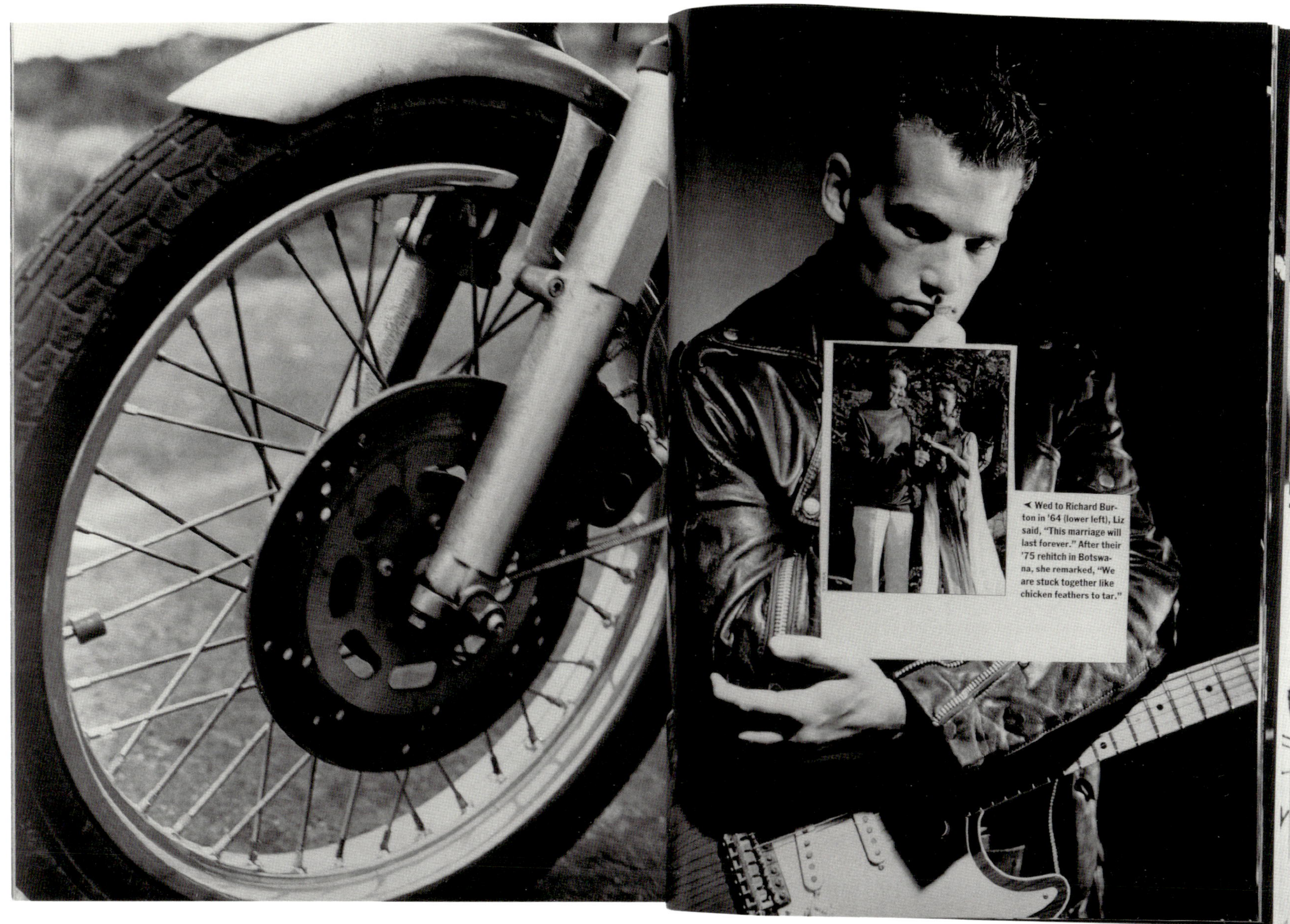

RICHARD HAWKINS

Bruce/People, 1991

ANDY WARHOL

Untitled (self-portrait), 1963-64

©The Estate of Andy Warhol

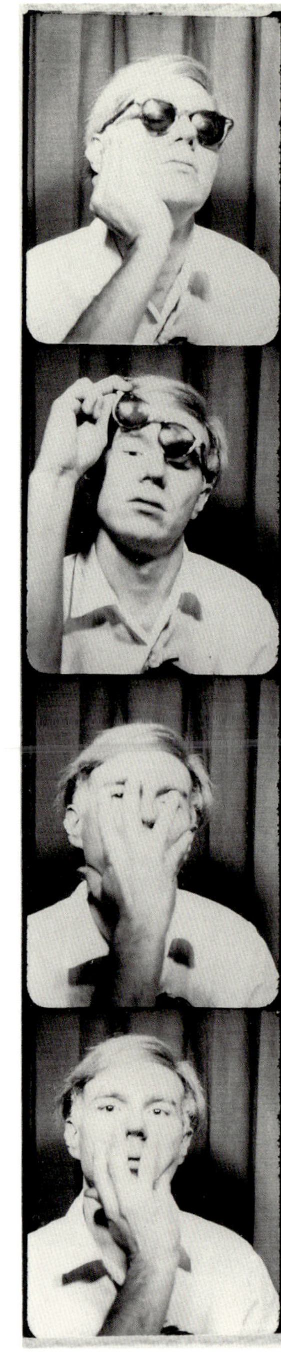

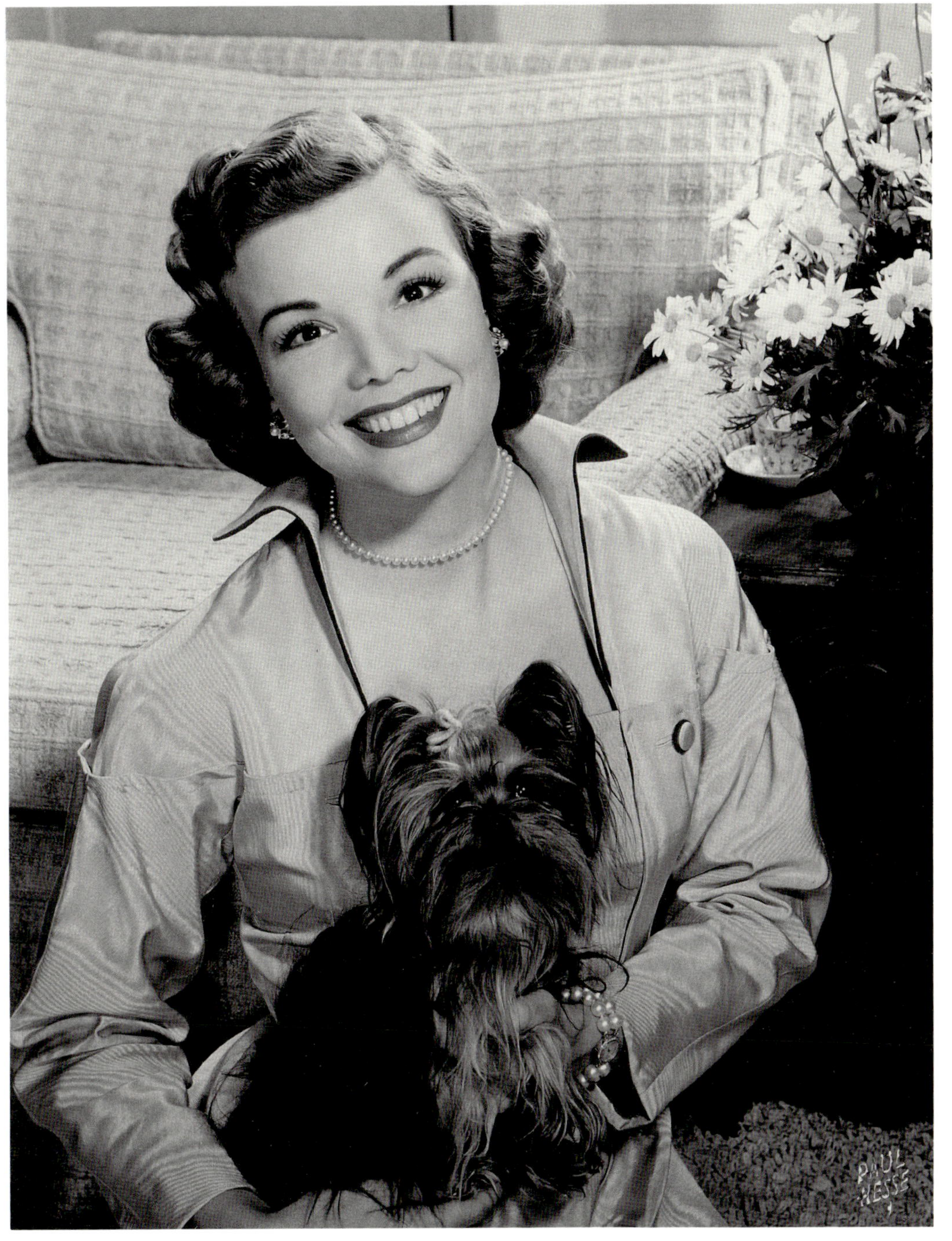

PAUL HESSE

Nanette Fabray, c. 1959

Exhibition Checklist

All measurements are in inches unless otherwise noted. Height precedes width.

JAMES ABBE

1. *Charlie Chaplin in "The Pilgrim,"* 1923
Black and white print, 10 x 8
Courtesy of the Los Angeles County
Museum of Art; gift of the Sid and
Diana Avery Trust

TED ALLAN

2. *Eleanor Powell, "Broadway Melody of 1936,"* 1936
Black and white print, 11 x 14
Courtesy of the artist and Sid Avery,
Motion Picture and Television Photo
Archive, Los Angeles

3. *Jimmy Stewart*, n.d.
Black and white print, 14 x 11
Courtesy of Fahey/Klein Gallery,
Los Angeles

ANGELYNE

4. *Angelyne Billboard*, 1992
Enamel on wood, aprox. 11' x 36'
Artist: Scott A. Hennig
Photographer: Larry L. Lombardi
Courtesy of Angelyne Incorporated,
Los Angeles

MAX MUNN AUTREY

5. *Warner Baxter, Fox Films*, n.d.
Black and white print, 10 x 8½
Courtesy of Fahey/Klein Gallery,
Los Angeles

6. *Max M. Autrey with 11 Portraits*, c. 1947
Black and white print, 8 x 10
Courtesy of the Los Angeles County
Museum of Art; gift of the Hollywood
Photographers Archive

SID AVERY

7. *Jayne Mansfield Signing Autographs in
front of Dino's Restaurant on the Sunset
Strip in Los Angeles*, 1961
Black and white print, 16 x 20

8. *Sammy Davis Jr. with Ex-wife Loray White
at the Premiere of "Can Can,"* 1960
Black and white print, 20 x 16
Both courtesy of Ron Avery, Motion
Picture and Television Photo Archive,
Los Angeles

JOHN BALDESSARI

9. *Two Dwarfs*, 1990
Two black and white prints
82 x 89½ overall
Courtesy of Alan Hergott and
Curt Shepard

NANCY BARTON
AND MICHAEL GLASS

10. *Untitled* (from the show *Butter Wouldn't
Melt in My Mouth*), 1990
Two color prints, 30 x 24, 20 x 24
Courtesy of the artists and American
Fine Arts, Co., New York

CECIL BEATON

11. *Orson Welles (with Bust of Shakespeare)*,
1936
Black and white print, 10 x 8
Courtesy of the Los Angeles County
Museum of Art; gift of the Hollywood
Photographers Archive

CINDY BERNARD

12. *Ask the Dust: North by Northwest
(1959/1990)*, 1990
Color print, 12½ x 23
Courtesy of the artist and Richard
Kuhlenschmidt Gallery, Santa Monica

13. *Ask the Dust: Dirty Harry (1971/1990)*,
1990
Color print, 11½ x 23
Courtesy of Marjorie and
Leonard Vernon

JOHN BOSKOVICH

14. *Self-portrait*, 1986-87
Black and white print, gouache
42¼ x 44
Courtesy of the artist and Rosamund
Felsen Gallery, Los Angeles

JOHN BRUMFIELD

15. *Robert Posing Coyly as a Hollywood Star*,
1977
Black and white print, 20 x 16
Courtesy of the artist

CLARENCE SINCLAIR BULL

16. *Nancy Carroll in Leon Gordon's Drama
"Undesirable Lady,"* n.d.
Black and white print, 10 x 8
Courtesy of Fahey/Klein Gallery,
Los Angeles

KATHE BURKHART

17. *Kathe Burkhart by Elizabeth Taylor (from
the Elizabeth Taylor Series)*, 1989
Acrylic and marker on paper, 50 x 44
Courtesy of the artist and Shoshana
Wayne Gallery, Santa Monica

NANCY BURSON

18. *Baby Marilyn*, 1988
Polacolor print, 24 x20
Courtesy of Jan Kesner

ROBERT COBURN

19. *Rita Hayworth and Glenn Ford*, c. 1946
Black and white print, 19¼ x 15

20. *William Holden and Kim Novak*, c. 1955
Black and white print, 19¼ x 15¼

21. *Charlie McCarthy and Edgar Bergen*, n.d.
Black and white print, 12 x 9¼

22. *Vanity (Rita Hayworth in "Cover Girl")*,
1944
Hand-colored dye transfer print,
16 x 12⅞

23. *Orson Welles*, 1952
Black and white print, 20 x 16
All courtesy of Robert Coburn II and
Fahey/Klein Gallery, Los Angeles

ROBERT COBURN II

24. *Kim Novak (Columbia Pictures)*, 1957
Black and white print, 11 x 14
Courtesy of the artist and Fahey/Klein
Gallery, Los Angeles

EILEEN COWIN

25. *Untitled*, 1986
Polacolor print, 24 x 20

26. *Untitled*, 1986
Polacolor print, 24 x 20
Both courtesy of the artist and Roy
Boyd Gallery, Santa Monica

LOUISE DAHL-WOLFE

27. *Lauren Bacall*, 1943
Black and white print, 12 x 12
Courtesy of the Los Angeles County
Museum of Art; gift of the Hollywood
Photographers Archive

JIMMY DESANA

28. *Aluminum Foil #3*, 1986
Color print, 10 x 8

29. *Aluminum Foil #4*, 1986
Color print, 10 x 8

30. *Bubblegum*, 1985
Color print, 20 x 16
All courtesy of Pat Hearn Gallery and
the Jimmy DeSana Estate, New York

MAX DUPAIN

31. *Greta Garbo*, 1940
Black and white print, 18 x 15
Courtesy of the Los Angeles County
Museum of Art; gift of the Hollywood
Photographers Archive

JOHN ENGSTEAD

32. *Sugar 'n' Spice (Peggy Lee)*, n.d.
Record album cover, 12½ x 12½
Courtesy of Marjorie Richardson

JOHN FLOREA

33. *Marilyn Monroe*, 1953
Color print, 16 x 20

34. *Doris Day (You Were Never Lovelier)*, 1953
Color print, 20 x 16
Both courtesy of the artist and
Fahey/Klein Gallery, Los Angeles

GREG GORMAN

35. *Divine*, 1984
Black and white print, 24 x 20

36. *Divine Close-up*, 1984
Black and white print, 24 x 20

37. *Divine with Bulldogs, Personal Publicity,
Los Angeles*, 1984
Black and white print, 24 x 20
All courtesy of the artist

EDMUND GOULDING

38. *Greta Garbo in "Grand Hotel,"* c. 1932
Black and white print, 7 x 8½
Courtesy of Anne and David Fahey

PHILIPPE HALSMAN

39. *Jean Simmons, Laughing*, 1950
Black and white print, 14 x 11

40. *Jean Simmons, Crying*, 1950
Black and white print, 14 x 11
Both courtesy of the Los Angeles
County Museum of Art; gift of
Sanford Robertson

RICHARD HAWKINS

41. *Bruce/People*, 1991
Magazine collage, 10⅞ x 16⅜
Courtesy of Barry Sloane

PAUL HESSE

42. *Nanette Fabray*, c. 1959
Black and white print, 16 x 12⅜
Courtesy of the Los Angeles County
Museum of Art; gift of Yves Mieszala
and Joyce Essex Mieszala

43. *Marlene Dietrich*, c. 1950
Color print, 20 x 25
Courtesy of Donald Hesse

GEORGE HURRELL

44. *Edwina Booth*, 1932
Black and white print, 14 x 11

45. *Joan Crawford and Franchot Tone in
"Dancing Lady,"* 1931
Black and white print, size 13 x 10

46. *Joan Crawford*, 1930
Black and white print, 13 x 10

47. *Joan Crawford*, 1932
Black and white print, 13 x 10
All courtesy of Fahey/Klein Gallery,
Los Angeles

PAUL JASMIN

48. *Rodney*, 1991
Black and white print, 14 x 11

49. *Kathy*, 1991
Black and white print, 14 x 11
Both courtesy of the artist

LARRY JOHNSON

50. *Untitled (Movie Stars on Clouds–
James Dean)*, 1983
Color print, 20 x 24

51. *Untitled (Movie Stars on Clouds–
Montgomery Clift)*, 1983
Color print, 20 x 24

52. *Untitled (Movie Stars on Clouds–
Clark Gable)*, 1983
Color print, 20 x 24

53. *Untitled (Movie Stars on Clouds–
Sal Mineo)*, 1983
Color print, 20 x 24

54. *Untitled (Movie Stars on Clouds–
Marilyn Monroe)*, 1983
Color print, 20 x 24

55. *Untitled (Movie Stars on Clouds–
Natalie Wood)*, 1983
Color print, 20 x 24
All courtesy of the artist and Stuart
Regen Gallery, Los Angeles

TOM KELLEY

56. *Marilyn Monroe*, 1949
Color print, 37 x 29½
Courtesy of Tom Kelley, Jr., and
Mirage Editions, Inc., Santa Monica

DOUGLAS KIRKLAND

57. *Judy Garland*, 1961
Color print, 20 x 16

58. *Peter O'Toole*, 1964
Color print, 16 x 20
Both courtesy of the artist

JEFF KOONS

59. *Art Magazine Ads*, Portfolio of 4,
1988-89
Lithographs, 45 x 37¼
Courtesy of the artist and Daniel
Weinberg Gallery, Santa Monica

LOUISE LAWLER

60. *Recognition Maybe, May Not Be Useful*,
1990
ArtScribe magazine cover, 11 x 8½
Original photograph ©Maureen Lambray
Courtesy of Fred Fehlau

RUTH HARRIET LOUISE
61. *Greta Garbo, Metro-Goldwyn-Mayer*, n.d.
Black and white print, 10 x 8
Courtesy of Anne and David Fahey

ROBERT MAPPLETHORPE
62. *Almasi*, 1981
Black and white print, 19 x 15
63. *Untitled*, 1980
Black and white print, 15½ x 15
Both courtesy of Richard Green
Gallery, Santa Monica, and the
Robert Mapplethorpe Estate

CHRISTIAN MARCLAY
64. *Absolutely*, 1991
Record covers, 20 x 12½
Courtesy of Max Lang

ANDREW MASULLO
65. *#2222*, 1990
Oil, photo and frame
14⅞ x 11 x ½
66. *#2249*, 1989-90
Mixed media and frame
10 x 8½ x ½
Both courtesy of the artist

ANGUS McBEAN
67. *Woman's Head under Chair*, c. 1940
Black and white print, 13 x 10
Courtesy of the Los Angeles County
Museum of Art; gift of the Hollywood
Photographers Archive

MARK MORRISROE
68. *Nathan Shapiro*, 1984
Color print, 20 x 16
69. *Portrait of Chi-Chi*, 1985
Color print, 20 x 16
70. *American Beauty Still Life #2*, 1985
Color print, 16 x 20
71. *Nympho Maniac Still*, 1983-84
Color print, 16 x 20
All courtesy of Pat Hearn Gallery and
the Mark Morrisroe Estate, New York

WILLIAM MORTENSEN
72. *Jean Harlow*, c. 1927
Black and white print, 12¾ x 10⅛
Courtesy of Deborah Irmas

JANE O'NEAL
73. *On the Set of "Impulse,"* 1989
Black and white print, 16 x 20
Courtesy of the artist

RUTH ORKIN
74. *Lana Turner at Famous Party Given by
Marion Davies, Esther Williams, Fernando
Lamas, and Ben Gage*, 1952
Black and white print, 11 x 14
Courtesy of the Los Angeles County
Museum of Art; gift of the Hollywood
Photographers Archive

THERESA PENDLEBURY
75. *Untitled ("An American in Paris")*, 1988
Photo and palette, 12 x 16½
Courtesy of Jorge Pardo

JACK PIERSON
76. *Excalibur*, 1992
Color print, 29¼ x 30¼
Courtesy of Stanley Soble
77. *Slow Dive*, 1992
Color print, 30 x 34¼
Courtesy of Alan Hergott and
Curt Shepard

FRANK POWOLNY
78. *Tony Perkins*, c. 1960
Color print, 14 x 11
Courtesy of the Kobal Collection,
New York

RICHARD PRINCE
79. *Untitled (mixed couple—men)*, 1977-78
Color print, 20 x 24
Courtesy of Councilman Joel Wachs
and Barbara Gladstone Gallery

EUGENE ROBERT RICHEE
80. *Gary Cooper in an Armchair*, 1931
Black and white print, 14 x 11
81. *Tallulah Bankhead*, n.d.
Black and white print, 14 x 11
Both courtesy of the Los Angeles
County Museum of Art; gift of the
Hollywood Photographers Archives

HERB RITTS
82. *Sylvester Stalone and Brigette Nielson in
Long Island*, 1985
Black and white print, 19 x 12¾
83. *Jack Nicholson, L.A.*, 1986
Black and white print, 19 x 15
84. *Pee-wee Herman*, 1987
Black and white print, 19 x 15
85. *Madonna, Tokyo*, 1987
Black and white print, 17⅛ x 15⅛
All courtesy of the artist and
Fahey/Klein Gallery, Los Angeles

DAVID ROBBINS
86. *And*, 1991
Bookjacket, 14 x 27¾
Courtesy of Mr. & Mrs. Michael Hopkins

MATTHEW ROLSTON
87. *Meredith Salenger and Clayton Rohner*,
1985
Black and white print, 16 x 20
Courtesy of the artist and Fahey/Klein
Gallery, Los Angeles

CHARLES ROSHER
88. *Mary Pickford in "Tess of the Storm Country,"*
1922
Black and white print, 11½ x 9½
Courtesy of the Los Angeles County
Museum of Art; gift of the Sid and
Diana Avery Trust

ANNE ROWLAND
89. *Untitled (Jacqueline Kennedy)*, 1986
Color print, 20 x 16
90. *Untitled (Frank Sinatra)*, 1987
Color print, 20 x 16
Both courtesy of the artist and Jan
Kesner Gallery, Los Angeles

RENÉ SANTOS
91. *Untitled*, 1984
Color print, 20 x 30½
Courtesy of the René Santos Estate and
Feature, New York

ROCKY SCHENCK
92. *Randy Allen*, 1989
Black and white print, 14 x 11
93. *Jimmy James*, 1989
Black and white print, 14 x 11
94. *Charles Pierce*, 1989
Black and white print, 14 x 11
95. *Phranc*, 1989
Color print, 14 x 11
All courtesy of the artist

BONNIE SCHIFFMAN
96. *Sandra Bernhard*, 1991
Black and white print, 14 x 11
97. *Sandra Bernhard*, 1991
Black and white print, 14 x 11
98. *Angelyne*, 1987
Color print, 30 x 40
All courtesy of the artist

CINDY SHERMAN
99. *Untitled Film Still (#6–black bra)*, 1978
Black and white print, 8 x 10
100. *Untitled Film Still (#34–black bed with
book)*, 1978
Black and white print, 10 x 8
101. *Untitled Film Still (#52–on bed in slip)*,
1979
Black and white print, 8 x 10
102. *Untitled Film Still (#54–blond in rain)*,
1980
Black and white print, 8 x 10

103. *Untitled (#180–Michael Jackson face)*,
1987
Two color prints, 96 x 60 each
All courtesy of the Eli and Edythe L.
Broad Foundation, Santa Monica

LAURIE SIMMONS
104. *English Lady*, 1987
Color print, 35 x 24
Courtesy of Marsha Kleinman

ALEXIS SMITH
105. *Miss April*, 1992
Mixed media, 26½ x 23½ x 3
106. *Your Name Here*, 1975
Mixed Media, 34 x 22 x 20
Both courtesy of the artist and Margo
Leavin Gallery, Los Angeles

ALICE SPRINGS
107. *My Husband (Monte Carlo)*, 1987
Black and white print, 24 x 20
Courtesy of the artist and Shoshana
Wayne Gallery, Santa Monica

JOHN SWOPE
108. *Mr. and Mrs. Oscar Levant and Hope Lange*,
1968
Black and white print, 11 x 14
109. *Elsa Maxwell, Tyrone Power and the Duke
of Windsor*, 1942
Black and white print, 11 x 14
Both courtesy of the Los Angeles
County Museum of Art; gift of the
Hollywood Photographers Archive;
the John Swope Estate

DAVID AND TIM TATTU
110. *Self-portraits*, 1992
Two black and white prints, 10 x 8 each
Courtesy of the artists

ANDY WARHOL
111. *Untitled (self-portrait)*, 1963-64
Black and white print, 7¾ x 1½
Courtesy of Robert Miller Gallery,
New York

WILLIAM WEGMAN
112. *Island Way*, 1990
Polacolor print, 24 x 20
Courtesy of the artist and Linda
Cathcart Gallery, Santa Monica

CHRISTOPHER WILLIAMS
113. *Andra Millian, Women and Roses* (detail),
1986
Black and white print, 8¾ x 7½
Courtesy of the artist and Galerie
Crousel-Robelin, Paris

LASZLO WILLINGER
114. *Susan Hayward*, n.d.
Black and white print, 14 x 11
115. *Robert Montgomery*, 1949
Black and white print, 14 x 11
Both courtesy of the Los Angeles
County Museum of Art; gift of the
Hollywood Photographers Archive

BOB WILLOUGHBY
116. *Marilyn Monroe*, 1960
Black and white print, 14 x 9½
117. *Elizabeth Taylor in "Raintree County,"*
1956
Black and white print, 14 x 20
118. *Anne Bancroft and Dustin Hoffman in
"The Graduate,"* 1967
Black and white print, 16 x 20
All courtesy of the Los Angeles County
Museum of Art; gift of the Sid and
Diana Avery Trust

GARRY WINOGRAND
119. *Marilyn Monroe, "Seven Year Itch"
Location*, c. 1957
Black and white print, 17 x 14
Courtesy of the Museum of
Contemporary Art, Los Angeles; gift of
the Graham Nash Collection

MAX YAVNO
120. *Betty Grable's Legs*, n.d.
Black and white print, 10 x 8
121. *Premiere at Cathay Circle*, 1949
Black and white print, 13½ x 10⅜
Both courtesy of the Museum of
Contemporary Art, Los Angeles; the
Max Yavno Collection

BRUCE AND NORMAN YONEMOTO
122. *Made in Hollywood*, 1989
¾" video, 58 minutes
Courtesy of the artists

UNIDENTIFIED ARTIST(S)
123. *Fred Astaire, Dancing*, n.d.
Black and white print, 14 x 11
124. *Fred Astaire, Dancing*, n.d.
Black and white print, 11 x 14
125. *Rita Hayworth From "Loves of Carmen,"*
1948
Color print, 14 x 11
126. *Paul Newman and Joanne Woodward Filmed
against a Back Projection for "From
the Terrace,"* 1960
Color print, 11 x 14
127. *Jean Simmons*, 1954
Color print, 14 x 11
All courtesy of the Kobal Collection,
New York

Selected Biographies

The following partial listing compiles a wide variety of information of differing biographical methods. Whenever possible, the first one-person exhibitions in individual galleries (in the United States and abroad) are listed along with a selection of one-person museum and related group exhibitions. In the interest of brevity, these institutions are listed as follows: Institute of Contemporary Art, ICA; Los Angeles Contemporary Exhibitions, LACE; Los Angeles County Museum of Art, LACMA; Los Angeles Institute of Contemporary Art, LAICA; Massachussetts Institute of Technology, MIT; Museum of Contemporary Art, MOCA; Museum of Modern Art, MoMA. At the end of this section a catalogue and book list is provided.

JAMES ABBE

Born 1883, Alfred, ME
Died 1973
Selected exhibitions:
1987 *Hollywood Photographers*, LACMA, Los Angeles
1985 *Das Aktfoto*, Fotomuseum im Stadtmuseum, Munich
1983 *Figure della Danza, 1859-1982*, Teatro R.Valli, Reggio Emilia, Italy
1979 *Amerika Fotografie, 1920-1940*, Kunsthaus, Zürich
       Fleeting Gestures: Dance Photographs, International Museum of Photography, George Eastman House, Rochester, NY
1977 *The History of Fashion Photography*, International Museum of Photography, George Eastman House, Rochester, NY
1975 *Fashion 1900-1939*, Victoria and Albert Museum, London
Selected solo exhibitions:
1978 *Dictatorship in the '30s*, Washburn Gallery, New York
1977 The Photographers' Gallery, London
1976 *Stars of the '20s*, Canon Photo Gallery, Amsterdam
       Fashions of the '20s, Washburn Gallery, New York
1975 Washburn Gallery, New York
1972 *Photographs of the '20s*, Lexington Lab Gallery, New York
Selected publications:
James Abbe: Stars of the '20s, with text by Mary Dawn Earley, London, 1975
Around the World in Eleven Years by Patience, James and Richard Abbe, London, 1936
I Photograph Russia, by James Abbe, New York, 1934

TED ALLAN

Born 1910, Clifton, AZ
Lives in Los Angeles
Selected exhibitions:
1987 *Masters of Starlight*, LACMA, Los Angeles
1983 *The Art of the Great Hollywood Portrait Photographers*, Smithsonian Institution, Washington, D.C.

ANGELYNE

No birth date given
Lives in Beverly Hills
A visual phenomenon, a living icon, and famous for the magic she possesses. . . ANGELYNE, Hollywood Billboard Queen—the new Love Goddess of the future! A 10-story mural of Angelyne graced a building on the corner of Hollywood & Vine for over three years, bringing her international attention! For those who come to Hollywood in hopes of catching a glimpse of some celebrity, an Angelyne sighting is an unforgettable experience. Angelyne has appeared in many magazine articles, talk and entertainment shows, and music videos. She has her own music video titled *My List* and four albums to her credit. Angelyne has also written her own script titled *Angelyne—The Movie* which chronicles the adventures of a Sex Goddess in Hollywood and beyond!

Although she has all this to her credit, Angelyne says, "I just want to be famous for the magic I possess." A true Hollywood Icon! From Jean Harlow to Marilyn and Jayne Mansfield, the tradition of the Blonde Bombshell is carried on in grand style, in a new high-tech form of the future!!!
—*Angelyne Press Release, 1992*

MAX MUNN AUTREY

Born 1898, Dallas, TX
Died 1971
Selected exhibitions:
1983 *The Art of the Great Hollywood Portrait Photographers*, Smithsonian Institution, Washington, D.C.
1963 *Creative Photography, 1826 to the Present: An Exhibition from the Gernsheim Collection*, Wayne State University, Detroit
Selected solo exhibitions:
1988 *Max Munn Autrey*, University Art Museum, California State University, Long Beach
Selected publications:
Max Munn Autrey: One Photographer's Hollywood, by Constance W. Glenn and Wendell Eckholm, University Art Museum, California State University, Long Beach, 1988

SID AVERY

Born 1918, Akron, OH
Lives in Los Angeles
Selected exhibitions:
1988 *The Art of Persuasion: A History of Advertising Photography*, International Museum of Photography, George Eastman House, Rochester, NY
1987 *Masters of Starlight*, LACMA, Los Angeles
1963 *Photography in the Fine Arts*, Metropolitan Museum of Art, New York
Selected solo exhibitions:
1991 Vision Gallery, San Francisco
       Academy of Motion Picture Arts and Sciences, Los Angeles
       G. Ray Hawkins, Santa Monica, CA
       Catherine Edelman Gallery, Chicago
1990 Staley/Wise Gallery, New York
       Museum of Art, Birmingham, AL
       Parco Gallery, Tokyo
       Melbourne Festival of Art, Melbourne
       Kathleen Ewing Gallery, Washington, D.C.
1983 Focus Gallery, San Francisco
1982 Gallery 70, New York
1981 Susan Spiritus Gallery, Newport Beach, CA
1962 California Museum of Science and Industry, Los Angeles
Selected publications:
Hollywood At Home, A Family Album, 1950-1965, by Richard Schickel, New York, 1990
Founder:
Hollywood Photographers Archive, Los Angeles

JOHN BALDESSARI

Born 1931, National City, CA
Lives in Los Angeles
Selected exhibitions:
1992 *Knowledge: Aspects of Conceptual Art*, University Art Museum, University of California at Santa Barbara; Santa Monica Art Museum, Santa Monica, CA
1989 *Invention and Continuity in Contemporary Photographs*, Metropolitan Museum of Art, New York
1988 *Layers: Media and Culture*, Hewlett Gallery, Carnegie Mellon University College of Fine Arts, Pittsburgh, PA
1987 *L.A. Hot and Cool: Pioneers*, Bank of Boston Art Gallery, Boston
       Photography and Art: 1946-1986, LACMA, Los Angeles
       Avant-Garde in the Eighties, LACMA, Los Angeles
1986 *Individuals: A Selected History of Contemporary Art, 1945-1986*, MOCA, Los Angeles
       The Art of Our Time, Art Center College of Design, Pasadena, CA
       TV Generations, LACE, Los Angeles
1985 *Systems of Response*, The Art Institute of Chicago, Chicago
       Extending the Perimeter of Twentieth Century Art, San Francisco Museum of Modern Art, San Francisco
1984 *Verbally Charged Images*, Queens Museum, New York
1983 *Photography Used in Contemporary Art, In and Around the '70s*, National Museum of Modern Art, Tokyo
1981 *Contemporary Issues: Visual Articulation of Idea*, Visual Studies Workshop, Rochester, NY
       Instant Photography, Stedelijk Museum, Amsterdam
       Erweiterte Fotographie, 5th Vienna International Biennale, Vienna
       The Museum as Site: Sixteen Artists, LACMA, Los Angeles
1980 *Situational Imagery*, Fine Arts Gallery, University of California at Irvine
1979 *Words*, Museum Bochum-Kunstsammlung, Bochum, Germany
       Narrative Art, Dartmouth College, Hanover, NH
       Attitudes: Photographs of the 1970s, Santa Barbara Museum of Art, Santa Barbara, CA
       Altered Photography, P.S. 1, Long Island City, Queens, NY
       Concept, Narrative, Document, Museum of Contemporary Art, Chicago
       American Photography in the 1970s, Art Institute of Chicago, Chicago
1978 *Wit & Wisdom: Works by Baldessari, Hudson, Levine and Oppenheim*, ICA, Boston
       Art About Art, Whitney Museum of American Art, New York
       Narration, ICA, Boston
       American Narrative/Story Art: 1967-1977, Contemporary Art Museum, Houston
1977 *Contemporary American Photographic Works*, Museum of Fine Arts, Houston
       Words, Whitney Museum Downtown, New York
       Photography as Art Form, John and Mable Ringling Museum of Art, Sarasota, FL
       New Aspects of the Self in American Photography, Herbert F. Johnson Museum of Art, Cornell University, Ithaca, NY
1976 *Rooms*, P.S. 1, Long Island City, Queens, NY
       Artists Use Photography, Hallwalls, Buffalo, NY
1975 *(photo)(photo) 2 ...(photo)n*, University of Maryland Art Gallery, Baltimore
       The Extended Document, International Museum of Photography, George Eastman House, Rochester, NY
1973 *Southern California Attitudes*, Pasadena Art Museum, Pasadena, CA
1972 *Pier 18*, MoMA, New York
1970 *Information*, MoMA, New York
1969 *Konzeption-Conception*, Staditschen Museum, Leverkusen, Germany
       The Vanishing Edge, Newport Harbor Art Museum, Newport Beach, CA
       Pop Art Redefined, Hayward Gallery, London
Selected solo exhibitons:
1991 Donald Young Gallery, Chicago
1990 *John Baldessari*, MOCA, Los Angeles
1989 *John Baldessari: Ni por ésas ("Not Even So")*, Centro de Arte Reina Sofia, Madrid
1988 Lisson Gallery, London
       John Baldessari: The Life and Opinions of Tristram Shandy, Gentleman, an exhibition celebrating publication of the book by Arion Press, Margo Leavin Gallery, Los Angeles
1987 *John Baldessari*, Centre National d'Art Contemporain de Grenoble
1986 *John Baldessari: California Viewpoints*, Santa Barbara Museum of Art, Santa Barbara, CA
       John Baldessari: MATRIX BERKELEY 94, University Art Museum, University of California at Berkeley
1985 *John Baldessari*, Le Consortium, Centre d'Art Contemporain, Dijon
1984 Galerie Peter Pakesh, Vienna
       Margo Leavin Gallery, Los Angeles
1983 Stampa Gallery, Basel, Switzerland
1982 Contemporary Art Center, Cincinnati, OH
       Contemporary Arts Museum, Houston
1981 *John Baldessari: Work 1966-1980*, The New Museum, New York
       John Baldessari, Municipal Van Abbemuseum, Eindhoven and Museum Folkwang, Essen
       John Baldessari: New Work, CEPA Gallery, Buffalo, NY
1980 *Fugitive Essays*, Sonnabend Gallery, Los Angeles
1978 *Baldessari: New Films*, Whitney Musem of American Art, New York
       ICA, Boston
1977 Galerie Massimo Velsecchi, Milan
       Robert Self Gallery, London
1976 James Corcoran Gallery, Los Angeles
       Institute of Modern Art, Brisbane, Australia
       ICA, Sydney
1975 Stedelijk Museum, Amsterdam
       The Kitchen, New York
1974 Art and Project/Galerie MTL, Antwerp
1973 Sonnabend Gallery, New York
       Galerie Sonnabend, Paris
1972 Galerie MTL, Bruxelles
1971 Galerie Konrad Fischer, Düsseldorf
       Art and Project, Amsterdam
1970 Richard Feigen Gallery, New York
       Eugenia Butler Gallery, Los Angeles
1968 Molly Barnes Gallery, Los Angeles
1962 Southwest College, Chula Vista, CA
1960 La Jolla Museum of Art, La Jolla, CA

Selected publications:
John Baldessari, by Coosje van Bruggen, published in conjunction with the retrospective exhibition organized at MOCA, Los Angeles, Rizzoli Publications, New York, 1990
Ni por ésas/Not Even So, Centro de Arte Reina Sofia, Madrid, 1989
The Life and Opinions of Tristram Shandy, by John Baldessari (photographic reproductions), San Francisco, 1988
John Baldessari: California Viewpoints, by Hunter Drohojowska, Santa Barbara Museum of Art, Santa Barbara, CA, 1986
John Baldessari, by Baldessari, Van Abbemuseum, Eindhoven, 1986
Close-Cropped Tales, by John Baldessari; (photographic reproductions), CEPA Gallery, Albright-Knox Art Gallery and Hallwalls, Buffalo, 1981
John Baldessari, by Marcia Tucker and Robert Pincus-Witten and an interview with Nancy Drew, The New Museum, New York and University Art Galleries, Wright State University, Dayton, OH, 1981
A Talk with Baldessari, by James Hugunin in *Photography and Language*, edited by Lew Thomas, San Francisco, 1977
Brutus Killed Caesar, by John Baldessari (photographic reproductions), Emily H. Davis Art Gallery, University of Akron with Sonnabend Gallery and Ohio State University, Columbus, 1976
Four Events and Reactions, by John Baldessari, published in connection with exhibition held at Stedelijk Museum, Amsterdam, 1975-1976

NANCY BARTON

Born 1957, Hollywood, CA
Lives in Los Angeles
Selected exhibitions:
1989 *Materiality*, CEPA Gallery, Buffalo, NY
       Remaking Make Believe, (7 California Photographers), MoMA, New York
       Intersection for the Arts, San Francisco
1988 *Recent Art from L.A.*, Cleveland Center for Contemporary Art, Cleveland, OH
       Image and Text, with Laurel Beckman, The Woman's Building, Los Angeles
1987 *L.A. Hot and Cool*, MIT List Visual Arts Center, Boston
1984 Alternate Routes, RTD Bus System, Los Angeles
Selected solo exhibitions:
1990 *Butter Wouldn't Melt in my Mouth*, (in collaboration with Michael Glass), American Fine Arts Co., New York; Hallwalls, Buffalo, NY
1988 American Fine Arts Co., New York
       XS Gallery, Carson City, NV
1987 SF Camerawork, San Francisco
1986 New Langton Arts, San Francisco
Selected publications:
New Langton Arts, San Francisco, 1986

CECIL BEATON

Born 1904, London
Died 1980
Selected exhibitions:
1987 *Hollywood Photographers*, LACMA, Los Angeles
1985 *Das Aktfoto*, Fotomuseum im Stadtmuseum, Munich
1983 *British Photography 1955-65*, The Photographers' Gallery, London
1980 *The Queen Mother: A Celebration*, National Portrait Gallery, London

1979 *Photographie als Kunst 1879-1979*, Tiroler Landesmuseum Ferdinanduem, Innsbruck
1977 *Fashion Photography*, International Museum of Photography, George Eastman House, Rochester, NY
1972 *Personal Views 1850-1970*, British Arts Council, London
1964 *The Painter and the Photograph: From Delacroix to Warhol*, University of New Mexico, Albuquerque
1959 *Hundert Jahre Photographie, 1839-1939*, Museum Folkwang, Essen
1929 *Film und Foto/Fifo*, Duetscher Werkbund, Stuttgart
Selected solo exhibitions:
1985 Barbican Art Gallery, London
1983 *Studied Beauty*, Smithsonian Institution, Washington, D.C.
1982 *Fotografie 1922-71*, Palazzo Fortuny, Venice
1980 Galerie Zabriskie, Paris
1974 Kodak Gallery, London
1973 *The First 10 Years*, Sonnabend Gallery, New York
Record of a Period, Draytons Gallery 12, Minneapolis, MN
1971 *Fashion: An Anthology*, Victoria and Albert Museum, London
1969 *600 Faces by Beaton 1928-69*, Museum of the City, New York
1968 *Portraits 1928-69*, National Portrait Gallery, London
Selected publications:
Cecil Beaton: The Royal Portraits, by Roy Strong, New York, 1988
Beaton, edited by James Danziger, New York, 1980
The Self-Portrait with Friends: The Selected Diaries of Cecil Beaton 1922-1974, edited by Richard Buckle, London and New York, 1979
Happy and Glorious: 130 Years of Royal Photographs, edited by Colin Ford, London, 1977
The Photographs of Sir Cecil Beaton, by Andrew Sproxton, New York, 1973
Fashion: An Anthology Compiled by Cecil Beaton, edited by Madeleine Ginsburg, London, 1971
The Best of Beaton, with an introduction by Truman Capote, London, 1968
Images, by Beaton with an introduction by Christopher Isherwood, London, 1959
The Face of the World, by Beaton, London and New York, 1957
The Glass of Fashion, by Beaton, London, 1954
Persona Grata, by Beaton and Kenneth Tynan, London, 1953
My Royal Past, by Baroness von Bulop as Told by Cecil Beaton (or Rather Written by Him), by Beaton, London, 1939
The Book of Beauty, by Beaton, London, 1930

CINDY BERNARD
Born 1959, Los Angeles
Lives in Los Angeles
Selected exhibitions:
1992 *Exhibit A*, Serpentine Gallery, London
Molteplici Culture, Casa della Citta, Rome
Tattoo Collection, Air de Paris (à Paris), Paris
1990 *Spiel der Spur*, Shedhalle, Zürich
Biennial I, California Museum of Photography, Riverside, CA
1989 *Whitney Biennial*, Whitney Museum of American Art, New York

Photography of Invention: American Pictures of the 1980s, National Museum of American Art, Washington, D.C.
Abstraction In Contemporary Photography, Fred L. Emerson Gallery, Hamilton College, Clinton, NY; Anderson Gallery, Virginia Commonwealth University, Richmond
1988 *CalArts: Skeptical Belief(s)*, Newport Harbor Art Museum, Newport Beach, CA
Recent Art from Los Angeles, Cleveland Center for Contemporary Art, Cleveland, OH
After Abstract, Art Center College of Design, Pasadena, CA
1987 *The Hallucination of Truth*, P.S.1, Long Island City, Queens, NY
Spiral of Artificiality, Hallwalls, Buffalo, NY
CalArts: Skeptical Belief(s), The Renaissance Society, Chicago
1986 *T.V. Generation*, LACE, Los Angeles
1985 *Women Photographers in America*, The Woman's Building, Los Angeles
1984 *The Cotton Exchange Show*, LACE, Los Angeles
Selected solo exhibitions:
1992 Richard Kuhlenschmidt Gallery, Santa Monica, CA
1991 Air de Paris, Nice, France
1990 Richard Kuhlenschmidt Gallery, Santa Monica, CA
1988 Michael Kohn Gallery, Los Angeles
Selected publications:
Cindy Bernard: Ask the Dust, text by Benjamin Weissman, Richard Kuhlenschmidt Gallery, Santa Monica, CA, 1990
Spiel der Spur: The Poetry of Chance, Shedhalle, Zürich, 1990
Nachschub (Supply), The Köln Show and Spex Magazine, Köln, 1990
Women Photographers in America, The Woman's Building, Los Angeles, 1985

JOHN BOSKOVICH
Born 1956, Los Angeles
Lives in Los Angeles
Selected exhibitions:
1991 Rosamund Felsen Gallery, Los Angeles
1989 *Bruce Nauman, Cindy Sherman, John Boskovich*, Laurie Rubin Gallery, New York
Selected solo exhibitions:
1988 Rosamund Felsen Gallery, Los Angeles
Laurie Rubin Gallery, New York
Selected performances:
1988 *Without You I'm Nothing*, Orpheum Theater, New York
1986 *Without You I'm Nothing*, written by Sandra Bernhard and John Boskovich, directed by John Boskovich, performed at Dance Theater Workshop, New York; LACE, Los Angeles

JOHN BRUMFIELD
Born 1934, Hollywood, CA
Lives in Los Angeles
Mr. Brumfield has worked for such clients as General Motors, Carnation Farms, and the Bank of America. Selected exhibitions include: de Saisset Museum, Santa Clara University, Santa Clara, CA; Camerawork Gallery, San Francisco; G. Ray Hawkins Gallery, Los Angeles; LACMA, Los Angeles; San Francisco Museum of Modern Art, San Francisco; Santa Barbara Museum of Art, Santa Barbara, CA; Victoria and Albert Museum, London.

CLARENCE SINCLAIR BULL
Born 1895, Sun River, MT
Died 1979
Selected exhibitions:
1987 *Masters of Starlight*, LACMA, Los Angeles
1983 *The Art of the Great Hollywood Portrait Photographers*, Smithsonian Institution, Washington, D.C.
Selected publications:
The Man Who Shot Garbo: The Hollywood Photographs of C.S. Bull, by Terence Pepper and John Kobal, New York, 1989
The Faces of Hollywood, by Bull with Raymond Lee, Garden City, NJ, 1968

KATHE BURKHART
Born 1958, Martinsburg, WV
Lives in New York City
Selected exhibitions:
1991 *P.S.1 Studio Artists Exhibition*, P.S.1, Long Island City, Queens, NY
Original Sin, Hillwood Art Museum, Long Island University, Brookville, NY
1990 *Sex and Language*, Garnet Press Gallery, Toronto
Re: Framing Cartoons, Loughelton Gallery, New York
Brut 90, White Columns, New York
1989 *Vulgar Realism*, Hallwalls, Buffalo, NY
1988 *10 Painters*, White Columns, New York
Selected solo exhibitions:
1992 *Selected Work from the Liz Taylor Series*, Shoshana Wayne Gallery, Santa Monica, CA
1991 *More Paintings from the Liz Taylor Series*, Feature, New York
1989 *Kathe Burkhart by Elizabeth Taylor: Paintings from the Liz Taylor Series*, Feature, New York
1988 *Paintings from the Liz Taylor Series*, Greathouse, New York

NANCY BURSON
Born 1948, St. Louis, MO
Lives in New York City
Selected exhibitions:
1991 *Power: Its Myth, Icons & Structures in American Culture, 1961-1991*, Indianapolis Museum of Art, Indianapolis, IN
80th Annual Exhibition: Focus on Photography 1890-1990, Maier Art Museum, Lynchberg, VA
Practicing Beauty, Art Gallery of Hamilton, Hamilton, Ontario, Canada
1990 *Seductive Deceptions: The Theatrical Image*, University Gallery, University of Florida, Gainesville, FL
Rien Que La Chose Exhorbitée..., Galerie Michele Chomette, Paris
Critical Realism, Perspektief, Rotterdam
Another View: A Selection of Contemporary Prints, Fosdick-Nelson Gallery, Alfred University, Alfred, NY
Identities: Portraiture in Contemporary Photography, Philadelphia Art Alliance, Philadelphia
Tendencies Multiples (videos of the '80s), Centre Georges Pompidou, Paris
1989 *Image World: Art and Media Culture*, Whitney Museum of American Art, New York
The Photography of Invention: American Pictures of the 1980s, Smithsonian Institution, Washington, D.C.
Photography Now, Victoria and Albert Museum, London
Fotografie, Wissenschaft und Neuetechnologien, Kunstmuseum, Düsseldorf
New Portraiture, Clarence Kennedy Gallery, Boston
Self and Shadow, Burden Gallery, New York
1988 *Fabrication: Staged, Altered and Appropriated Photographs*, Carpenter Center, Harvard University, Cambridge, MA
Acceptable Entertainment, The Everson Museum, Syracuse, NY; Municipal Art Gallery, Los Angeles; Alberta College of Art, Alberta, Canada
Lifelike, Lorence Monk Gallery, New York
Female Reproduction, White Columns, New York
About Faces, a video/computer installation, Rubin Fleet Science Center, San Diego, CA
1987 *Fake*, The New Museum, New York
The Spiral of Artificiality, Hallwalls, Buffalo, NY
1986 *Stills: Cinema and Video Transformed*, Seattle Art Museum, Seattle, WA
Television's Impact on Contemporary Art, Queens Museum, Queens, NY
Cinema/Object, City Gallery, New York
1985 *Signs of the Times, Some Recurring Motifs in 20th Century Photography*, San Francisco Museum of Modern Art, San Francisco
Past and Future Perfect, Hallwalls, Buffalo, NY
Identity, Palais de Tokyo, Paris
1984 *Seven Women Artists*, Zürich Art Fair
1983 Video Show, Kunsthalle, Düsseldorf
1982 *Androgyny*, Emily Lowe Gallery, Hofstra University, Long Island, NY
documenta 7, videotape presentation with Fashion Moda, Kassel
Selected solo exhibitions:
1992 Denver Fine Arts Museum, Denver, CO
Contemporary Arts Museum, Houston
1991 Galerie Michele Chomette, Paris
1990 Museum of Contemporary Photography, Columbia College, Chicago
List Visual Arts Center, MIT, Cambridge, MA
Jayne H. Baum Gallery, New York
1989 Jan Kesner Gallery, Los Angeles
1987 Torino Fotographia, Turin, Italy
New Britian Museum of Contemporary Art, New Britian, CT
1986 Greathouse Gallery, New York
Chrysler Museum, Norfolk, VA
1985 International Center for Photography, New York
ICA, Boston
Baker Gallery, Kansas City, MO
1984 Holly Solomon Gallery, New York
Bruce Velick Gallery, San Francisco
1978 C.W. Post College, Long Island, NY
1977 Hal Bromm Gallery, New York
1974 Bertha Urdang Gallery, New York
Selected publications:
Rien Que La Chose Exhorbitée..., by Regis Durand, Marval, Cahiers de la Creation Contemporaine, Paris, 1990
Artificial Nature, by Jeffery Dietch, Athens, Greece, 1990
In Our Own Image, by Fred Ritchin, *Aperture*, New York, 1990
Nancy Burson: "The Age Machine" and Composite Portraits, by Dana Friis-Hansen, Cambridge, MA, 1990

ROBERT COBURN
Born 1900, Chateau, MT
Died 1990
Selected exhibitions:
1987 *Masters of Starlight*, LACMA, Los Angeles
1983 *The Art of the Great Hollywood Portrait Photographers*, Smithsonian Institution, Washington, D.C.

ROBERT COBURN II
Born 1928, Hollywood, CA
Lives in Los Angeles
Selected exhibitions:
1987 *Masters of Starlight*, LACMA, Los Angeles

EILEEN COWIN
Born 1947, Brooklyn NY
Lives in Santa Monica, CA
Selected exhibitions:
1992 *Quotations: The Second History of Art*, Aldrich Museum of Contemporary Art, Ridgefield, CT
1991 *Erotic Desire*, Perspektif, Rotterdam
Pleasures and Terrors of Domestic Comfort, MoMA, New York
1990 *Odalisque*, Jayne H. Baum Gallery, New York
1987 *Photography and Art: Interactions Since 1945*, LACMA, Los Angeles,
Frames of Time and Content: The Development of Photographic Ideas, Security Pacific Bank, Los Angeles
1986 *Stills: Cinema and Video Transformed*, Seattle Art Museum, Seattle, WA
1985 *Eileen Cowin and John Divola: Recent Work, No Fancy Titles*, La Jolla Museum of Contemporary Art, La Jolla, CA
1983 *WhitneyBiennial*, Whitney Museum of American Art, New York
1982 *The Image Scavengers*, ICA, Philadelphia
Selected solo exhibitions:
1991 Roy Boyd Gallery, Santa Monica, CA
Jayne H. Baum Gallery, New York
Museum of Contemporary Photography, Chicago
1989 Roy Boyd Gallery, Santa Monica, CA
1988 Jayne H. Baum Gallery, New York
Cleveland Museum of Art, Cleveland, OH
1987 MIN Gallery, Tokyo
1985 LACMA, Los Angeles
Viviane Esders Gallery, Paris
1977 O.K. Harris Gallery, New York
1976 Light Gallery, New York
1971 Witkin Gallery, New York
Selected publications:
DET iscenesatt Fotographie, by Mette Sandbye, Amsterdam, 1992
The Photographic: Two Points of View, by Judi Freeman, California State University, Fullerton, 1989
Eileen Cowin, by Mark Johnstone, MIN Gallery, Tokyo, 1987
Eileen Cowin and John Divola: Recent Work, No Fancy Titles, La Jolla Museum of Contemporary Art, La Jolla, CA, 1985

LOUISE DAHL-WOLFE
Born 1895, Alameda, CA
Lives in Flemington, NJ
Selected exhibitions:
1987 *Hollywood Photographers*, LACMA, Los Angeles
1986 *The Animal in Photography, 1843-1985*, The Photograpers' Gallery, London
1982 *Color as Form*, International Museum of Photography, George Eastman House, Rochester, NY

1980 *Fashion Photographs*, Tennessee Fine Arts
      Museum at Cheekwood, Nashville
1979 *Recollections: 10 Women of Photography*,
      International Center of Photography,
      New York
1977 *The History of Fashion Photography*, International
      Museum of Photography, George Eastman
      House, Rochester, NY
1975 *Women of Photography: An Historical Survey*,
      San Francisco Museum of Modern Art,
      San Francisco
1961 *Fashion: 7 Decades*, Hofstra University,
      Hempstead, NY
1937 *Photography 1839-1937*, MoMA, New York
Selected solo exhibitions:
1986 Center for Creative Photography, University
      of Arizona, Tucson
1985 *Louise Dahl-Wolfe: A 90th Birthday Salute*,
      Museum of Contemporary Photography,
      Columbia College, Chicago
1983 Staley-Wise Gallery, New York
      Grey Art Gallery, New York University,
      New York
1965 *Louise Dahl-Wolfe: Photographs / Meyer Wolfe:
      Sculpture and Drawings*, Country Art Gallery,
      Westbury, Long Island, NY
Selected publications:
A Photographer's Scrapbook, by Louise Dahl-Wolfe,
      New York, 1984

JIMMY DeSANA
      Born 1950, Detroit, MI
      Died 1990
Selected exhibitions:
1990 *Photomodern: Issues in Photography*, Atlanta
      Arts Festival, GA
      Hollywoodland, fiction/nonfiction, New York
      Against Interpretation, CEPA Gallery/Hallwalls,
      Buffalo, NY
1989 *Abstraction in Contemporary Photography*,
      Fred L. Emerson Gallery, Hamilton
      College, Clinton, NY
      Double Take, Contemporary Art Center,
      Cincinnati, OH
      *The Photography of Invention: American Pictures of
      the 1980s*, Smithsonian Institution,
      Washington, D.C.
1988 *The Photography Show*, Paterson Museum,
      Paterson, NJ
      Nassau County Museum of Fine Arts, NY
1987 *Poetic Injury*, Alternative Museum, New York
1986 *Staging the Self: Photography 1840-1985*,
      National Portrait Gallery, London
1985 American Academy in Rome
      Psycho Pueblo, Vijande, Madrid
1984 *Lower East Side*, Santa Barbara Museum of Art,
      Santa Barbara, CA
      The New Portraits, P.S. 1, Long Island
      City, Queens, NY
1983 *Subculture*, Group Material, New York
      Franklin Furnace, New York
1982 *New Figuration in America*, Milwaukee Art
      Museum, Milwaukee, WI
      Image Scavengers, ICA, Philadelphia
1981 *New York, New Wave*, P.S. 1, Long Island City,
      Queens, NY
      Kenneth Anger Retrospective, Whitney Museum
      of American Art, New York
      Couches, Diamonds and Pie, P.S. 1, Long Island
      City, Queens, NY
      Pictures and Promises, The Kitchen, New York

Love is Blind, Castelli Graphics, New York
Auto Portraits, Musée d'Art Moderne,
      Ville de Paris (ARC), Paris
1980 *Movin'*, MoMA, New York
      Times Square Show, New York
      Dubbed in Glamor, The Kitchen, New York
1979 *Artist Postcard Show*, Musée d'Art Moderne,
      Ville de Paris (ARC), Paris
      Stefanotti, New York
1978 *Punk Art Exhibition*, Washington Project for
      the Arts, Washington, D.C.
Selected solo exhibitions:
1989 Galerie Jablonka, Köln
1987 Pat Hearn Gallery, New York
1986 CCD, Düsseldorf
      Hillman Holland, Atlanta, GA
1984 Oggi Domani, New York
      OAE Gallery, Minneapolis, MN
1983 R. Appleton, Aspen, CO
      Arthur Roger, New Orleans
1982 Stefanotti/Bonlow, New York
1981 Museum of the 20th Century, Vienna
      CEPA Gallery, Buffalo, NY
      Galerie Jaques De Windt, Brussels
1980 Galleria Trisoria, Naples
1979 Stefanotti, New York
Selected publications:
Jimmy DeSana, edited by William S. Bartman with an
      interview by Laurie Simmons, and
      an introduction by Roberta Smith, A.R.T.
      Press, Los Angeles, 1990
Quotations from Jimmy DeSana, Pat Hearn Gallery,
      New York, 1988
Wrongrong, Pat Hearn Gallery, New York, 1988
Psycho Pueblo, by Robert Pincus-Witten and Carlo
      McCormick, Madrid, 1985
Submission, Scat Publications, New York, 1980
101 Nudes, New York, 1972

MAX DUPAIN
      Born 1911, Sydney, Australia
      Lives in Sydney
Selected exhibitions:
1987 Staley-Wise Gallery, New York
1981 Photographers' Gallery, London
1955 *Six Photographers*, Sydney
Selected solo exhibitions:
1980 Art Gallery of New South Wales, Sydney
Selected publications:
Max Dupain: Photographs, Australian National Gallery,
      Canberra, 1992
Max Dupain's Australia, Viking, 1986
Max Dupain, Art Gallery of New South Wales,
      Sydney, 1980

JOHN ENGSTEAD
      Born 1912, Los Angeles
      Died 1984
Selected exhibitions:
1987 *Masters of Starlight*, LACMA, Los Angeles
Selected publications:
Star Shots, by Engstead, New York, 1978

JOHN FLOREA
      Born 1916, Alliance, OH
      Lives in Hollywood, CA
Selected exhibitions:
1991 Fahey/Klein Gallery
1987 *Masters of Starlight*, LACMA, Los Angeles
1955 *The Family of Man*, MoMA, New York

MICHAEL GLASS
      Born 1961, Los Angeles
      Lives in Los Angeles
Selected exhibitions:
1991 *Situations*, New Langton Arts, San Francisco
1990 *Law of Desire*, Future Perfect, Los Angeles
1989 *No Stomach*, Installation, San Diego, CA
1988 *Against Nature*, LACE, Los Angeles
1984 *Alternate Routes*, RTD Bus System,
      Los Angeles
Selected solo exhibitions:
1991 New Langton Arts, San Francisco
1990 *Butter Wouldn't Melt in my Mouth*, (in
      collaboration with Nancy Barton)
      American Fine Arts Co., New York;
      Hallwalls, Buffalo, NY
1986 LACE Bookstore, Los Angeles
1984 CalArts, Valencia, CA
Selected publications:
New Langton Arts, San Francisco, 1991

GREG GORMAN
      Born 1949, Kansas City, MO
      Lives in Los Angeles
Mr. Gorman has produced covers for *Life*, *Rolling
Stone*, *US*, *Ms.*, *American Film*, *People*, and *Interview*
magazines. He has photographed such celebrities as
Barbra Streisand, Dustin Hoffman, Burt Reynolds,
David Bowie, and Bette Midler. He was still
photographer for such films as *Tootsie*, *The Big Chill*,
The River, *Cannonball Run*, and *Lust in the Dust*.
Selected publications:
Greg Gorman, Volume One, by Gorman, CPC
      Publishing, 1990
Visual Aid, by Gorman, Pantheon, 1986

EDMUND GOULDING
      Born 1891 in England
      Died 1959
Mr. Goulding, a British expatriate in Hollywood,
directed the major woman stars of the '30s and '40s.
His films include *Reaching for the Moon*, 1930;
Grand Hotel, 1932; *The Flame Within*, 1935; *Dark
Victory*, 1939; *Till We Meet Again*, 1940;
Of Human Bondage, 1946; *The Razor's Edge*, 1946;
and *Teenage Rebel*, 1956.

PHILIPPE HALSMAN
      Born 1906, Riga, Latvia
      Died 1979
Selected exhibitions:
1984 *Sammlung Gruber*, Museum Ludwig, Köln
1983 *Photography in America 1910-1982*, Tampa
      Museum, Tampa, FL
1982 *Lichtbildnisse: Das Porträt in der Fotografie*,
      Rheinisches Landesmuseum, Bonn
1980 *Photography of the '50s*, International Center
      of Photography, New York
1979 *Fleeting Gestures: Dance Photographs*,
      International Center of Photography,
      New York
      Life: The First Decade 1936-1945, Grey Art
      Gallery, New York University, New York
1978 *Photos from the Sam Wagstaff Collection*,
      Corcoran Gallery of Art, Washington, D.C.
1965 *12 International Photographers*, Gallery of
      Modern Art, New York
1951 *Memorable Life Photographs*, MoMA, New York
1936 *Exposition Internationale de la Photographie
      Contemporaine*, Musée des Arts Décoratifs,
      Paris

Selected solo exhibitions:
1985 Galerie zür Stockeregg, Zürich
1981 Foto Galerij Paule Pia, Antwerp, Belgium
1979 International Center of Photography,
      New York
Selected publications:
Halsman at Work, by Yvonne Halsman,
      New York, 1989
Portraits / Halsman, by Yvonne Halsman,
      New York, 1983
Halsman, with an introduction by Owen Edwards,
      New York, 1979
Photographers on Photography, edited by Jerry C.
      LaPlante, New York, 1979
Halsman, with an introduction by Owen Edwards,
      New York, 1979
Halsman: Sight and Sound, New York, 1972
Halsman on the Creation of Photographic Ideas,
      New York and London, 1961
Philippe Halsman's Jump Book, New York and
      London, 1959
*Dali's Mustache: A Photographic Interview with Salvador
      Dali*, by Halsman, New York, 1954

RICHARD HAWKINS
      Born 1961, Mexia, TX
      Lives in Los Angeles
Selected exhibitions:
1992 *In Pursuit of a Devoted Repulsion*, Roy Boyd
      Gallery, Santa Monica, CA; Feature, New York
      Trouble Over So Much Skin, Feature, New York
      The Mud Club..., Center for the Arts,
      Dupage, IL
      True Grit, B.B. La Femme Gallery,
      San Diego, CA
      Jory Felice, Richard Hawkins, B. Wurtz, Roy Boyd
      Gallery, Santa Monica, CA
1991 *Presenting Rearwards*, Rosamund Felsen
      Gallery, Los Angeles
      Stussy, Feature, New York
      Situation, New Langton Arts, San Francisco
      The Rock Show, Southern Exposure,
      San Francisco
      Examples Cool & Lonely, Roy Boyd Gallery,
      Santa Monica, CA
1990 *Que Overdose!* Mincher/Wilcox Gallery,
      San Francisco
1989 *HoHoHoMo*, Feature, New York
Selected solo exhibitions:
1992 Roy Boyd Gallery, Santa Monica, CA
      Mincher/Wilcox Gallery, San Francisco

PAUL HESSE
      Born 1896, New York City
      Died 1973
Selected exhibitions:
1987 *Masters of Starlight*, LACMA, Los Angeles
Selected publications:
Hollywood's Photographic Ziegfeld, by Susan Stowen
      (manuscript), 1980

GEORGE HURRELL
      Born 1904, Cincinnati, OH
      Died 1992
Selected exhibitions:
1987 *Masters of Starlight*, LACMA, Los Angeles
1983 *The Art of the Great Hollywood Portrait
      Photographers*, Smithsonian Institution,
      Washington, D.C.
1981 *The Hollywood Portrait Photographers 1921-1941*,
      MoMA, New York
1976 *Dreams for Sale*, Municipal Art Gallery,
      Los Angeles

1965 *Glamour Noses*, MoMA, New York
Selected solo exhibitions:
1980 Laguna Beach Museum of Art, Laguna
      Beach, CA
Selected publications:
The Hurrell Style, by Hurrell with Whitney Stine,
      New York, 1977
The Portfolios of George Hurrell, by Gene Thornton,
      Santa Monica, CA, 1991

PAUL JASMIN
      Born 1935, Helena, MT
      Lives in Los Angeles
Mr. Jasmin has produced images for *Esquire*, *Vogue*,
Interview, *Taxi*, *L.A. Style*, *French Glamour*, and *GQ* mag-
azines. He has photographed such celebrities as
Daryl Hannah, Richard Gere, Deborah Winger, Liza
Minelli, Barbra Streisand, Melanie Griffith, Truman
Capote, Isabella Rossellini, and others. He has
exhibited in the *Festival Due Monde*, Spoleto, Italy,
and in Los Angeles and New York. He also works
extensively in the field of fashion photography.

LARRY JOHNSON
      Born 1959, Long Beach, CA
      Lives in Los Angeles
Selected exhibitions:
1991 *A Dialogue about Recent American and European
      Photography*, MOCA, Los Angeles
      Words & #'s, Museum of Contemporary Art,
      Wright State University, Dayton, OH
      Whitney Biennial, Whitney Museum of
      American Art, New York
      Word as Image: American Art 1960-1990,
      Contemporary Arts Museum, Houston
      Ausenraum-Innenstadt, Sprengel Museum,
      Hannover, Germany
      *Just What Is It That Makes Today's Homes So
      Different, So Appealing?* The Hyde
      Collection, Glen Falls, NY
1990 *Charade of Mystery*, Whitney Museum
      Downtown, New York
      Language in Art, The Aldrich Museum of
      Contemporary Art, Ridgefield, CT
      Word as Image: American Art 1960-1990,
      Milwaukee Art Museum, Milwaukee, WI
      Drinking and Driving, Cleveland Center for
      Contemporary Art, Cleveland, OH
1989 *Image World: Art and Media Culture*, Whitney
      Museum of American Art, New York
      *A forest of SIGNS: Art in the Crisis of
      Representation*, MOCA, Los Angeles
      California Photography: Remaking Make-Believe,
      MoMA, New York
      Beyond Family of Man, Northeastern University
      Art Gallery, Boston
      *The Photography of Invention: American Pictures of
      the 1980s*, Smithsonian Institution,
      Washington, D.C.
1988 *UtopiaPostUtopia*, ICA, Boston
      Aperto: Venice Biennale, Venice
      Modes of Address: 25 Years of Language in Art,
      Whitney Museum of American Art,
      New York
1987 *The Castle*, installation by Group Material at
      documenta 8, Kassel
      Industrial Icons, San Diego State University,
      San Diego, CA
      CalArts: Skeptical Belief(s), The Renaissance
      Society, Chicago; Newport Harbor Art
      Museum, Newport Beach, CA
      Contemporary Diptych: Divided Vision, Whitney
      Museum of American Art, Stamford, CT

On View, with Willian Anastasi, New Museum, New York

Perverted by Language, Hillwood Art Gallery, Long Island University, New York

1986 *Uplifted Atmospheres, Borrowed Taste*, Hallwalls, Buffalo, NY

1985 *Proof and Perjury*, LAICA, Los Angeles

Synaesthetics, P.S.1, Long Island City, NY

Selected solo exhibitions:

1991 Johnen & Schottle, Köln
Rena Bransten Gallery, San Francisco

1990 Stuart Regen Gallery, Los Angeles

1989 Le Case d'Arte, Milan

1987 Kuhlenschmidt/Simon Gallery, Los Angeles
Galerie Isabella Kacprzak, Köln

1986 303 Gallery, New York

TOM KELLEY

Born 1911, Philadelphia, PA
Died 1984

Mr. Kelley worked for *Town & Country* magazine during the early 1930s. By 1949, he was a celebrity photographer working in Hollywood. His "Red Velvet" photo session with Marilyn Monroe in 1949 brought him tremendous notoriety after which he maintained his own photographic studio for nearly five decades. His work has appeared in galleries and several major museums including the Smithsonian Institution.

DOUGLAS KIRKLAND

Born 1934, Toronto, Canada
Lives in Los Angeles

Mr. Kirkland worked as an assistant for Irving Penn in the early 1960s. He became a staff photographer for *Look* Magazine and later, in 1971, for *Life* Magazine. Kirkland currently works for such publications as *Town & Country, Newsweek, New York* Magazine, and *Paris Match*. His work has been widely exhibited in North America, Europe, and Asia.

Selected publications:

Icons, to be published in 1993

Light Years: 30 Years Photographing Among the Stars, New York, 1990

JEFF KOONS

Born 1955, York, PA
Lives in New York City and Munich

Selected exhibitions:

1992 *Quotations: The Second History of Art*, Aldrich Museum of Contemporary Art, Ridgefield, CT

1991 *Metropolis*, Martin-Gropius-Bau, Berlin

Just What is it That Makes Today's Homes So Different, So Appealing? The Hyde Collection, Glen Falls, NY

1990 *High and Low: Modern Art and Popular Culture*, MoMA, New York

Aperto: Venice Biennale, Italy

Objectives: The New Sculpture, Newport Harbor Museum, Newport Beach, CA

Word as Image in American Art: 1960-1990, Milwaukee Art Museum, Milwaukee, WI

1989 *Horn Of Plenty*, Stedelijk Museum, Amsterdam

Image World: Art and Media Culture, Whitney Museum of American Art, New York

A forest of SIGNS: Art in the Crisis of Representation, MOCA, Los Angeles

Conspicuous Display, Stedman Art Gallery, Rutgers University, Camden, NJ

1988 *Carnegie International*, Pittsburgh, PA

BiNATIONAL, ICA, Chicago

NY Art Now II, Saatchi Collection, London

1987 *Avant-Garde in the Eighties*, LACMA, Los Angeles

New York Art Now, The Saatchi Collection, London

Collection Sonnabend, Centro d'Arte Reina Sofia, Madrid; CAPC, Bordeaux

1986 *New Sculpture*, The Renaissance Society, Chicago

Damaged Goods, The New Museum, New York

Endgame: Reference and Simulation in Recent Painting and Sculpture, ICA, Boston

Paravision, Margo Leavin Gallery, Los Angeles

1984 *Objectivity*, Hallwalls, Buffalo, NY

1983 *Science Fiction*, John Weber Gallery, New York

1982 *A Fatal Attraction: Art and the Media*, The Renaissance Society, Chicago

Selected solo exhibitions:

1989 *Jeff Koons–Nieuw Werk* Kunststichting, Rotterdam

1988 Sonnabend Gallery, New York
Museum of Contemporary Art, Chicago
Donald Young Gallery, Chicago
Galerie Max Hetzler, Köln

1986 Daniel Weinberg Gallery, Los Angeles

1985 International With Monument, New York
Feature Gallery, Chicago

1980 *The New*, The New Museum, New York

Selected publications:

Jeff Koons, by Michael Danoff, Museum of Contemporary Art, Chicago, 1988

LOUISE LAWLER

Born 1947, Bronxville, NY
Lives in New York City

Selected exhibitions:

1992 *Quotations: The Second History of Art*, Aldrich Museum of Contemporary Art, Ridgefield, CT

Knowledge: Aspects of Conceptual Art, University Art Museum, University of California at Santa Barbara, Santa Barbara; Santa Monica Art Museum, Santa Monica, CA

1991 *Whitney Biennial*, Whitney Museum of American Art, New York

1990 *Word As Image*, Contemporary Arts Museum, Houston

The Decade Show, The New Museum, New York

To Be and Not To Be, Centre d'Arte Santa Monica, Barcelona

1989 *Moscow-Vienna-New York*, The Vienna Festival, Vienna

In Other Words: Wort und Schrift in Bildern der Konzeptuellen Kunst, Museum an Ostwall, Dortmund, Germany

Confronting the Uncomfortable: Questioning Truth and Power, Yale University Art Gallery, New Haven, CT

Filling the Gap, Feigen and Co., Chicago

Visual Paradox: Truth and Fiction in the Photographic Image, John Michael Kohler Arts Center, Sheboygan, WI

Tenir l'Image à Distance, Musée d'Art Contemporain de Montreal, Montreal

Fictive Strategies: Actuality and Originality in Contemporary Photography, The Squibb Gallery, Princeton, NJ

A forest of SIGNS: Art in the Crisis of Representation, MOCA, Los Angeles

The Photography of Invention: American Pictures of the 1980s, Smithsonian Institution, Washington, D.C.

Conspicuous Display, Stedman Art Gallery, State University of New Jersey, Rutgers Camden Campus

What Does She Want? Carleton College Art Gallery, Northfield, MN

1988 *Re: Placement*, LACE, Los Angeles

Modes of Address: Language in Art Since 1960, Whitney Museum Downtown, New York

Sexual Difference: Both Sides of the Camera, Wallach Art Gallery, Columbia University, New York

1987 *Implosion: A Postmodern Perspective*, Moderna Museet, Stockholm

Nothing Sacred, Margo Leavin Gallery, Los Angeles

Photography and Art: Interactions Since 1946, LACMA, Los Angeles

This Is Not A Photograph: Twenty Years of Large-Scale Photography, The John and Mable Ringling Museum of Art, Sarasota, FL

Resistance (Anti-Baudrillard) by Group Material, White Columns, New York

1986 *The Fairy Tale: Politics, Desire and Everyday Life*, Artists Space, New York

l'oeuvre et son accrochage, Centre Georges Pompidou, Paris

Rooted Rhetoric, Una Tradizione nell'Arte Americana, Pallazzina Centrale, Castel dell'Ovo, Naples

The Real Big Picture, Queens Museum, Flushing, NY

The Law and Order Show, Castelli, Gladstone and Weber Galleries, New York

Damaged Goods, The New Museum, New York

The Real Big Picture, Queens Museum, Flushing, NY

1985 *The Art of Memory / The Loss of History*, The New Museum, New York

1984 *Natural Genre*, Fine Arts Gallery, Florida State University, Tallahassee, FL

Re-place-ment, Hallwalls, Buffalo, NY

Masking/Unmasking: Aspects of Post Modernist Photography, The Friends of Photography, Carmel, CA

Multiple Choice, P.S.1, Long Island City, Queens, NY

Borrowed Time, Baskerville & Watson Gallery, New York

1982 *Public Vision*, White Columns, New York

1981 *Extended Photography*, Secessionist Museum, Vienna

Photo, Metro Pictures, New York

A PICTURE IS NO SUBSTITUTE FOR ANY THING is the title of collaborative work of Louise Lawler and Sherrie Levine, Harold Rivkin Gallery, New York

Selected solo exhibitions:

1991 *For Sale*, Metro Pictures, New York

1990 *A Vendre*, Galerie Yvon Lambert, Paris

"The Enlargement of Attention, No One Between the Ages of 21 and 35 is Allowed," Connections: Louise Lawler, Museum of Fine Arts, Boston

1989 *How Many Pictures*, Metro Pictures, New York

The Show Isn't Over, Photographic Resource Center, Boston

1988 *Vous Avez Déjà Vu Ça*, Galerie Yvon Lambert, Paris

Les Objets, Galerie Meert-Rihoux, Brussels

1987 *It Remains to Be Seen*, Metro Pictures, New York

The Big Top is Up, Kuhlenschmidt/Simon, Los Angeles

"Enough," Projects: Louise Lawler, MoMA, New York

As Serious as a Circus, Isabella Kacprzak, Stuttgart

1985 *Interesting*, Nature Morte, New York

1984 *Home/Museum-Arranged Living and Viewing*, Matrix, The Wadsworth Atheneum, Hartford, CT

1982 *Another Gallery*, Anna Leonowens Gallery II, Halifax, Nova Scotia

An Arrangement of Pictures, Metro Pictures, New York

1981 *Jancar/Kuhlenschmidt*, Jancar/Kuhlenschmidt Gallery, Los Angeles

1979 *A Movie Will Be Shown Without The Picture*, FAR, Aero Theater, Santa Monica, CA

Selected publications:

What Is the Same: Louise Lawler, by Claude Gintz, Maison de la Culture et de la Communication de Saint-Etienne, 1990

Untitled, by Lawler, New York, 1978

Untitled, by Lawler and Janelle Reiring, New York, 1978

RUTH HARRIET LOUISE

Born 1906, New York City
Died 1944

Selected exhibitions:

1987 *Masters of Starlight*, LACMA, Los Angeles

1983 *The Art of the Great Hollywood Portrait Photographers*, Smithsonian Institution, Washington, D.C.

ROBERT MAPPLETHORPE

Born 1946, Long Island, NY
Died 1989

Selected exhibitions:

1991 *Fashion Photography Since 1945*, Victoria and Albert Museum, London

1990 *Altered Truths*, New Orleans Museum of Art, New Orleans

1989 *Photography Now*, Victoria and Albert Museum, London

150 Years of Photography, National Gallery of Art, Washington, D.C.

1988 *First Person Singular: Self-Portrait Photography, 1840-1986*, The High Museum, Georgia-Pacific Center, Atlanta

Identity: Representations of the Self, Whitney Museum Downtown, New York

1986 *Staging the Self*, National Portrait Gallery and Plymouth Arts Centre, London

Art and Advertising: Commercial Photography by Artists, International Center of Photography, New York

Intimate/INTIMATE, Turman Gallery, Indiana State University, Terre Haute, IN

Rules of the Game: Culture Defining Gender, Mead Art Institute, Amherst College, Amherst, MA

1985 *Picture Taking: Weegee, Walker Evans, Sherrie Levine, Robert Mapplethorpe*, Mary and Leigh Block Gallery, Northwestern University, Evanston, IL

1984 *The Heroic Figure*, Contemporary Arts Musem, Houston

Face to Face: Recent Portrait Photography, ICA, Philadelphia

Radical Photography: The Bizarre Image, Nexus Gallery, Atlanta

1983 *Self-Portraits*, Linda Farris Gallery, Seattle, WA; Municipal Art Gallery, Los Angeles

Photography in America 1910-1983, The Tampa Museum, Tampa, FL

1982 *Points of View*, University of Oklahoma Museum of Art, Norman

1981 *Surrealist Photographic Portraits 1920-1980*, Marlborough Gallery, London

Inside Out: Self Beyond Likeness, Newport Harbor Art Museum, Newport Beach, CA

1980 *Presences: The Figure and Manmade Environments*, Freedman Gallery, Albright College, Reading, PA

1979 *American Portraits of the Sixties and Seventies*, Center for the Visual Arts, Aspen, CO

Attitudes, Santa Barbara Museum of Art, Santa Barbara, CA

1978 *Mirrors and Windows*, MoMA, New York

The Collection of Sam Wagstaff, Corcoran Gallery of Art, Washington, D.C.

Selected solo exhibitions:

1988 *Robert Mapplethorpe: The Perfect Moment*, ICA, Philadelphia

Mapplethorpe Portraits, National Portrait Gallery, London

Robert Mapplethorpe, Stedelijk Museum, Amsterdam

1987 *Robert Mapplethorpe 1986*, Galerie Kicken-Pauseback, Köln

1986 *Robert Mapplethorpe Photographs 1976-1985*, South Yarra, Melbourne

1985 *Robert Mapplethorpe, Black Flowers*, Galerie Comicos, Lisbon

1984 *Lady*, Hara Museum of Contemporary Art, Tokyo

Robert Mapplethorpe Photographs, 1978-1984, John A. Schweitzer Gallery, Montreal

Robert Mapplethorpe Fotografias 1970-1983, Galeria Fernando Vijande, Madrid

Processes, Barbara Gladstone Gallery, New York

1983 *Robert Mapplethorpe 1970-1983*, ICA, London

New Works, Watari Gallery, Tokyo

Lady, Lisa Lyon, Leo Castelli Gallery, New York

1982 *Robert Mapplethorpe*, Contemporary Art Center, New Orleans

Robert Mapplethorpe, Recent Work, Galerie Jurka, Amsterdam

1981 *Robert Mapplethorpe*, Kunstverein, Frankfurt am Mein

1980 *Black Males*, Galerie Jurka, Amsterdam

1979 Galerie Jurka, Amsterdam

Robert Mapplethorpe 1970-1975, Robert Samuel Gallery, New York

Contact, Robert Miller Gallery, New York

1978 The Corcoran Gallery of Art, Washington, D.C.

LAICA, Los Angeles

Film and Stills, Robert Miller Gallery, New York

The Chrysler Museum, Norfolk, VA

1977 *Erotic Pictures*, The Kitchen, New York

Portraits, Holly Solomon Gallery, New York

Selected publications:

Robert Mapplethorpe: Early Works 1970-1975, edited by John Cheim, New York, 1991

Flowers, by Mapplethorpe, foreword by Patti Smith, Boston-Toronto-London, 1990

Some Women, by Mapplethorpe, introduction by Joan Didion, Boston-Toronto-London, 1989

Robert Mapplethorpe: The Perfect Moment, text by Janet Kardon, David Joselit, Kay Larson, Patti Smith, ICA, Philadelphia, 1988

Robert Mapplethorpe, edited by Richard Marshall with essays by Richard Howard and Ingrid Sischy, New York, 1988

Mapplethorpe Portraits, text by Peter Conrad, National Portrait Gallery, London, 1988

Robert Mapplethorpe, text by Els Barents, Stedelijk Museum, Amsterdam, 1988

Robert Mapplethorpe 1986, interview with Anne Horton, Galerie Kicken-Pauseback, Köln, 1986

Robert Mapplethorpe Photographs 1976-1985, text by Paul Foss, South Yarra, Melbourne, 1986

The Power of Theatrical Madness, by Mapplethorpe with Jan Fabre, ICA, London, 1986
Picture Taking:Weegee, Walker Evans, Sherrie Levine, Robert Mapplethorpe, text by William Olander, Mary and Leigh Block Gallery, Northwestern University, Evanston, IL, 1985
Certain People: A Book of Portraits, by Mapplethorpe with Susan Sontag, Twelvetrees Press, Pasadena, CA, 1985
Robert Mapplethorpe 1970-1983, text by Stuart Morgan and Alan Hollinghurst, ICA, London, 1983
Lady: Lisa Lyon, by Mapplethorpe with text by Bruce Chatwin and forward by Sam Wagstaff, Viking Press, New York, 1983
New Works, text by Sam Wagstaff, Watari Gallery, Tokyo, 1983
Robert Mapplethorpe, texts by Sam Wagstaff and Peter Weiermeir, Kunstverein, Frankfurt am Mein, 1981
Black Males, text by Edmund White, Galerie Jurka, Amsterdam, 1980
Robert Mapplethorpe, text by Rein von der Fuhr, Galerie Jurka, Amsterdam, 1979
Robert Mapplethorpe, text by Mario Amaya, The Chrysler Museum, Norfolk, VA, 1978

CHRISTIAN MARCLAY
Born 1955, San Rafael, CA
Lives in New York City
Selected exhibitions:
1992 Israel Museum, Jerusalem
1991 *The Savage Garden*, Fundacion Caja de Pensiones, Madrid
Fluxus Attitudes, Hallwalls, Buffalo, NY
Whitney Biennial, Whitney Museum of American Art, New York
Spy Stories, Galleria il Campo, Rome
Just What Is It That Makes Today's Homes So Different, So Appealing? The Hyde Collection, Glen Falls, NY
1990 *Status of Sculpture*, Espace Lyonnais d'Art Contemporain, Lyon
Assembled, University Art Galleries, Wright State University, Dayton, OH
Regarding Art; Artworks About Art, John Michael Kohler Arts Center, Madison, WI
New Work For New Spaces: Into the '90s, Wexner Center, Columbus, OH
1989 Musée de Carouge, Geneva
Strange Attractors: Signs of Chaos, The New Museum, New York
1988 *Redefining the Object*, University Art Galleries, Wright State University, Dayton, OH
Cleveland Center for Contemporary Art, Cleveland, OH
Group Material Politics and Election, Dia Art Foundation, New York
1985 *On the Wall/On the Air: Artists Make Noise*, Hayden Gallery, MIT, Cambridge, MA
Visual Sound, Brattleboro Museum, Brattleboro, VT
1983 *Sound Seen*, Washington Project for the Arts, Washington, D.C.
Selected solo exhibitions:
1992 Galleria Valentina Moncade, Rome
1991 *Abstract Music*, Trans Avant-Garde Gallery, San Francisco
Galerie Isabella Kacprzak, Köln
Interim Art, London
1990 Hirshhorn Museum, Washington, D.C.
1989 Shedhalle, Zürich
Galerie Rivolta, Lausanne

1988 *One Thousand Records*, Gelbe Musik, Berlin
Tom Cugliani Gallery, New York
1987 *850 Records*, Clocktower, New York
Selected publications:
Directions: Christian Marclay, essay by Amada Cruz, Hirshhorn Museum, Washington, D.C., 1990
Christian Marclay, essays by Harm Lux and Dennis Cooper, Shedhalle, Zürich, 1989

ANDREW MASULLO
Born 1957, Elizabeth, NJ
Lives in New York City
Selected exhibitions:
1991 *Departures: Photography 1924-1989*, Cantor Gallery, Worcester, MA
Just What is it That Makes Today's Homes So Different, So Appealing? The Hyde Collection, Glen Falls, NY
The Library of Babel, Hallwalls, Buffalo, NY and White Columns, New York
1990 *Word as Image: American Art 1960-1990*, Milwaukee Art Museum, Milwaukee, WI
Word/Image, Bard College, Annandale-on-Hudson, NY
Regarding Art: Artworks About Art, John Michael Kohler Arts Center, Sheboygan, WI
The Milky Way, Shoshana Wayne Gallery, Santa Monica, CA
1986 *Small Works*, Sculpture Center, New York
1985 *Funeral Rites*, White Columns, New York
1984 *Still Life With Transaction: Former Objects, New Moral Arrangements, and the History of Surfaces*, International With Monument, New York
Selected solo exhibitions:
1990 Asher-Faure Gallery, Los Angeles
1988 fiction/non-fiction, New York
1987 Bockley Gallery, Minneapolis
1986 Paulo Salvador Gallery, New York
Andrew Masullo at Chartwell, Chartwell Booksellers, New York
Selected publications:
Andrew Masullo, fiction/nonfiction, New York, 1989

ANGUS McBEAN
Born 1904, Newbridge, Monmouthshire, South Wales
Lives in England
Selected exhibitions:
1984 *Sammlung Gruber*, Museum Ludwig, Köln
1980 *Modern British Photography 1919-1939*, Museum of Modern Art, Oxford
1959 *Hundert Jahre Photographie 1839-1939*, Folkwang Museum, Essen
Selected solo exhibitions:
1984 The Photograpers' Gallery, London
1980 *Photographs 1934-1960*, Rex Irwin Gallery, Sydney
1976 *A Darker Side of the Moon*, Impressions Gallery, York, England
Selected publications:
Angus McBean, with text by Adrian Woodhouse, London, 1982
Angus McBean in Islington, edited by Mary Cosh, London, 1982

MARK MORRISROE
Born 1959, Malden, MA
Died 1989
Selected exhibitions:
1989 *In the Valley of the Shadow*, Artists Space, New York
1987 *The Spiral of Artificiality*, Hallwalls, Buffalo, NY

History of the Male Nude in Photography, Pinacoteca Di Ravenna, Italy
1985 *Split Vision*, Artists Space, New York
Travelling Scholars, Museum of Fine Arts, Boston
1984 *Local Visions IV: Portraits*, Hayden Art Gallery, MIT, Cambridge, MA
1982 Museum of Fine Arts, Boston
Selected publications:
1987 Valorie Furlano Gallery, Providence, RI
1986 Pat Hearn Gallery, New York
1984 *Inside the Boy Next Door*, Vision Gallery, Boston
1982 Fogg Art Museum, Cambridge, MA
Selected publications:
The Hidden Image, by Peter Weiermair, Cambridge, MA, 1988
Nude 2, by Toshiharu Itoh and Allen Frame, Tokyo, 1988

WILLIAM MORTENSEN
Born 1897, Park City, UT
Died 1965
Selected exhibitions:
1987 *Masters of Starlight*, LACMA, Los Angeles
1977 *California Pictorialism*, San Francisco Museum of Modern Art, San Francisco
Selected solo exhibitions:
1979 Los Angeles Center for Photographic Studies, Los Angeles
1948 Smithsonian Institution, Washington, D.C.
Selected publications:
The Photographic Magic of William Mortensen, by Deborah Irmas, Los Angeles, 1979
Monsters and Madonnas, Camera Craft, San Francisco, 1936
The Command to Look, Camera Craft, San Francisco, 1937
The Model, Camera Craft, San Francisco, 1937
Mortensen on the Negative, San Francisco, 1940
Outdoor Portraiture, San Francisco, 1940
Founder: Mortensen School of Photography, 1930-1960, Laguna Beach, CA

JANE O'NEAL
Born 1945, San Diego, CA
Lives in Los Angeles
Selected exhibitions:
1985 *Modern Art at Harvard*, Fogg Museum, Harvard University, Cambridge, MA
1982 *Critic's Choice*, Eaton-Shoen Gallery, San Francisco
1981 *Photoflexion*, Municipal Art Gallery, Los Angeles
1980 *10 California Photographers*, San Francisco Museum of Modern Art, San Francisco
1979 Cirrus Gallery, Los Angeles
Photographic Directions, L.A., Security Pacific Bank, Los Angeles
1978 *Place, Product, Advertising*, Cooper-Hewitt Museum, New York
Postcard Show, Green Collection Gallery, Tokyo
Fogg Museum, Harvard University, Cambridge, MA
1977 *Interiors, Exteriors*, Municipal Art Gallery, Los Angeles
1976 *Soho/Cameraworks*, Los Angeles
L.A. Photographers, Secessionist Gallery, Victoria, B.C., Canada
Selected solo exhibitions:
1985 Arizona State University, Phoenix
1978 Evergreen State College, Olympia, WA Foto, New York
1977 Soho/Cameraworks, Los Angeles

Selected publications:
Annie on Camera, Nine Photographers, Abbeville Press, New York, 1982
Unit still photography on feature films:
To Live and Die in L.A.; Desert Heart; Peggy Sue Got Married; River's Edge; Lost Boys; Impulse; Joe vs. the Volcano; Delirious; The Search for Intelligent Life in the Universe; One Good Cop; Warshawski; Singles; Back to the Future III

RUTH ORKIN
Born 1922, Boston, MA
Died 1986
Selected exhibitions:
1987 *Masters of Starlight*, LACMA, Los Angeles
1986 *Women Photographers Now*, A.I.R. Gallery, New York
1985 *American Images 1945-80*, Barbican Art Gallery, London
1981 *Art of the Olmstead Landscape*, Metropolitan Museum of Art, New York
1978 *Photographic Crossroads: The Photo League*, National Gallery of Canada, Toronto
1963 *Photography in the Fine Arts*, Metropolitan Museum of Art, New York
1955 *The Family of Man*, MoMA, New York
1950 *Young Photographers*, MoMA, New York
Selected solo exhibitions:
1985 *Memorial Exhibition*, Witkin Gallery, New York
1981 *A Photo Journal*, International Center of Photography, New York
A Photo Journal, Witkin Gallery, New York
1980 Atlanta Gallery of Photography
1979 *Window Photographs*, International Center of Photography, New York
Afterimage Gallery, New York
Ruth Orkin: Exhibition of 100 Photographs, Rizzoli Gallery, Chicago
1978 *New York–New York*, G. Ray Hawkins Gallery, Los Angeles
1974 Witkin Gallery, New York
Selected publications:
More Pictures from My Window, New York, 1983
A Photo Journal: Ruth Orkin, New York, 1981
Legacy of Love, illustrations of poems by Allen Ginsburg, New York, 1971
A World through My Window: Photographs by Ruth Orkin, New York, 1974

THERESA PENDLEBURY
Born 1950, Blackfoot, ID
Lives in Los Angeles
Selected exhibitions:
1992 *Summer Lighting*, London and Los Angeles
1991 *L.A. Times*, Boise Museum of Art, Boise, ID
1989 *Eyesores: Rehearsing the Death of the Image*, New Langton Arts, San Francisco
Self-Evidence, (installation titled, *Personal Work*, Anne Castle, Curator), LACE, Los Angeles
1987 *Nothing Sacred*, Margo Leavin Gallery, Los Angeles
Projections in Public, FAR, West Hollywood, CA
1984 *The Bus Show*, RTD Buses, FAR, Los Angeles
Selected solo exhibitions:
1991 *Jane McElheney: Theresa Pendlebury*, Thomas Solomon's Garage, Los Angeles
1990 *She's Not There*, Genovese Gallery, Boston
1989 *Why Go Outside When the Door is So Pretty?* Thomas Solomon's Garage, Los Angeles
1986 *Media Shelter: The Closer You Get the Better It Looks*, bus shelters located throughout Los Angeles, FAR, Los Angeles

Selected publications:
Self-Evidence, essay by Lawrence Rinder, Los Angeles, 1989
New Langton Arts, 1990, New Langton Arts, San Francisco 1990
L.A. Times, essay by Jacqueline Crist, Boise Museum of Art, Boise, ID, 1991
Jane McElheney: Theresa Pendlebury, essay by Colin Gardner, Thomas Solomon's Garage, Los Angeles, 1991

JACK PIERSON
Born 1960, Plymouth, MA
Lives in New York City
Selected exhibitions:
1991 *Presenting Rearwards*, Rosamund Felsen Gallery, Los Angeles
Situations, New Langton Arts, San Francisco
Someone or Somebody, Meyers/Bloom Gallery, Santa Monica, CA
Something Pithier and More Psychological, Simon Watson Gallery, New York
Phillip Lorca Di Corcia, Nan Goldin and Jack Pierson, York University, Toronto
Selected solo exhibitions:
1992 Tom Cugliani Gallery, New York
1991 Richard Kuhlenschmidt Gallery, Santa Monica, CA
Pat Hearn Gallery, New York
1990 Simon Watson Gallery, New York

FRANK POWOLNY
Born 1901, Vienna, Austria
Died 1986
Selected exhibitions:
1987 *Masters of Starlight*, LACMA, Los Angeles
Mr. Powolny began his career as an assistant cameraman. Between 1926 and 1966, he was a studio photographer at 20th Century Fox, where he photographed a variety of celebrities. In 1943 he created the famous Betty Grable pin-up.

RICHARD PRINCE
Born 1949, Panama Canal Zone
Lives in New York City
Selected exhibitions:
1991 *Metropolis*, Neuer Berliner Kunstverein, Berlin
1990 *Life Size: A Sense of the Real in Recent Art*, The Israel Museum, Jerusalem
Word as Image: American Art 1960-1990, Milwaukee Museum of Art, Milwaukee, WI
The Charade of Mastery, Whitney Museum Downtown, New York
Art et Publicité, Centre Georges Pompidou, Paris
The Decade Show: Frameworks of Identity in the '80s, The New Museum, New York
1989 *Wittgenstein–The Play of the Unsayable*, Palais voor Schöne Kunsten, Brussels
Image World: Art and Media Culture, Whitney Museum of American Art, New York
A forest of SIGNS: Art in the Crisis of Representation, MOCA, Los Angeles
Moskau–Wien–New York, Festival of Vienna, Vienna
Prospect Photographie, Frankfurter Kunstverein, Frankfurt
In Other Words: Wort und Schrift in Bildern der Konzeptuellen Kunst, Museum an Ostwall, Dortmund, Germany
D & S Ausstellung, Kunstverein in Hamburg, Hamburg

The Photography of Invention: American Pictures of the 1980s, Smithsonian Institution, Washington, D.C.
Suburban Home Life: Tracking the American Dream, Whitney Museum Downtown, New York
Nocturnal Visions in Contemporary Painting, Whitney Museum of American Art at the Equitable Center, New York
Prospect '89, Frankfurter Kunstverein, Frankfurt
Through a Glass Darkly, University Galleries, Illinois State University, Normal, IL
Photography Now, Victoria and Albert Museum, London
Horn of Plenty: Sixteen Artists from New York City, Stedelijk Museum, Amsterdam
Amerikarma, Hallwalls, Buffalo, NY
1988 *BiNATIONALE: Deutsche / Amerikanische Kunst der 80er Jehre*, Stadt. Kunsthalle, Kunstsammlung Nordrhein-Westfalen, Kunstverein fur d. Rheinlande u. Westfalen, Düsseldorf
Modes of Address: Language in Art Since 1960, Whitney Museum Downtown, New York
The Object of the Exhibition, Centre National des Arts Plastiques, Paris
Nostalgia as Resistance, Clocktower, New York
Sexual Difference: Both Sides of the Camera, Wallach Art Gallery, Columbia University, New York
Photographic Truth, The Bruce Museum, Greenwich, CT
1987 *Photography and Art: Interactions since 1946*, LACMA, Los Angeles
1986 *As Found*, ICA, Boston
TV Generations, LACE, Los Angeles
The Real Big Picture, Queens Museum, Flushing, NY
1985 *The Art of Memory / The Loss of History*, The New Museum, New York
1984 *New York: Ailleurs et Autrement*, ARC / Musée d'Art Moderne, Ville de Paris
The Magazine Stand, Washington Project for the Arts, Washington, D.C.
The Heroic Figure, Contemporary Arts Museum, Houston
Drawings: After Photography, Allen Memorial Art Museum, Oberlin College, Oberlin, OH
1983 *Language, Drama, Source and Vision*, The New Museum, New York
1982 *Image Scavengers*, ICA, Philadelphia
Face It, The Contemporary Arts Center, Cincinnati, OH
((" ' ")) Frames of Reference, Whitney Museum Downtown, New York
Art and Media, The Renaissance Society, Chicago
1981 *New Voices 2: Six Photographers Concept / Theater / Fiction*, Allen Memorial Art Museum, Oberlin College, Oberlin, OH
Erweiterte Fotografie, 5th Weiner Internationale Biennale, Wiener Secession, Vienna
Body Language, Hayden Gallery, MIT, Cambridge, MA
1980 *Ils se disent peintres, Ils se disent photographes*, ARC / Musée d'Art Moderne, Ville de Paris
Pictures and Promises, The Kitchen, New York
1979 *Imitation of Life*, Hartford Art School, University of Hartford, CT
Selected solo exhibitions:
1992 *Richard Prince Retrospective*, Whitney Museum of American Art, New York

1991 Barbara Gladstone Gallery, New York
Stuart Regen Gallery, Los Angeles
1990 *Richard Prince: Jokes, Gangs, Hoods*, Galerie Rafael Jablonka and Galerie Gisela Capitain, Köln
Richard Prince, Galerij Micheline Szwajcer, Antwerp
Arthur Roger Gallery, New Orleans
1989 *Spiritual America*, IVAM Centre del Carme, Valencia, Spain
Richard Prince–Sculpture, Barbara Gladstone Gallery and Jay Gorney Modern Art, New York
Richard Prince–Paintings, Jay Gorney Modern Art and Barbara Gladstone Gallery, New York
1988 Centre National d'Art Contemporain de Grenoble (MAGASIN), Grenoble, France
Le Case d'Arte, Milan
Tell Me Everything, One Times Square, Spectacolor Lightboard installation sponsored by the Public Art Fund, Inc., New York
Galerie Ghislaine Hussenot, Paris
1987 Guttenbergstrasse 62a e.V., Stuttgart
Daniel Weinberg Gallery, Los Angeles
1985 International With Monument, New York
1984 Riverside Studios, London
Feature, Chicago
1983 Le Nouveau Musée, Lyon, France
ICA, London
Baskerville & Watson, New York
1981 Metro Pictures, New York
Richard Kuhlenschmidt Gallery, Los Angeles
1980 Artists Space, New York
CEPA Gallery, Buffalo, NY
Selected publications:
Richard Prince Retrospective, edited by Lisa Phillips, Whitney Museum of American Art, New York, 1992
Richard Prince: Jokes, Gangs, Hoods, by Prince, Jablonka Galerie and Galerie Gisela Capitaine, Köln, 1990
Inside World, Kent Fine Art and Thea Westreich, 1989
Spiritual America, by Prince, New York, 1989
Untitled Artist's Book, by Prince, Barbara Gladstone Gallery, New York, 1988
Richard Prince, MAGASIN, Grenoble, France, 1988
Richard Prince, by Kate Linker, Lyon, France, 1983
Menthol Wars, by Prince, CEPA Gallery, Buffalo, NY, 1980

EUGENE ROBERT RICHEE
Born 1895, Denver, CO
Died 1972
Selected exhibitions:
1987 *Masters of Starlight*, LACMA, Los Angeles

HERB RITTS
Born 1952, Los Angeles
Lives in Los Angeles
Selected exhibitions:
1989 *The Christmas Show*, Staley-Wise Gallery, New York
Censorship, Couturier Gallery, Los Angeles
Arthur Roger Gallery, New Orleans
Selected solo exhibitions:
1991 *Le Printemps de la Photo*, Cahors, France
Robert Koch Gallery, San Francisco
Allene LaPides Gallery, Sante Fe, NM
PPS Gallery, Hamburg
1990 Arthur Roger Gallery, New Orleans
Jane Corkin Gallery, Toronto
Catherine Edelman Gallery, Chicago

PPS Gallery, Hamburg
Hamilton's Gallery, London
1988 *Pictures*, Fahey/Klein Gallery, Los Angeles
Parco Gallery, Tokyo
Staley-Wise Gallery, New York
Selected publications:
Herb Ritts: Portraits, Little Brown, New York, 1992
Herb Ritts: Duo, Twin Palms, Pasadena, CA, 1991
Herb Ritts: Men/Women, Twin Palms, Pasadena, CA, 1989
Herb Ritts: Pictures, Twin Palms, Pasadena, CA, 1988

DAVID ROBBINS
Born 1957, Whitefish Bay, WI
Lives in New York City
Selected exhibitions:
1991 *The Private Eye*, Arti et Amicitiae, Amsterdam
Neighborhood, Artists International Research, Amsterdam
1990 *Against Interpretation (Towards a Non-Representational Photography)*, CEPA, Buffalo, NY
In The Beginning…, Cleveland Center for Contemporary Art, Cleveland, OH
1989 *Image World: Art and Media Culture*, Whitney Museum of American Art, New York
The Photography of Invention: American Pictures of the 1980s, Smithsonian Institution, Washington, D.C.
Abstraction in Contemporary Photography, Fred L. Emerson Gallery, Hamilton College, Clinton, NY; ICP Midtown, New York
Double Take, Contemporary Arts Center, Cincinnati, OH
A Climate of Site, Barbara Farber Gallery, Amsterdam
1988 *McCollum, Prince, Robbins*, PPS Galerie, Hamburg
International Landscape, Forum Stadtpark, Graz, Austria
Works, Concepts, Processes, Situations, Information, Galerie Hans Mayer, Düsseldorf
1987 *Fake*, The New Museum, New York
Beyond the Image, First Street Forum, St. Louis
Perverted by Language, Hillwood Art Gallery, C.W. Post Campus, Brookville, NY
The Spectre of Saturation, McIntosh/Drysdale Gallery, Washington, D.C.
Constitution, The Temple Gallery, Tyler School of Art, Temple University, Philadelphia
1986 *When Attitudes Become Forms*, Bess Cutler Gallery, New York
Uplifted Atmospheres, Borrowed Taste, Hallwalls, Buffalo, NY
Rooted Rhetoric, Castel dell'Ovo, Naples
1985 *Talking Back to the Media*, Aorta, Amsterdam
Personae non Gratae, Daniel Weinberg Gallery, Los Angeles
Objects in Collision, The Kitchen, New York
Paravision, Postmasters, New York
Infotainment, Texas Gallery, Houston
1984 *Semi(op)tics*, International With Monument, New York
The New Capital, White Columns, New York
1981 *REAL LIFE Magazine Presents*, White Columns, New York
Selected solo exhibitions:
1991 Gallerie Christian Nagel, Köln
Galerie Claire Burrus, Paris
Feature Gallery, New York
1990 Galerie Hufkens, Bruxelles
Galerie Kubinski, Stuttgart

1989 American Fine Arts, New York
Galerie Daniel Bucholz, Köln
Diagramma, Milan
1988 Galerie Dorrie / Priess, Hamburg
Galerie Christoph Durr, Munich
1987 Nature Morte, New York
303 Gallery, New York
Cable Gallery, New York (in collaboration with Clegg and Guttman)
1986 Nature Morte, New York
Selected publications by Robbins:
The Camera Believes Everything, Editions Patricia Schwarz, Stuttgart, 1988
Another World, in *Special Effects*, Milan, 1989
Solid Light in *Made in Camera*, Stockholm, 1988
Stars in *Aperture*, Spring, 1988
Search for Tomorrow in *Information as Ornament*, Feature Gallery, Chicago, 1988
Hollywood Out-takes and Rare Footage in *Picture This*, Hallwalls, Buffalo, NY, 1987
Artificial Intelligence in *Rooted Rhetoric*, Guida Editori, Naples, 1986

MATTHEW ROLSTON
Born 1957, Los Angeles
Lives in Los Angeles
Selected exhibitions:
1988 *Fashion and Surrealism*, F.I.T. Collection, New York; Victoria and Albert Museum, London
1987 *New Nudes*, G. Ray Hawkins Gallery, Los Angeles
1985 *Working in LA*, with Herb Ritts and Greg Gorman, G. Ray Hawkins Gallery, Los Angeles
1984 *Modern Masters*, Hokin-Kaufman Gallery, Chicago
Selected solo exhibitions:
1991 *Big Pictures*, Fahey/Klein Gallery, Los Angeles
Big Pictures, Staley-Wise Gallery, New York
Big Pictures, Arthur Roger Gallery, New Orleans
1987 Govinda Gallery, Washington, D.C.
1982 Jennifer Dumas Gallery, Los Angeles
New Hollywood Portraiture, FOTO Gallery, New York
Selected publications:
Big Pictures: A Book of Photographs, Boston, 1991

CHARLES ROSHER
Born 1885
Died 1974
Mr. Rosher was an American cinematographer. His films include *The Clown*, 1916; *Sunrise*, 1927; *What Price Hollywood?* 1932; *Little Lord Fauntleroy*, 1936; *Kismet*, 1944; *The Yearling*, 1946; *Show Boat*, 1951; *Kiss Me Kate*, 1953; and *Young Bess*, 1954.

ANNE ROWLAND
Born 1957, Washington, D.C.
Lives in West Redding, CT
Selected exhibitions:
1991 *Objectional Beauty*, Jan Kesner Gallery, Los Angeles
Maier Museum of Art, Lynchburg, VA
1990 *Signs of the Self: Changing Perceptions*, Woodstock Artists Association, Woodstock, NY
1989 *The Photography of Invention: American Pictures of the 1980s*, Smithsonian Institution, Washington, D.C.

Photography: A Contemporary View, Newport Art Museum, Newport, RI
Photography and Performance, Photographic Resource Center, Boston
Unconventional Perspectives, G. Ray Hawkins Gallery, Los Angeles
Assumed Identities, Zoe Gallery, Boston
Taken: Photography and Death, The Tartt Gallery, Washington, D.C.
1987 *Boston Baroque: Elements of Drama in Contemporary Art*, Vault Gallery, Boston
1986 *50th Anniversary Celebration*, ICA, Boston
1985 *Boston Now: Photography*, ICA, Boston
No Shadows: Recent Photographic Self-Portraiture, Laurence Miller Gallery, New York
1984 *Twelve on 20 x 24*, The School of the Museum of Fine Arts, Boston
Flash: An Aesthetic, Second Street Gallery, Charlottesville, VA
Contemporary Color Photography, Sioux City Art Center, Sioux City, IA
1983 *Rated X*, Neikrug Photographica, New York
Photographs in Color, Gallery East, The Art Institute of Boston, Boston
1981 *Surrealism in Photography*, Intuitiveye Gallery, Washington, D.C.
Selected solo exhibitions:
1991 *Dictu Sanctificare*, Greg Kucera Gallery, Seattle, WA; Zoe Gallery, Boston
1990 *Dictu Sanctificare*, The Tartt Gallery, Washington, D.C.
Houston Center for Photography, Houston
1988 *Persona*, Robert B. Menschel Gallery, Syracuse, NY
1986 Zoe Gallery, Boston
1984 Burlington County College, Pemberton, NJ
School of Art, University of Denver, CO
1983 Hera Cooperative Gallery, Wakefield, RI
Selected publications:
Boston Now: Photography, by Elizabeth Sussman, ICA, Boston, 1985

RENÉ SANTOS
Born 1954, Puerto Rico
Died 1986
Selected exhibitions:
1989 *Office Party*, Feature, New York
1985 *The Art Of Memory, The Loss of History*, The New Museum, New York
Engagement, Feature, New York
TV Pictures, The New Museum, New York
1984 *Opposing Force*, Hallwalls, Buffalo, NY
Drawings: After Photography, Allen Memorial Art Museum, Oberlin College, Oberlin, OH
Great Values, Feature, Chicago
1982 *Face It:10 Contemporary Artists*, Contemporary Arts Center, Cincinnati, OH
1981 *New Voices 2: Six Photographers; Concept / Theater / Fiction*, Allen Memorial Art Museum, Oberlin College, Oberlin, OH
Selected solo exhibitions:
1986 *Venice Biennale*, Venice
New Paintings, Feature, Chicago
New Paintings, Diane Brown Gallery, New York
1985 *Dog Show*, Grey Art Gallery and Study Center, New York University, New York
Real/Reel, Joseph Gross Gallery, University of Arizona, Tucson
1984 *Dog Show*, Feature, Chicago

ROCKY SCHENCK
Born 1955, Dripping Springs, TX
Lives in Hollywood, CA
Selected exhibitions:
1989 Tom Cugliani Gallery, New York
1987 Self, Photo Impact Gallery, Los Angeles
Selected solo exhibitions:
1991 Fotek, Los Angeles
1988 Tom Cugliani Gallery, New York
1986 Photo Impact Gallery, Los Angeles
Filmography:
Mr. Schenck has directed over sixty music videos, short films, and experimental clips, including projects with Joni Mitchell, The Cramps, Devo, Ann Magnunson, Faster Pussycat, Alice in Chains, etc.
Stage direction:
My Rotten Life, A Bitter Operetta, by Susan Tyrell

BONNIE SCHIFFMAN
Born 1950, Los Angeles
Lives in Los Angeles
Within Ms. Schiffman's twenty-year career, her photographs of celebrities have been published in such magazines as Rolling Stone, Vanity Fair, Woman's Sport, Playboy, Gentleman's Quarterly and Forbes.
Selected publications:
The Rolling Stone Book of Comedy, photographs by Bonnie Schiffman, Los Angeles and New York, 1991

CINDY SHERMAN
Born 1954, Glen Ridge, NJ
Lives in New York City
Selected exhibitions:
1992 Quotations: The Second History of Art, Aldrich Museum of Contemporary Art, Ridgefield, CT
1990 Louise Lawler, Cindy Sherman, Laurie Simmons, Metro Pictures, New York
Culture and Commentary, The Hirshhorn Museum, Washington, D.C.
The Decade Show, The New Museum, New York
Energies, The Stedelijk Museum, Amsterdam
Affinities and Intuitions: The Gerald S. Elliot Collection of Contemporary Art, The Art Institute of Chicago, Chicago
1989 The Photographer's Eye: A Selection by Chris Kellep, Victoria and Albert Museum, London
Three Decades: The Oliver Hoffman Collection, Museum of Contemporary Art, Chicago
Surrogate Selves, The Corcoran Gallery of Art, Washington, D.C.
Making Their Mark: Women Artists Move Into the Mainstream, 1970-1985, Cincinnati Art Museum, Cincinnati, OH
Peinture Cinéma Peinture, Centre de la Ville Charité, Musée de Marseille
The Photography of Invention: American Pictures of the 1980s, Smithsonian Institution, Washington, D.C.
Photography Now, Victoria and Albert Museum, London
A forest of SIGNS: Art in the Crisis of Representation, MOCA, Los Angeles
Tenir l'image à distance, Musée d'Art Contemporain de Montreal, Montreal
Invention and Continuity in Contemporary Photography, Metropolitan Museum of Art, New York
Moscow-Vienna-New York, The Vienna Festival, Vienna
Image World: Art and Media Culture, Whitney Museum of American Art, New York
1988 Matris, Malmö Konsthall, Sweden
Sexual Difference: Both Sides of the Camera, Wallach Art Gallery, Columbia Universtiy, New York
The Pop Project, The Clocktower, New York
1988: The World of Art Today, Milwaukee Art Museum, Milwaukee, WI
Presi per Incantamento, Padiglione d'Arte Contemporanea di Milano, Milan
1987 L'Epoque, la Mode, la Morale, La Passion: Aspects de l'Art d'Aujourd'hui, 1977-1987, Centre Georges Pompidou, Paris
Avant-Garde in the Eighties, LACMA, Los Angeles
This Is Not a Photograph 1966-1986, The John and Mable Ringling Museum of Art, Sarasota, FL
Photography and Art: Interaction Since 1946, LACMA, Los Angeles
Implosion: A Postmodern Perspective, Moderna Museet, Stockholm
1986 The American Exhibition, The Art Institute of Chicago, Chicago
Eve and the Future, Hamburg Kunsthalle, Hamburg
Prospect 86, Frankfurter Kunstverein, Frankfurt
Art and Its Double: A New York Perspective, Fundacio Caixa de Pension, Barcelona
Individuals: A Selected History of Contemporary Art 1945-1986, MOCA, Los Angeles
Staging the Self: Self-Portrait Photography 1840s-1980s, National Portrait Gallery, London
1985 Self-Portrait, MoMA, New York
Carnegie International, Museum of Art, Pittsburgh, PA
Content: A Contemporary Focus, 1974-1984, Hirshhorn Museum, Washington, D.C.
1984 The Heroic Figure, Contemporary Arts Museum, Houston
Alibis, Centre Georges Pompidou, Paris
1983 Big Pictures by Contemporary Photographers, MoMA, New York
1982 New Figuration in America, Milwaukee Art Museum, Milwaukee, WI
((" ")) Frames of Reference, Whitney Museum Downtown, New York
A Fatal Attraction: Art and the Media, The Renaissance Society, Chicago
Eight Artists: The Anxious Edge, Walker Art Center, Minneapolis, MN
Lichtbildnisse: The Portrait in Photography, Rheinisches Landesmuseum, Bonn
1981 Body Language: Figurative Aspects of Recent Art, Hayden Gallery, MIT, Cambridge, MA
Autoportraits, Centre Georges Pompidou, Paris
1980 Pictures and Promises, The Kitchen, New York
Ils se disent peintres, Ils se disent photographes, ARC/Musée d'Art Moderne, Ville de Paris
1978 Four Artists, Artists Space, New York
1976 Albright-Knox Art Gallery, Buffalo, NY
Hallwalls, Artists Space, New York
Selected solo exhibitions:
1992 Linda Cathcart Gallery, Santa Monica, CA
1989 Galerie Crousel-Robelin, Paris
Galerie der Wiener Secession, Vienna
Galerie Pierre Hubert, Geneva
1988 La Maquina Espanola, Madrid
Lia Rumma, Naples, Italy
1987 HoffmanBorman Gallery, Los Angeles
Provincial Museum, Hasselt, Belgium
1986 Jenny Holzer/Cindy Sherman, The Contemporary Arts Center, Cincinnati, OH
Portland Art Museum, Portland, OR
Wadsworth Atheneum, Hartford, CT
Aldrich Museum of Contemporary Art, Ridgefield, CT
1985 Westfälischer Kunstverein, Münster, Germany
1984 Seibu Gallery of Contemporary Art, Tokyo
Akron Art Museum, Akron, OH
Galerie Monika Spruth, Köln
1983 Currents 20, Cindy Sherman, The St. Louis Art Museum, St. Louis, MO
Galerie Schellmann & Kluser, Munich
Cindy Sherman, Fine Arts Center Gallery, State University of New York at Stony Brook, NY
Rhona Hoffman Gallery, Chicago
Cindy Sherman, Musée d'Art et d'Industrie de Saint Etienne, France
1982 Texas Gallery, Houston
Galerie Chantal Crousel, Paris
Larry Gagosian Gallery, Los Angeles
Stedelijk Museum, Amsterdam
1981 Young/Hoffman Gallery, Chicago
1980 Cindy Sherman: Photographs, Contemporary Arts Museum, Houston
The Kitchen, New York
Metro Pictures, New York
1979 Hallwalls, Buffalo, NY
Selected publications:
Cindy Sherman, Untitled Film Stills, by Arthur C. Danto, New York, 1990
Cindy Sherman, Parco Co., Ltd., Tokyo, 1987
Cindy Sherman, essays by Peter Schjeldahl and Lisa Phillips, Whitney Museum of American Art, New York, 1987
Cindy Sherman, essay by Marianne Stockebrand, Westfälischer Kunstverein, Münster, 1985
Currents 20, Cindy Sherman, by Jack Cowart, St. Louis Art Museum, St. Louis, MO, 1983
Cindy Sherman, by Thom Thompson, Fine Arts Center Gallery, State University of New York at Stony Brook, NY, 1983
Cindy Sherman: Photographs, by Linda Cathcart, Contemporary Arts Museum, Houston, 1980

LAURIE SIMMONS
Born 1949, Long Island, NY
Lives in New York City
Selected exhibitions:
1992 More Than One Photography, MoMA, New York
1991 The Surrogate Figure: Intercepted Identities in Contemporary Photography, The Center for Photography, Woodstock, NY
Pleasures and Terrors of Domestic Comfort, MoMA, New York
1990 To Be and Not To Be, Centre d'Arte Santa Monica, Barcelona
Modern Detour, Vienna Secession, Vienna
1989 Surrogate Selves, Corcoran Gallery of Art, Washington, D.C.
Making Their Mark: Women Artists Move Into the Mainstream, 1970-1985, Cincinnati Art Museum, Cincinnati, OH
The Photography of Invention: American Pictures of the 1980s, Smithsonian Institution, Washington, D.C.
A forest of SIGNS: Art in the Crisis of Representation, MOCA, Los Angeles
The Desire of the Museum, Whitney Museum Downtown, New York
Image World: Art and Media Culture, Whitney Museum of American Art, New York
1988 Media Post Media, Scott Hansen Gallery, New York
Female (Re)production, White Columns, New York
1987 Photography and Art: Interactions Since 1946, LACMA, Los Angeles
Implosion: A Postmodern Perspective, Moderna Museet, Stockholm
1986 The Real Big Picture, Queens Museum, New York
Photographic Fiction, Whitney Museum of American Art, Fairfield County, Stamford, CT
Art and Advertising: Commercial Photography by Artists, International Center for Photography, New York
The Fashionable Image: Unconventional Fashion Photography, The Mint Museum of Art, Charlotte, NC
1985 Persona non Grata, Daniel Newburg Gallery, New York
Remembrances of Things Past, Long Beach Museum of Art, Long Beach, CA
Infotainment, Texas Gallery, Houston
1984 Visions of Childhood: A Contemporary Iconography, Whitney Museum Downtown, New York
A Decade of New Art, Artists Space, New York
Between Here and Nowhere, Riverside Studios, London
Disarming Images, Contemporary Arts Center, Cincinnati, OH
Masking/Unmasking: Aspects of Post-Modernist Photography, The Friends of Photography, Carmel, CA
1983 Images Fabriqués, Centre Georges Pompidou, Paris
In Plato's Cave, Marlborough Gallery, New York
1982 The Image Scavengers, ICA, Philadelphia
Staged Photo Events, Lijnbaancentrum, Rotterdam
Public Vision, White Columns, New York
1981 Couches, Diamonds and Pie, P.S. 1, Long Island City, Queens, NY
Photo, Metro Pictures, New York
Body Language: Figurative Aspects of Recent Art, Hayden Gallery, MIT, Cambridge, MA
Erweiterte Fotografie, 5., Wiener Internationale Biennale, Wiener Secession, Vienna
1980 Pictures and Promises, The Kitchen, New York
Invented Images, University Art Musuem, University of California at Santa Barbara, Santa Barbara
1979 Photographie als Kunst, Innsbruck Museum, Ninz Gras, Austria
Selected solo exhibitions:
1992 Orangerie München, Munich
1991 Galerie Carola Mosch, Berlin
1990 San Jose Museum of Art, San Jose, CA
1989 Daniel Weinberg Gallery, Los Angeles
Galerie Jablonka, Köln
1985 Actual Photos (collaboration with Allan McCollum) Nature Morte, New York and Josh Baer Gallery, New York
1984 International With Monument, New York
Galerie Tanja Grunert, Stuttgart
1983 CEPA Gallery, Buffalo, NY
1981 Metro Pictures, New York
Diane Brown Gallery, Washington, D.C.
1979 P.S. 1, Long Island City, Queens, NY
Selected publications:
Laurie Simmons, by Dan Cameron, San Jose Museum of Art, San Jose, CA, 1990
Laurie Simmons, by Ronald Jones, Galerie Jablonka, Köln, 1989
Laurie Simmons, Parco, Tokyo, 1987
In and Around the House: Photographs 1976-1979, by Simmons, CEPA Gallery, Buffalo, NY, 1983

ALEXIS SMITH
Born 1949, Los Angeles
Lives in Los Angeles
Selected exhibitions:
1992 Songs of Innocence, Songs of Experience: Meg Cranston, Mike Kelley, Collier Schorr, Jim Shaw, Gary Simmons, Alexis Smith, Whitney Museum of American Art at the Equitable Center, New York
1991 20th Century Collage, Margo Leavin Gallery, Los Angeles
1990 Word as Image, American Art 1960-1990, Milwaukee Art Museum, Milwaukee, WI
1989 Image World: Art and Media Culture, Whitney Museum of American Art, New York
A Brave New World: John Baldessari, Vernon Fisher, Stephen Prina, Ed Ruscha, Alexis Smith, Karsten Schubert Ltd., London
1988 Striking Distance, MOCA, Los Angeles
1987 Avant-Garde in the Eighties, LACMA, Los Angeles
comic iconoclasm, ICA, London
1986 Individuals: A Selected History of Contemporary Art 1945-1986, MOCA, Los Angeles
Remembrances of Things Past, Long Beach Museum of Art, Long Beach, CA
Spectrum: In Other Works, Corcoran Gallery of Art, Washington, D.C.
1984 An International Survey of Recent Painting and Sculpture, MoMA, New York
Verbally Charged Images, Queens Museum, Flushing, NY
1983 The Comic Art Show, Whitney Museum Downtown, New York
New Directions 1983, Hirshhorn Museum, Washington, D.C.
1981 Words as Images, The Renaissance Society, Chicago
Humor in Art, LAICA, Los Angeles
1980 Views Over America, MoMA, New York
Tableau, LAICA, Los Angeles
1979 Decade in Review, Whitney Museum of American Art, New York
Words and Images, Philadelphia College of Art, Philadelphia
Paper on Paper, San Francisco Museum of Art, San Francisco
1978 Southern California Styles of the '60s and '70s, La Jolla Museum of Contemporary Art, La Jolla, CA
Narration, ICA, Boston
1977 Narrative Themes/Audio Works, LAICA, Los Angeles
Paris Biennale, Musée d'Arte Moderne, Ville de Paris
1976 Autobiographical Fantasies, LAICA, Los Angeles
1972 Southern California Attitudes, Pasadena Museum of Modern Art, Pasadena, CA
Selected solo exhibitions:
1991 Alexis Smith: Public Works, Mandeville Gallery, University of California at San Diego, La Jolla, CA
Alexis Smith, Whitney Museum of American Art, New York; MOCA, Los Angeles

1990 *Past Lives* (collaboration with Amy Gerstler),
Josh Baer Gallery, New York
1989 *Past Lives* (collaboration with Amy Gerstler),
Santa Monica Museum of Art, Santa
Monica, CA
1987 *Alexis Smith & Joseph Cornell: Parallels*, Aspen
Art Center, Aspen, CO
Same Old Paradise, Grand Lobby installation,
The Brooklyn Museum, Brooklyn, NY
1986 *Viewpoint: Alexis Smith*, Walker Art Center,
Minneapolis, MN
Currents: Alexis Smith, ICA, Boston
1985 *Jane*, Margo Leavin Gallery, Los Angeles
1982 *Christmas Eve, 1943*, Margo Leavin Gallery,
Los Angeles
Chinese Junk, Clocktower, New York
1981 *Stardust*, Bing Theater, LACMA, Los Angeles;
La Jolla Museum of Contemporary Art,
La Jolla, CA
1979 De Appel, Amsterdam
1978 *The Art Of Magic, Close-up* (performance with
Tony DeLap) Baxter Art Gallery, California
Institute of Technology, Pasadena, CA
Rosamund Felsen Gallery, Los Angeles
1977 Holly Solomon Gallery, New York
Nicholas Wilder Gallery, Los Angeles
1975 Long Beach Museum of Art, Long Beach, CA
1974 Riko Mizuno Gallery, Los Angeles
Selected publications:
Alexis Smith, by Richard Armstrong, Whitney
Museum of American Art, New York;
MOCA, Los Angeles, 1991
Past Lives, (collaboration with Amy Gerstler),
Santa Monica Museum of Art, Santa Monica,
CA, 1989
Alexis Smith & Joseph Cornell: Parallels, Aspen Art
Center, Aspen, CO, 1987
Viewpoint: Alexis Smith, Walker Art Center,
Minneapolis, MN, 1986
Jane, Margo Leavin Gallery, Los Angeles, 1985

ALICE SPRINGS
No birth date given
Lives in Monte Carlo
Selected exhibitions:
1991 Paris Audiovisual, French Photographers
Museum of Modern Art, Bratislava,
Czechoslovakia
Selected solo exhibitions:
1992 Shoshana Wayne Gallery, Santa Monica, CA
1991 Rheinisches Landesmuseum, Bonn
1990 Musée Contemporaneo, Mexico City
1988 Gerfiollet, Amsterdam
National Portrait Gallery, London
Olympus Galerie, Hamburg
Musée d'Art Moderne, Paris
1987 Fotoform, Frankfurt/Main
1986 Espace Photographie de la Ville de Paris/
Paris Audiovisual, Paris
1985 Musée de Sainte Croix, Poitiers, France
Center Culturel, Orléans, France
Documenta Gallery, Turin, Italy
1984 Musée Cheret, Nice, France
1983 Olympus Gallery, London
Galerie de France, Paris
1982 David Heath Gallery, Atlanta, GA
The Yuen Lui Gallery, Seattle, WA
1980 Duc et Camroux, Paris
1978 Canon Gallery, Amsterdam
Selected publications:
Alice Springs Portraits, Schirmer & Mosel, 1991
Alice Springs Portraits, Twelvetrees Press, Pasadena,
CA, 1986

Alice Springs Portraits, Musée Saint Croix,
Poitiers, 1985
Alice Springs Portraits, Edition du Regard, Paris, 1983

JOHN SWOPE
Born 1908, New Brunswick, NJ
Died 1979
Selected exhibitions:
1987 *Masters of Starlight*, LACMA, Los Angeles
1973 *Henry Moore in America*, LACMA, Los Angeles
1963 Joslyn Art Museum, Omaha, NE
1952 *People and Places*, Albright-Knox Art Gallery,
Buffalo, NY
Selected solo exhibitions:
1953 Santa Barbara Museum of Art, Santa
Barbara, CA
Selected publications:
Autobiography of a Princess, by James Ivory, with
photos by Swope, New York, 1975
Bombs Away, by John Steinbeck, with photos by
Swope, New York, 1942
Camera Over Hollywood, by Swope with Leland
Hayward, New York, 1938

DAVID TATTU
Born 1963, Santa Cruz, CA
Lives in Los Angeles

TIM TATTU
Born 1964, Hermosa Beach, CA
Lives in Los Angeles

ANDY WARHOL
Born 1928, McKeesport, PA
Died 1987
Selected exhibitions:
1986 *Ooghoogte*, Stedelijk van Abbemuseum,
Eindhoven
1985 *Transformations in Sculpture*, the Solomon R.
Guggenheim Musuem, New York
1982 *Lichtbildnisse: das Portraits in der Fotografie*,
Rheinisches Landesmuseum, Bonn
Painter as Photographer, John Hansard Gallery,
Southampton, England
1980 *La Photo Polaroid*, Musée d'Art Moderne, Paris
Instantanes, Centre Georges Pompidou, Paris
1978 *Mirrors and Windows: American Photography since
1960*, MoMA, New York
Art about Art, Whitney Museum of American
Art, New York
1977 *Paris-New York*, Centre Georges Pompidou,
Paris
1975 *Photographic Process as Medium*, Rutgers
University, New Brunswick, NJ
1971 *Photo/Graphics*, International Museum of
Photography, George Eastman House,
Rochester, New York
1969 *Pop Art*, Hayward Gallery, London
1966 *The Photographic Image*, the Solomon R.
Guggenheim Museum, New York
1964 *The Painter and The Photograph: From Delacroix to
Warhol*, University of New Mexico,
Albuquerque
Selected solo exhibitions:
1990 *Andy Warhol, ange ou demon?* Centre Georges
Pompidou, Paris
1989 *Andy Warhol: A Retrospective*, MoMA,
New York
1987 Galerie Thaddaeus Ropac, Salzberg
1986 Anthony D'Offay Gallery, London
1984 Judith Goldberg Gallery, New York
Flow Ace Gallery, Los Angeles
1983 Fraenkel Gallery, San Francisco

1982 Galerie Daniel Templon, Paris
1981 Städtische Galerie im Lenbachhaus, Munich
Portrait Screenprints 1965-1980,
Gloucestershire College of Arts and
Technology, Cheltenham, England
1980 *Andy Warhol: Photos*, Lisson Gallery, London
Stedelijk Museum, Amsterdam
1979 *Andy Warhol: Portraits of the '70s*, Whitney
Museum of American Art, New York
1978 ICA, London
Kunsthaus, Zürich
1976 Württembergischer Kunstverein, Stuttgart
1975 Baltimore Museum of Art, Baltimore
1973 Margo Leavin Gallery, Los Angeles
1972 Multiples Gallery, New York
1971 Galerie Bruno Bischofberger, Zürich
ICA, London
1970 Tate Gallery, London
Museum of Contemporary Art, Chicago
Stedelijk van Abbemuseum, Eindhoven,
Netherlands
Musée d'Art Moderne, Ville de Paris
Pasadena Museum of Art, Pasadena, CA
1969 Neue Nationalgalerie der Staatlichen Museen
Preussischer Kulturbesitz, West Berlin
Irving Blum Gallery, Los Angeles
1968 Stedelijk Museum, Amsterdam
Kunstnernes Hus, Oslo
Moderna Musset, Stockholm
1967 Galerie Rudolf Zwirner, Köln
1966 Gian Enzo Sperone Arte Moderna, Milan
ICA, Boston
Contemporary Arts Center, Cincinnati, OH
Ferus Gallery, Los Angeles
1965 Gian Enzo Sperone Arte Moderna, Milan
ICA, Philadelphia
1964 Leo Castelli Gallery, New York
Galerie Sonnabend, Paris
1962 Stable Gallery, New York
Ferus Gallery, Los Angeles
1956 Bodley Gallery, New York
1952 Hugo Gallery, New York
Selected publications:
Andy Warhol Diaries, by Pat Hackett, New York, 1991
Andy Warhol: A Retrospective, by Kynast McShine,
MoMA, New York, 1991
Holy Terror: Andy Warhol Close Up, by Bob Colacello,
New York, 1990
Absolute Warhol, by Brian Wallis, New York, 1989
Andy Warhol: Photographs, by Stephen Koch, New
York, 1986
America, by Warhol, New York, 1985
Andy Warhol, by Carter Radcliff, New York, 1983
Pop-ism: The Warhol '60s, by Warhol with Pat
Hackett, New York, 1980
*The Philosophy of Andy Warhol (from a to b and back
again)*, by Warhol, New York, 1975
Andy Warhol: Films and Paintings, by Peter Gidal, New
York, 1971
The Autobiography and Sex Life of Andy Warhol, by John
Wilcock, New York, 1971
Andy Warhol, by John Coplans, Pasadena, CA, 1970
A: A Novel, by Warhol, New York, 1968
Andy Warhol's Index Book, by Warhol, New York, 1967

WILLIAM WEGMAN
Born 1942, Holyoke, MA
Lives in New York City
Selected exhibitions:
1990 *Photography Until Now*, MoMA, New York
1989 *Fantasies, Fables and Fabrications*, Fine Arts
Center, University of Massachusetts,
Amherst

Images of American Pop Culture Today, LaForet
Art Museum, Tokyo
Photography Now, Victoria and Albert
Museum, London
Image World: Art and Media Culture, Whitney
Museum of American Art, New York
1988 *First Person Singular: Self-Portrait Photography
1840-1987*, High Museum at Georgia
Pacific Center, Atlanta
Photography and Art, 1946-1986, LACMA,
Los Angeles
Identity: Representations of the Self, Whitney
Museum Downtown, New York
*Fabrications: Staged, Altered and Appropriated
Photographs*, Carpenter Center for the Arts,
Harvard University, Cambridge, MA
1987 *Poetic Injury: The Surrealist Legacy in Post-Modern
Photography*, The Alternative Museum,
New York
Portrait: Faces of the '80s, Virginia Museum of
Fine Art, Richmond, VA
1986 *Television's Impact on Contemporary Art*, Queens
Museum, New York
The Real Big Picture, Queens Museum,
New York
Altered Egos, Phoenix Art Museum, Phoenix, AZ
Text and Image: The Wording of American Art,
Holly Solomon Gallery, New York
Advertising: Commercial Photography by Artists,
International Center for Photography,
New York
Prospect 86, Frankfurter Kunstverein, Düsseldorf
1984 *Exposition Alibis*, Musée National d'Art
Moderne, Paris
Visions of Childhood: Contemporary Iconography,
Whitney Museum Downtown, New York
Alibis, Centre Georges Pompidou, Paris
1983 *Subjective Vision: The Lucinda W. Bunnen
Collection of Photographs*, High Museum of
Art, Atlanta
Contemporary Self-Portraiture in Photography,
Hayden Gallery, MIT, Cambridge, MA
Funny/Strange, ICA, Boston
Big Pictures, MoMA, New York
1982 *Faces Photographed*, Grey Art Gallery,
New York University, New York
Momentbild Kunstlerfotografie, Kestner-
Gesellschaft, Hannover, Germany
1981 *Not Just for Laughs; The Art of Subversion*, The
New Museum, New York
Lichtbildnisse–Das Portrait in der Fotografie,
Rheinisches Landesmuseum, Bonn
1980 *Ils se disent peintres, Ils se disent photographes*,
Musée d'Art Moderne, Ville de Paris
Invented Images, University Art Museum,
University of California at Santa Barbara,
Santa Barbara, CA
1979 *The Altered Photograph*, P.S. 1, Long Island
City, Queens, NY
Images of the Self, Hampshire College Gallery,
Amherst, MA
1978 *Contemporary American Photo Works*, Museum of
Fine Arts, Houston; Museum
of Contemporary Art, Chicago
1977 *The Word As Image*, Museum of Contemporary
Art, Chicago
1976 *American Family Portraits*, Philadelphia
Museum of Art, Philadelphia
1969 *When Attitudes Become Form*, Bern
Sign, Signal, Symbol, Moreau Art Gallery, St.
Mary's College, Notre Dame University,
South Bend, IL

Selected solo exhibitions:
1992 The Whitney Museum of American Art,
New York
Contemporary Arts Museum, Houston
Columbus Museum of Art, Columbus, OH
1991 ICA, Boston
Sperone Westwater Gallery, New York
John and Mable Ringling Museum, Sarasota, FL
1990 *William Wegman: Paintings, Drawings,
Photographs, Videotapes*, Kunstmuseum,
Lucerne, Switzerland
William Wegman: New Photographs, Linda
Cathcart Gallery, Santa Monica, CA
1989 *William Wegman: Photographies*, Baudoin
Lebon, Paris
1988 *William Wegman: Polaroids and Videos*, San
Francisco Museum of Modern Art,
San Francisco
Thomas Solomon's Garage, Los Angeles
1986 *Improved Photographs*, Daniel Wolf Gallery,
New York
William Wegman: Color Photographs, Cleveland
Museum of Art, Cleveland, OH
1985 *William Wegman's Instant Miami*, Lowe
Museum of Art, Miami
1982 Southeastern Center for Contemporary Art,
Winston-Salem, NC
Wegman's World, Walker Art Center,
Minneapolis, MN
1981 Clarence Kennedy Gallery (with Willard van
Dyke and Olivia Parker), Cambridge, MA
1980 *William Wegman: Selected Works, 1970-1979*,
University of Colorado Art Gallery,
Boulder
1979 *William Wegman: Retrospective*, Fine Arts
Galleries, University of Wisconsin,
Milwaukee, WI
Holly Solomon Gallery, New York
1978 Rosamund Felsen Gallery, Los Angeles
1977 Bruno Soletti Gallery, Milan
1976 The Kitchen, New York
1974 112 Greene Street, New York
1973 LACMA, Los Angeles
Francoise Lambert and Claire Copley
Gallery, Los Angeles
1972 Sonnabend Gallery, New York
Situation, London
Galerie Konrad Fisher, Düsseldorf
1971 Galerie Sonnabend, Paris
Pomona College, Claremont, CA
Selected publications:
*William Wegman: Paintings, Drawings, Photographs,
Videotapes*, by Martin Kunz and David Ross,
New York, 1990
William Wegman, Whitney Museum Downtown,
New York, 1984
Man's Best Friend, by Wegman, New York, 1983
William Wegman, Southeastern Center for
Contemporary Art, Winston-Salem, NC, 1982
Wegman's World, by Lisa Lyons, Walker Art Center,
Minneapolis, MN, 1982

CHRISTOPHER WILLIAMS
Born 1956, Los Angeles
Lives in Los Angeles
Selected exhibitions:
1992 *Knowledge: Aspects of Conceptual Art*, University
Art Museum, University of California at
Santa Barbara, Santa Barbara; Santa
Monica Art Museum, Santa Monica, CA
1991 *Carnegie International*, Carnegie Museum of
Art, Pittsburgh, PA

Facing the Finish: Some Recent California Art, San Francisco Museum of Modern Art, San Francisco; Santa Barbara Contemporary Arts Forum, Santa Barbara, CA; Art Center College of Design, Pasadena, CA
Castello di Rivera, Torino
Enclosure, Municipal Art Gallery, Los Angeles
1990 *Artedomani: 1990/Point of View*, Musei di Spoleta, Rome
1989 *Constructing a History: A Focus on MOCA's Permanent Collection*, MOCA, Los Angeles
Wittgenstein and the Art of the 20th Century, The Vienna Secession, Vienna; Palais des Beaux-Arts, Brussels
A forest of SIGNS: Art in the Crisis of Representation, MOCA, Los Angeles
1987 *L.A. Hot and Cool: The Eighties*, List Visual Arts Center, MIT, Cambridge
CalArts: Skeptical Belief(s), The Renaissance Society, Chicago; Newport Harbor Art Museum, Newport Beach, CA
1986 *TV Generations*, LACE, Los Angeles
Rooted Rhetoric, Una Tradizione nell 'Arte Americana, Castel dell' Ovo, Naples, Italy
1985 *The Art of Memory, The Loss of History*, The New Museum, New York
Selected solo exhibitons:
1992 Galerie Gisela Capitain, Köln
1991 Galerie Nelson, Lyon, France
Galerie Crousel-Robelin/BAMA, Paris
Galerie Max Hetzler, Köln
1990 Luhring Augustine Hetzler, Santa Monica, CA
1989 Luhring Augustine Gallery, New York
Galerie Crousel-Robelin/BAMA, Paris
Shedhalle, Zürich
1985 *Selections From Adweek: Western Advertising News, Vol. XXXIV, No. 20, April 30, 1984*, programmed with Herbert Gold, Beyond Baroque, Venice, CA
1982 *Source, The Photographic Archive, John F. Kennedy Library…*, Jancar/Kuhlenschmidt Gallery, Los Angeles
Selected publications:
Chris Williams, Angola to Vietnam, Ghent, 1989
Chris Williams, Shedalle, Zürich, 1989
Realism and the Cinema, edited by Williams, London, 1980

LASZLO WILLINGER
Born 1909, Budapest
Lives in Los Angeles
Selected exhibitions:
1987 *Masters of Starlight*, LACMA, Los Angeles
1983 *The Art of the Great Hollywood Portrait Photographers*, Smithsonian Institution, Washington, D.C.
1982 *Faces and Fabrics/Feathers and Furs*, International Museum of Photography, George Eastman House, Rochester, NY
Selected publications:
Berlin, Berlin, 1927
London, Berlin, 1927

BOB WILLOUGHBY
Born 1927, Los Angeles
Lives in Cork County, Ireland
Selected exhibitions:
1987 *Masters of Starlight*, LACMA, Los Angeles
1985 *Stars of the British Screen*, National Portrait Gallery, London
1973, 1968, 1964, *World Exhibition of Photography*, (privately organized travelling exhibition)

1959 *Photography at Mid-Century*, International Museum of Photography, George Eastman House, Rochester, NY
1955 *The Family of Man*, MoMA, New York
Selected solo exhibitions:
1979 American Cultural Center, Paris
Selected publications:
The Platinum Years, by Willoughby with Richard Schickel, New York, 1974
Voices from Ancient Ireland, London, 1981

GARRY WINOGRAND
Born 1928, New York City
Died 1984
Selected exhibitons:
1987 *Photography and Art 1946-86*, LACMA, Los Angeles
1985 *American Images, 1945-80*, Barbican Art Gallery, London
1982 *Floods of Light*, Photographers' Gallery, London
1979 *Fleeting Gestures: Dance Photographs*, International Museum of Photography, George Eastman House, Rochester, NY
1968 *5 Photographers*, Sheldon Memorial Art Gallery, University of Nebraska, Lincoln
1967 *Photography in the 20th Century*, National Gallery of Canada, Ottawa
1966 *Contemporary Photography since 1950*, International Museum of Photography, George Eastman House, Rochester, NY
1963 *Photography '63*, International Museum of Photography, George Eastman House, Rochester, NY
1959 *Photographer's Choice*, Workshop Gallery, New York
1955 *The Family of Man*, MoMA, New York
Selected solo exhibitions:
1986 *Little Known Photographs*, Fraenkel Gallery, San Francisco
1985 Williams College Museum of Art, Williamstown, MA
1984 Zabriskie Gallery, New York
1983 *Celebrities 1960-80*, Fraenkel Gallery, San Francisco
1979 Orange Coast Gallery, Costa Mesa, CA
1977 *Public Relations*, MoMA, New York
1976 Light Gallery, New York
1969 *The Animals*, MoMA, New York
1967 *New Documents*, with Diane Arbus and Lee Friedlander, MoMA, New York
1963 MoMA, New York
1960 Image Gallery, New York
Selected publications:
Stock Photographs: Fort Worth Fat Stock Show and Rodeo, by Winogrand, with introduction by Ron Tyler, Austin, TX, 1980
Public Relations, by Winogrand, with texts by Tod Papageorge and John Szarkowski, New York, 1977
Garry Winogrand, Grossmont College, El Cajon, CA, 1976
Women Are Beautiful, by Winogrand, with text by Helen Gary Bishop, New York, 1975
A Photographer Looks at Evans, by Winogrand, Austin, TX, 1974
The Animals, by Winogrand, with text by John Szarkowski, New York, 1969

MAX YAVNO
Born 1911, New York City
Died 1985
Selected exhibitions:
1984 *Photography in California 1945-1980*, San Francisco Museum of Modern Art, San Francisco
1979 *New Directions*, MoMA, New York
The Photograph as Artiface, Independent Curators, Inc., New York
Photographic Directions: L.A. 1979, Security Pacific Bank, Los Angeles
1977 *Photographic Crossroads: The Photo League*, Boston Museum of Fine Arts, Boston
Cityscapes, Fine Arts Museum, San Francisco
1976 *Exposing: Photographic Definitions*, LAICA, Los Angeles
1947 *Seventeen American Photographers*, LACMA, Los Angeles
1939 *Pictorial Photographers of America*, New York
Selected solo exhibitions:
1980 Equivalents Gallery, Seattle, WA
G. Ray Hawkins Gallery, Los Angeles; Fine Arts Museum, San Diego
Simon Lowinsky Gallery, San Francisco
1979 Gallery for Photographic Arts, North Olmstead, OH
Marcuse Pfiefer Gallery, New York
1978 Gallery for Fine Photography, New Orleans
1977 Halsted Gallery, Burmingham, MI
1948 California Palace of the Legion of Honor, San Francisco
1946 American Contemporary Gallery, Los Angeles
Selected publications:
The Photography of Max Yavno, with text by Ben Maddow, Berkeley, CA, 1981
Portfolio One: Image as Poem, by Yavno with introduction by Ben Maddow, Los Angeles, 1977
Faces: A Narrative History of the Portrait in Photography, by Ben Maddow, Boston, 1977
Silver See, portfolio, intoduction by Victor Landweber, Los Angeles, 1977
Exposing: Photographic Definitions, introduction by Robert Mautner, Los Angeles, 1976
The Los Angeles Book, by Yavno with Lee Shippey, Boston, 1950
The San Francisco Book, by Yavno with Herb Caen, Boston, 1948

BRUCE YONEMOTO
Born 1948, San Jose, CA
Lives in Los Angeles

NORMAN YONEMOTO
Born 1946, Chicago
Lives in Santa Monica, CA
Selected exhibitions:
1992 *Relocations and Visions: The Japanese Internment Reconsidered*, Long Beach Museum of Art, Long Beach, CA
1991 *Televisions: Channels for Changing TV*, Long Beach Museum of Art, Long Beach, CA
1990 *Traversals: Instructions to the Double*, Long Beach Museum of Art, Long Beach, CA
American Film Institute Video Festival
1989 *World Wide Video Festival*, Kijkhuis, The Hague
New California Video: A Survey of Open Channels, Long Beach Museum of Art, Long Beach, CA
1988 *Videonale Festival*, Bonn
Spirit of Place, The Learning Channel, PBS
Newport Harbor Art Museum, Newport Beach, CA

1987 *Terrorising the Code: Recent U.S. Video*, Australian Video Festival
1986 *Ghosts in the Machine*, Channel 4, Great Britian
1985 *Video From Vancouver to San Diego*, MoMA, New York
Whitney Biennial, Whitney Museum of American Art, New York
1984 *World Wide Video Festival*, Kijkhuis, The Hague
New Narrative: Recent Video Acquisitions, MoMA, New York
1983 *The New Soap*, ICA, Boston
1980 *California Video*, 11me Biennal de Paris
N/A Vision, Long Beach Museum of Art, Long Beach, CA
Selected two-man exhibitions:
1992 *Land of Projection*, Japanese American Cultural Community Center, Los Angeles
United States Information Service, American Embassy, Tokyo
1990 LACMA, Los Angeles
The Kitchen, New York
ICA, Boston
Mandeville Gallery, University of California at San Diego, La Jolla, CA
Pacific Film Archive, University of California at Berkeley, Berkeley
1989 Long Beach Museum of Art, Long Beach, CA
Rosamund Felsen Gallery, Los Angeles
1988 Herbert F. Johnson Museum, Cornell University, Ithaca, NY
1987 Florida Atlantic University, Boca Raton, FL
1986 Baskerville & Watson, New York
1985 American Film Institute, Los Angeles
Hallwalls, Buffalo, NY
1984 Anthology Film Archive, New York
Image Forum, Tokyo
MOCA, Los Angeles
1982 Franklin Furnace, New York
Long Beach Museum of Art, Long Beach, CA
LACE, Los Angeles
1980 University Art Museum, University of California at Berkeley, Berkeley
Selected publications:
Relocations and Visions: The Japanese Internment Reconsidered, text by Noriko Gamblin, video catalogue by Carole Ann Klorindes, Long Beach Museum of Art, Long Beach, CA, 1992
Moving the Image: Independent Asian Pacific American Media Art, edited by Russell Leong, Los Angeles, 1991
The Medium is the Mess…Age, by Bruce and Norman Yonemoto, in *Illuminations: An Essential Guide to Video Art*, edited by Doug Hall and Sally Jo Fifer, San Francisco, 1991
Television and Video Text: A Crisis of Desire, by Beverle Houston, in *Resolution: A Critique of Video Art*, edited by Patti Podesta, LACE, Los Angeles, 1986

Selected Readings

About Faces, by Terry Landau, New York, 1989
Abstraction In Contemporary Photography, by Andy Grundberg and Jerry Saltz, Fred L. Emerson Gallery, Hamilton College, Clinton, NY; Anderson Gallery, Virginia Commonwealth University, Richmond, 1989
Acceptable Entertainment, by Andy Grundberg, New York, 1988
Alibis, curated by Bernard Blistène, additional texts by Yann Beauvais, Pascal Bonitzer and Jean-François Chevrier, Musée National d'Art Moderne, Centre Georges Pompidou, Paris
All Consuming Images: The Politics of Style in Contemporary Culture, by Stuart Ewen, New York, 1988
American Fashion, edited by Sarah Tomerlin, New York, 1975; London, 1976
American Images: Photography 1945-1980, edited by Peter Turner, London, 1985
American Portraits of the Sixties and Seventies, curated by Julie Augur, Center for the Visual Arts, Aspen, CO, 1979
The Anti-Aesthetic, Essays on Postmodern Culture, edited by Hal Foster, Bay Press, Port Townsend, WA, 1983
Appearances, text by Martin Harrison, published in conjunction with *Fashion Photography Since 1945*, Victoria and Albert Museum, London, 1991
Art and Advertising: Commercial Photography by Artists, curated by Willis Hartshorn, International Center of Photography, New York, 1986
Art and Its Double: A New York Perspective, curated by Dan Cameron, Centre Cultural de la Fundació Caixa de Pension, Barcelona, 1986
Art History of Photography, by Volker Kahmen, New York, 1973
The Art of the Great Hollywood Portrait Photographers, 1925-1940, by John Kobal, National Portrait Gallery, Smithsonian Institution, Washington, D.C., 1983
The Art of Memory, The Loss of History, curated by William Olander, additional texts by David Deitcher and Abigail Solomon-Godeau, The New Museum, New York, 1985
The Art of Photography: 1839-1989, Yale University Press, New Haven and London, 1989
Aspects of American Photography, St. Louis, MO, 1976
Assembled, curated by Barry A. Rosenberg, Wright State University, Dayton, OH, 1990
Autoportraits, Musée National d'Art Moderne, Centre Georges Pompidou, Paris, 1981
Avant-Garde in the Eighties, curated by Howard Fox, LACMA, Los Angeles, 1987
Beauty: Variations on the Theme, Women by Masters of the Camera—Past and Present, edited by L. Fritz Gruber, London and New York, 1965
Between Here and Nowhere, by Rosetta Brooks, Riverside Studios, London, 1984
Biennial I, California Museum of Photography, University of California at Riverside, 1990
Body Language: Figurative Aspects of Recent Art, curated by Roberta Smith, Hayden Gallery, MIT, Cambridge, MA, 1981
A Book of Photographs from the Collection of Sam Wagstaff, by Arne Lewis, New York, 1978
CalArts: Skeptical Belief(s), curated by Suzanne Ghez, additional texts by Susan A. Davis, Catherine Lord, Howard Singerman and others, The Renaissance Society at the University of Chicago, Chicago, and Newport Harbor Art Museum, Newport Beach, CA, 1987

The Charade of Mystery: Deciphering Modernism in Contemporary Art, Whitney Museum Downtown, New York, 1990

Color as Form: A History of Color Photography, with introduction by Robert Sobieszek, International Museum of Photography at George Eastman House, Rochester, NY, 1982

Concerning Photography, by Jonathan Bayer, Peter Turner, Ian Jeffery and Ainslie Ellis, London, 1977

Confronting the Uncomfortable: Questioning Truth and Power, curated by Mary Law, Yale University Art Gallery, New Haven, CT, 1989

Conspicuous Display, curated by Sid Sachs, Stedman Art Gallery, State University of New Jersey, Camden, NJ, 1989

Constructing a History: A Focus on MOCA's Permanent Collection, MOCA, Los Angeles, 1989

Contemporary Diptych: Divided Vision, curated by Roni Feinstein, Whitney Museum of American Art, New York, 1987

The Contest of Meaning: Critical Histories of Photography, edited by Richard Bolton, Cambridge, MA, 1989

Crisis of the Real: Writings on Photography 1974-1989, by Andy Grundberg, Aperture, New York, 1990

Critical Image: Essays on Contemporary Photography, edited by Carol Squires, Seattle, WA, 1990

Cult Heroes: How to be Famous for More than Fifteen Minutes, Deyan Sudjic, London, 1989

Damaged Goods: Desire and the Economy of the Object, curated by Brian Wallis, with additional texts by Deborah Bershad, Hall Foster, The New Museum, New York, 1986

The Decade Show: Frameworks of Identity in the '80s, The New Museum, New York, 1990

Departures: Photography 1924-1989, by Edmund Yankor, Independent Curators, Inc., New York, 1991

The Difficulty of Difference: Psychoanalysis, Sexual Difference and Film Theory, David Rodowick, New York, 1991

Drawings: After Photography, by William Olander and Andy Grundberg, Independent Curators, Inc., New York, 1984

Endgame: Reference and Simulation in Recent Painting and Sculpture, ICA, Boston, 1986

Erotic Desire, Perspektif, Rotterdam, 1991

Fabrications: Staged, Altered and Appropriated Photographs, by Anne H. Hoy, Abbeville Press, Inc., New York, 1987

Face It: 10 Contemporary Artists, curated by William Olander, Contemporary Arts Center, Cincinnati, OH, 1982

Face to Face: Recent Portrait Photography, curated by Paula Marincola, ICA, Philadelphia, 1984

Fake, The New Museum, New York, 1987

Fame: Famous Portraits of Famous People by Famous Photographers, edited by L. Fritz Gruber, London and New York, 1960

The Family of Man, edited by Edward Steichen, New York, 1955

Fantasies, Fables and Fabrications, Fine Arts Center, University of Massachusetts, Amherst, 1987

Fashion 1900-1939, by Valerie Lloyd and others, London, 1975

The Fashionable Image: Unconventional Fashion Photography, curated by Carol Squires and Henry Barendse, The Mint Museum of Art, Charlotte, NC, 1986

A Fatal Attraction: Art and the Media, text by Thomas Lawson, The Renaissance Society, Chicago, 1982

First Person Singular: Self-Portrait Photography, 1840-1986, curated by Ellen Dugan, The High Museum, Georgia-Pacific Center, Atlanta, 1988

Floods of Light: Flash Photography 1851-1981, by Rupert Martin, London, 1982

Fluxus Attitudes, edited by Cornelia Lauf and Susan Hapgood, Hallwalls, Buffalo, NY, 1991

A forest of SIGNS: Art in the Crisis of Representation, edited by Catherine Gudis, curated by Ann Goldstein and Mary Jane Jacobs, additional texts by Anne Rorimer and Howard Singerman, MOCA, Los Angeles, 1989

((" ' ")) Frames of Reference, curated by Nora Halpern, Whitney Museum Downtown, New York, 1982

Frames of Time and Content: The Development of Photographic Ideas, Security Pacific Bank, Los Angeles, 1987

The Frenzy of Renown: Fame and Its History, by Leo Braudy, New York and Oxford, 1986

Grand Illusions, by Richard Lawton, with additional text by Hugo Leckey, London, 1974

The Heroic Figure, curated by Linda Cathcart, additional text by Craig Owens, Contemporary Arts Museum, Houston, 1984

High and Low: Modern Art and Popular Culture, by Kirk Varnedoe and Adam Gopnick, MoMA, New York, 1990

The History of Fashion Photography, by Nancy Hall-Duncan, New York, 1977

Hundert Jahre Photographie 1839-1939, by Helmut and Alison Gersheim, Essen, 1959

A Hundred Years of Photography, 1839-1939, by Lucia Moholy, London, 1939

Identities: Portraiture in Contemporary Photography, Philadelphia Art Alliance, 1990

Ils se disent peintres, Ils se disent photographes, curated by Michael Nuridsany, ARC/Musée d'Art Moderne, Ville de Paris, 1980

Image Scavengers: Photography, curated by Paula Marincola, additional text by Douglas Crimp, ICA, Philadelphia, 1982

Image World: Art and Media Culture, curated by Marvin Heiferman and Lisa Phillips with John G. Hanhardt, Whitney Museum of American Art, New York, 1989

Images Fabriqués, Musée National d'Art Moderne, Centre Georges Pompidou, Paris, 1983

Images of the Self, Hampshire College Gallery, Amherst, MA, 1979

Implosion: A Postmodern Perspective, curated by Lars Nittve, additional texts by Germano Celant, Kate Linker and Craig Owens, Moderna Museet, Stockholm, 1987

Information as Ornament, Feature Gallery and Rezac Gallery, Chicago, 1988

Infotainment, texts by Thomas Lawson, David Robbins and George W.S. Trow, Aspen Art Museum, Aspen, CO, 1985

In Plato's Cave, curated by Abigail Solomon-Godeau, Marlborough Gallery, New York, 1984

In Other Words: Wort und Schrift in Bildern der Konzeptuellen Kunst, Museum an Ostwall, Dortmund, Germany, 1989

Inside Out: Self Beyond Likeness, curated by Lynn Gamwell, Newport Harbor Art Museum, Newport Beach, CA, 1981

Intimate/INTIMATE, curated by Charles S. Mayer and Bert Brouwer, Truman Gallery, Indiana State University, Terre Haute, 1986

Just What Is It That Makes Today's Homes So Different, So Appealing? The Hyde Collection, Glen Falls, NY, 1991

Knowledge: Aspects of Contemporary Art, curated by Phyllis Plous, University Art Museum, University of California at Santa Barbara, Santa Barbara, 1992

L.A. Hot and Cool: The Eighties, curated by Dana Friis-Hansen, additonal texts by Dennis Cooper, Rita Valencia and Benjamin Weissman, and a conversation between Christopher Knight and Howard Singerman, List Visual Arts Center, MIT, Cambridge, MA, and Bank of Boston Art Gallery, Boston, 1987

L'Epoque, La Mode, La Morale, La Passion: Aspects de l'Art d'Aujourd'hui, 1977-1987, Musée National d'Art Moderne, Centre Georges Pompidou, Paris, 1987

The Library of Babel, Hallwalls, Buffalo, NY and White Columns, New York, 1991

Lichtbildnisse: Das Portrait in der Fotografie, edited by Klaus Honnef, Köln, 1982

Life Size: A Sense of the Real in Recent Art, The Israel Museum, Jerusalem, 1990

LIFE: The First Decade 1936-1945, by Ralph Littman, Ralph Graves and Doris O'Neill, New York, 1979

The Magic Image: The Genius of Photography from 1839 to the Present Day, by Cecil Beaton and Gail Buckland, London and Boston, 1975

Masters and Masterpieces: Photographs from the George Eastman House, by Robert Sobieszak, Abbeville Press, 1986

Masters of Starlight: Photographers in Hollywood, by David Fahey and Linda Rich in collaboration with LACMA and Hollywood Photographers Archive (Sid Avery), Los Angeles, 1987

MediaPostMedia, curated by Tricia Collins and Richard Milazzo, Scott Hansen Gallery, New York, 1988

Memorable Life Photographs, by Edward Steichen, MoMA, New York, 1951

Metropolis, Neuer Berliner Kunstverein, Berlin, 1991

Mirrors and Windows: American Photography since 1960, curated by John Szarkowski, MoMA, New York, 1978

Modern British Photography, 1919-1939 by David Mellor, London, 1980

Modern Detour, by Dan Cameron and Hildegund Amanshauser, Vienna Secession, Vienna, 1990

Modes of Address: Language in Art Since 1960, Whitney Museum of American Art, New York, 1989

Momentbild: Kunstlerfotografie, Kestner-Gesellschaft, Hannover, Germany, 1982

More Than One Photography, MoMA, New York, 1992

Moscow-Vienna-New York, Vienna Festival, Vienna, 1989

Narration, ICA, Boston, 1978

Natural Genre, curated by Tricia Collins and Richard Milazzo, Fine Arts Gallery, Florida State University, Tallahassee, 1984

New American Photography, curated by Kathleen Gauss, LACMA, Los Angeles, 1985

New Directions 1983, curated by Phyllis Rosenzweig, Hirshhorn Museum, Smithsonian Institution, Washington, D.C., 1983

New Photography USA, by John Szarkowski, Arturo Quintavalle and Massimo Mussini, Parma, Italy, 1971

New Voices 2: Six Photographers; Concept/Theater/Fiction, curated by William Olander, Allen Memorial Art Museum, Oberlin College, Oberlin, OH, 1981

New York: Ailleurs et Autrement, curated by Suzanne Pagé and Béatrice Parent, text by Claude Gintz, ARC/Musée d'Art Moderne, Ville de Paris, 1984

Not Just for Laughs; The Art of Subversion, The New Museum, New York, 1981

The Object of the Exhibition, Centre National des Arts Plastiques, Paris, 1988

Paravision, curated by Tricia Collins and Richard Milazzo, Margo Leavin Gallery, Los Angeles, 1986

People Will Talk, by John Kobal, New York, 1985

Perverted by Language, curated by Robert Nickas, Hillwood Art Gallery, Long Island University, Greenvale, NY, 1987

Photographic Directions: L.A. 1979, by Robert Glenn Ketchum, Los Angeles, 1979

Photographic Fiction, Whitney Museum of American Art, Fairfield County, Stamford, CT, 1986

Photographic Surrealism, edited by Nancy Hall-Duncan, Cleveland, OH, 1979

Photographs: Sheldon Memorial Art Gallery Collection, introduction by Norman A. Geske, University of Nebraska, Lincoln, 1977

Photography in America 1910-1983, text by Julie M. Saul, The Tampa Museum, Tampa, FL, 1983

Photography and Art: Interactions Since 1946, curated by Andy Grundberg and Kathleen McCarthy-Gauss, LACMA, Los Angeles, 1987

Photography in the 20th Century, by Nathan Lyons, New York, 1967

Photography Now, by Mark Haworth-Booth, Victoria and Albert Museum, London, 1989

The Photography of Invention: American Pictures of the 1980s, essay by Joshua P. Smith, Smithsonian Institution, Washington D.C. and MIT Press, Cambridge, MA, 1989

Photography of the 1950s, by Helen Gee, Tucson, AZ, 1980

Photography Until Now, by John Szarkwoski, MoMA, New York, 1990

Picture Personalities: The Emergence of the Star Stystem in America, Richard deCordova, Chicago, 1990

Pictures and Promises, curated by Barbara Kruger, The Kitchen, New York, 1980

Pleasures and Terrors of Domestic Comfort, by Peter Galassi, MoMA, New York, 1991 and International Center of Photography Midtown, New York, 1990

Pop Art Redefined, by John Russel and Suzi Gablik, New York, 1969

Portrait: Faces of the '80s, Virginia Museum of Fine Art, Richmond, 1989

Post-Modern Currents, Art and Artists in the Age of Electronic Media, by Margot Lovejoy, New York, 1989

Presences: The Figure and Manmade Environments, curated by Bruce Sheftel, Freedman Gallery, Albright College, Reading, PA, 1989

The Privileged Eye, by Max Kozloff, University of New Mexico Press, 1987

Radical Photography: The Bizarre Image, curated by Eric Brookhardt, Nexus Gallery, Atlanta, GA, 1984

The Real Big Picture, curated by Marvin Heiferman, Queens Museum, Flushing, NY, 1986

Recollections: Ten Women of Photography, by Margaretta Mitchell, New York, 1979

Redefining the Object, curated by Dan Cameron, University Art Galleries, Wright State University, Dayton, OH, 1988

Regarding Art; Artworks About Art, curated by Stanley Grand, John Michael Kohler Arts Center, Madison, WI, 1990

Remembrances of Things Past, curated by Connie Fitzsimmons, Long Beach Museum of Art, Long Beach, CA

Rooted Rhetoric, Una Tradizione nell'Arte Americana, curated by Gabriele Guercio, additional texts by Benjamin H.D. Buchloh, Joseph Kosuth and others, Castel dell'Ovo, Naples, 1986

Rules of the Game: Culture Defining Gender, curated by Judith Barter and Anne Mochon, Mead Art Institute, Amherst College, Amherst, MA, 1986

Sammlung Gruber: Photographie des 20 Jahrhunderts, forward by Siegfried Gohr, Köln, 1984

The Savage Garden, curated by Dan Cameron, Fundacion Caja de Pensiones, Madrid, 1991

Sexual Difference: Both Sides of the Camera, curated by Abigail Solomon-Godeau, Wallach Art Gallery, Columbia University, New York, 1988

Signs of the Times, Some Recurring Motifs in 20th Century Photography, San Francisco Museum of Modern Art, San Francisco, 1985

The Spiral of Artificiality, Hallwalls, Buffalo, NY, 1987

Split Vision, Echo and Narcissus, Artists Space, New York, 1985

Staging the Self: Self-Portrait Photography 1840s-1980s, National Portrait Gallery, London, 1986

Star Texts: Image and Performance in Film and Television, edited by Jeremy G. Butler, Detroit, MI, 1991

Stardom: Industry of Desire, edited by Cristine Gledhill, London and New York, 1991

Stars, Richard Dyer, London, 1979/1990

Status of Sculpture, curated by Bernard Brunon, Espace Lyonnais d'Art Contemporain, Lyon, 1990

Strange Attractors: The Spectacle of Chaos, Kaos, Inc., Chicago, 1989

Striking Poses: Photographs from the Kobal Collection, Richard Schickel, New York and London, 1970

Subjective Vision: The Lucinda W. Bunnen Collection of Photographs, with introduction by A.D. Coleman, High Museum of Art, Atlanta, GA, 1983

Surrealist Photographic Portraits 1920-1980, curated by Dennis Longwell, Marlborough Gallery, London, 1981

The Surrogate Figure: Intercepted Identities in Contemporary Photography, The Center for Photography, Woodstock, NY, and Cooley Memorial Art Gallery, Reed College, Portland, OR, 1991

Tenir l'Image à Distance, by Real Lussier and Philippe Dubois, Musée d'Art Contemporain de Montreal, Montreal, 1989

This is Not a Photograph: Twenty Years of Large Scale Photography, 1966-1986, curated by Joseph Jacobs and Marvin Heiferman, The John and Mable Ringling Museum of Art, Sarasota, FL, 1987

Through a Glass Darkly, University Galleries, Illinois State University, Normal, 1984

To Be and Not To Be, curated by Dan Cameron, Centre d'Arte Santa Monica, Barcelona, 1990

TV Generations, curated by John Baldessari and Bruce Yonemoto, LACE, Los Angeles, 1986

Uplifted Atmospheres, Borrowed Taste, curated by Howard Halle, Hallwalls, Buffalo, NY, 1986

UtopiaPostUtopia, ICA, Boston, 1988

Visions and Images: American Photographers on Photography, edited by Barbaralee Diamonstein, New York, 1981

What Does She Want? Carleton College Art Gallery, Northfield, MN, and First Bank System Division of Visual Arts, Minneapolis, MN, 1989

Wittgenstein—The Play of the Unsayable, Palais des Beaux-Arts, Brussels, 1989

Women of Photography: An Historical Survey, San Francisco Museum of Modern Art, San Francisco, 1975

Word as Image: American Art 1960-1990, Milwaukee Museum of Art, Milwaukee, WI, 1990

Word as Image, Contemporary Arts Museum, Houston, 1991

Word/Image, Bard College, Annandale-on-Hudson, NY, 1990

Words as Images, The Renaissance Society, Chicago, 1981